Richard Binns'

Best of Britain

**All maps designed &
drawn by the author**

New York   ATHENEUM   1985

To
all British chefs
working honestly, striving hard to use fresh produce and preparing their
own home-made specialities. How much easier your task would be if every
one of your clients adopted this simple, happy philosophy:
enquire, encourage, enthuse and **enjoy**

And how much more quickly would that enquiring philosophy bring about
the downfall of 'cheating' cooks – serving 'out-of-the-bag' products
prepared in 'factories' far away from their own kitchens.

And to
all my 'mapoholic' readers
in the hope that not too many 'arguments' ensue when following the
recommended drives: remember – the more you run the risk of getting lost
the more certain you are of seeing the 'Best of Britain'.

Cover: *A Glimpse of the Chilterns* by Denis Pannett; a specially commissioned
watercolour and reproduced with his permission. Denis lives at 'Heathers', 1 Woodland
Drive, Beaconsfield, Bucks.

My thanks to Dick Millard and the English Tourist Board for all their help and
encouragement.

15 area maps: based on Ordnance Survey 1: 250 000 maps with the permission of the
Controller of Her Majesty's Stationery Office, Crown copyright reserved.

Contents

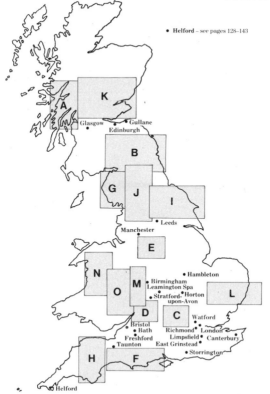

Helford – see pages 128–143

Glasgow
Gullane
Edinburgh
Leeds
Manchester
Hambleton
Birmingham
Leamington Spa
Stratford-upon-Avon
Horton
Bristol
Bath
Freshford
Taunton
Richmond
Watford
London
Limpsfield
East Grinstead
Canterbury
Storrington
Helford

As I go to press it seems likely that *Best of Britain* may well be the last book from my family's do-it-yourself publishing company, 'Chiltern House'. Why? A simple study of the chapter called *Profit and Loss Account for French Leave 3* – see pages 8 and 9 – explains the financial realities of the last 12 months. Why, to date, has our last book, *French Leave 3*, been a financial failure? There could be various reasons:

- the total costs were too excessive;
- the cover price of the book may have been too high – even though it simply reflected the total costs of production;
- not enough potential buyers knew that it was a greatly enlarged and much improved third edition of *French Leave*;
- perhaps readers only buy new editions of established guide books once every few years (confirmed by Michelin's market research for their own guides);
- perhaps the first two editions of *French Leave* should not have been such indestructible products – paperbacks do fall apart far more quickly;
- perhaps not enough bookshops stocked *French Leave 3* – see note 10 on page 9;
- a French 'backlash' in Britain – many UK retailers have commented on this unhappy 1984 phenomenon;
- finally, and I face this quite realistically, it may well be that the first *French Leave* and *French Leave 82/83* proved to be neither useful nor good enough to encourage users to buy *French Leave 3* – described by one reader as a 'quantum jump forward' from the previous two editions.

Whatever the reasons, a possible end to the publishing venture looms ahead; I will know where I stand within four months. I have kept my costs and sales targets low with *Best of Britain*; yet I may still pay a heavy financial price for my longstanding wish to publish my first British book. If *Best of Britain* and the remaining stock of *French Leave 3* fail to sell, this will then most certainly prove to be my last chance to thank you for your past support and encouragement; most of you live in the UK but a significant number reside overseas in North America and Europe. Hopefully, it will be an *au revoir* that I leave you with – rather than a final 'Goodbye'.

Despite the setback, I continue to stand by the principle – started with *Hidden France* two years ago – of limiting sales of our books to sensible maximums. When a book provides a modest number of hotel recommendations it is nonsense to let sales reach a six-figure total. I deplore the habit of linking massive TV coverage with books of unlimited sales potential but offering only a small number of hotel recommendations – a tactic about to be hit for a 'six' yet again in the UK during 1985 (a 'home run' to my North American readers); fine for the author, publisher, printer and booksellers – but hopeless for the book buyer. That's why *Hidden France*, *French Leave 3* and *Best of Britain* are not published in paperback or book club editions. The difficult 'trick' is to pass the all-important sales 'break-even' point – and beyond that to sell just enough books to provide a reasonable profit for 'Chiltern House'.

Key to Abbreviations – Price Bands – Maps & Text

Abbreviations

menus	range of cost of fixed-price menus. Often bar lunches only are available at midday; such establishments are clearly identified
alc	minimum cost of three courses from à la carte menu (only shown where no fixed-price menus available)
rooms	number of bedrooms and price band range (inclusive price for **the room**). Also includes cost of full cooked breakfast
cards	accepted: A – Access; AE – American Express; DC – Diners Club; Visa – as shown. (Always check with establishments)
closed	annual and weekly dates of closing (a **caveat** – check ahead); 'non-res' – closed to non-residents
post	full postal address and postal code where known
phone	STD code (in brackets) and number. Omit 0 if abroad
Mich	Michelin yellow map number on which recommendation is located ('400' series) and its map square co-ordinates

Price Bands

A	£5 to £10	**C**	£15 to £20
B	£10 to £15	**D**	Over £20

D2, D3, D4, D5: multiply D by figure indicated. All price bands include VAT and service (if latter not normally included 10 per cent has been added).

Maps & Text

Villages and towns in which recommended restaurants, inns and hotels are located are shown in one of three ways on each area map and in each area text; within the text the villages and towns are listed alphabetically.

Category 2 Name of village/town   Name of restaurant/inn/hotel
     CHURCH STRETTON   **Stretton Hall**

These are recommendations where, in my opinion, cooking ranges from modest, simple fare to an often very high standard. If the cooking is straightforward – identified by the symbol **(S)** – **do not expect marvels from the chef.** Other factors count in making the recommendation: value-for-money meals; perhaps the site; attractive local terrain; friendly hosts; or its usefulness as a 'base' (ignoring its restaurant). There is only one **category 1** entry included – of the *French Leave* 'no restaurant' type.

Category 3 Name of village/town   Name of restaurant/inn/hotel
     GREAT MILTON   **Le Manoir aux Quat'Saisons**

These are recommendations where, in my opinion, cuisine is of the very **highest** standard; they include both simple and luxury establishments. I have been very selective – as you will see from their limited number.
During my extensive travels in Britain during 1984 a few chefs cooked really outstanding meals – identified as **BEST MEAL IN 84.**

Some recommendations are personal favourites of mine: either they offer particularly good cuisine or they have some other attractive feature. Their entries are highlighted by the symbol ®. Some are quite exceptional – for varying reasons; their ® symbols are printed in red.
Some establishments offer clients particularly good value-for-money meals: the term **good value** is used to highlight these recommendations. (I have been unable to make any good-value recommendations for bedrooms.)
Do remember **simple** means what it says – for meals and rooms.

Places of special interest – towns, villages, rivers and other scenic attractions – referred to in each area text (in **bold** print) are shown on the maps as follows: • **Claverley**   • **Stourbridge**   **Severn**   **Wrekin**
Towns with Tourist Information Centres – open all year: • **Bridgnorth**
Towns with Tourist Information Centres – open summer only: •*Ironbridge*
Recommended drives are suggested in each area – see the detailed strip maps. On main area maps the drives are outlined as follows: ....
Some drives are special favourites: their headings are printed in red.

I would have loved my first book to have been *Best of Britain*. But four years ago it would have been commercial suicide to be so rash at the start of my family's do-it-yourself publishing venture – numerous guides on Britain were and still are available. Instead, five books on France came first from my pen.

Best of Britain may yet prove to be a financial mistake. However, one great merit accrues from the timing of this latest project: the enthusiastic message I convey to readers within these pages comes after spending so much of my time across the Channel during the last five years. For me *Best of Britain* is a celebration – a revealing and happy reminder to all those who turn their backs on this glorious land to stop and think again.

Britain is incomparably beautiful – **celebrate** and **enjoy** Nature's exquisite handiwork.

Britain is a treasure-chest of man-made riches – **celebrate** and **enjoy** the pleasures that await round every corner.

Britain, today, is endowed with a steadily improving base of inns, restaurants and hotels – many of which are privately owned. **Celebrate** and **enjoy** the vast change for the better that has taken place on the British culinary scene. Though we have a long way to go before we can match the sheer number of inexpensive, quality hotels and restaurants that one finds in France – the 'real' strength of French cooking – we can all play our part in changing the culinary status quo here in Britain.

I have many constructive comments to make in *Best of Britain* about the hotel and restaurant industry in Britain today. But first I want to implore readers to **support** the talented men and women who have brought about such a fundamental change in British culinary standards – particularly in **provincial** Britain. Celebrate the good news that there are now scores of British men and women who are doing their bit alongside the more famous established chefs, both British and European.

Enquire, encourage and **enthuse** whenever you visit any inn, hotel or restaurant. British cooking need not be a copy of all things French. The basic formula of marrying fresh, local produce to a simple, light, natural and creative style should become the rule, not the exception, in British cooking.

Only a handful of chefs in Britain come close to matching the genius of Girardet (a Swiss), Wynants (a Belgian), Robuchon (based in Paris), Pic, Guérard, Georges Blanc, Maximin or Meneau (all of whom work in the French provinces). That fact is of no importance at this stage of the British culinary metamorphosis. It is the improvement further down the prestige scale that is so encouraging in Britain.

In France, Michelin award their coveted stars to 642 restaurants – ludicrous, confetti-like generosity. In Britain, only 32 establishments win similar accolades. You would be absurdly wrong in assuming that the culinary gulf between the two nations is 20:1. Michelin inspectors in Britain are just that much harder to please – and quite rightly so, too.

By the end of this century Britain can get closer to matching French culinary standards – considered the best in the world – in quality, quantity and consistency. For that to become a reality it requires the **attitude** of British diners to become more demanding – though, hopefully, never as outrageously out of proportion as French attitudes; and it requires the hotel industry to make significant changes in its outlook, performance and pricing – particularly of bedrooms. More of that later.

So **enquire, encourage, enthuse** and **enjoy**. Celebrate all that is 'Best of Britain'. Surprise yourselves

Bouquets for . . . . . .

● Britain's rapidly increasing number of enterprising chefs – and three cheers for the steadily improving standards in the nation's hotels, restaurants and inns; the best of the British culinary revolution is happening, amazingly, north and west of Watford! Though outstanding chefs are relatively few in number – compared with France – Britain's cooks deserve your support and encouragement.

● Britain's incomparable countryside, man-made treasures, and her numerous alluring country lanes and rewarding footpaths.

● Britain's marvellous pubs. Most overseas visitors, who make the effort to journey beyond London, are captivated by the friendly atmosphere of our unique public houses. They rate them, together with pub lunches, British breakfasts, parish churches, our cathedral choirs, beautiful gardens, and our open-hearted welcome, as Britain's most beguiling assets.

● The Best Bed and Breakfast in the World. Though I criticise the high prices of hotel bedrooms elsewhere in this book, what does partly compensate are the numerous private houses and cottages, pubs, stately homes and friendly farmhouses providing value-for-money bed and breakfast accommodation.

● British restaurateurs who ask clients not to smoke in dining rooms – unheard of in France, where smoking is the norm.

● Last, but not least, that special welcome the British know how to give their guests. And I don't mean the half-hearted ones that are so common these days in London – but something quite different as you head north or west.

Brickbats & Boos for . . . . . .

● No – the gallows for all 'chefs' who serve frozen, pre-prepared meals from bags; the worst of all 'culinary cons'. These 'cheats' undermine the efforts of 'honest' cooks (**see page 23**).

● All those in the British hotel industry who have done nothing to ensure the large-scale provision of inexpensive bedrooms. Britain's tourist business would grow enormously if we could match the prices and numbers of strongly-established, value-for-money hotels that one finds in France; and, importantly, even more good chefs would surface and flourish in the UK.

   Why can't the UK have 140 one-star hotels like the new £60m. 'Balladins' chain in France? Cost of a double room? £13! Another 140 inexpensive hotels to add to thousands!

● All restaurateurs who fail to give English translations of French menus – so much time is wasted 'explaining'.

● All restaurateurs who prolong the life of the miserable *couvert* – cover charge. Kill it off! And let's have 'all-inclusive' prices – with VAT and service not added extras.

● All those sour bores with puritanical, guilt-ridden complexes about good cooking, good food and good eating.

● All those miseries who claim that food is fast becoming another British 'obsession'. How British cooks would love to be badgered daily by 'obsessed' clients taking an active interest in the fresh ingredients and local produce they use.

● The present level of Government support for our national parks – equivalent to 16p per person each year in Britain.

● Successive governments for allowing the rape of the British landscape to continue unabated: more woods, hedgerows, marshes and pools disappear every year. And put a stop to salmon 'netting', overgrazing and 'egg-poaching'.

● Airline and car hire firms: your UK prices are 'shockers'.

● All those French chefs who, on hearing of my British book, asked if it would only have five pages! Surprise, surprise . . . . . .

Profit & Loss Account for French Leave 3

Since the publication of *French Leave 3* – in which I explained how my family and I came to publish my own work – dozens of readers have enquired about the pitfalls, asking what the trials and tribulations are and seeking details on costs. Some of you may like to see what the Profit & Loss Account for *French Leave 3* looks like and to discover just what the financial hurdles are. What follows is a brief outline: on the opposite page you can study the financial realities – on this page I'll explain in note form what is involved, starting with the finished product at the point when it's ready for sale.

It does not take long to establish who the main groups of bookshops and wholesalers are in the UK and to discover the names of the 3,000 privately-owned bookshops – though probably no more than 500-700 make a serious job of it. Lists of these shops are easily obtained; then you set about mailing them all, announcing your product (along with 40,000 others each year). There are many freelance representatives who service bookshops for small publishers – they do splendid work.

Your first problem is the area of publicity. It would be nice to think – but childishly naïve – that books sell without reviews, features or interviews. **They don't.** You must find a way of getting the public into bookshops – my guess is that 70 per cent of all our sales have come after a media mention, the rest being 'impulse' sales. (I reckon that well over 2,000 UK bookshops have never 'stocked' our titles – being quite happy to order single copies if a buyer asks for one.) On average I send off about 250 review copies of each of my titles, leaving it to the editors and journalists who receive them to ignore the books or to write about them. Less than one in four do the latter. As an example, consider the travel editors of the major Fleet Street newspapers: only two of them have ever mentioned any one of the three editions of *French Leave*. But my greatest good fortune has been the opportunity offered me by the editors of four National Sundays to write articles for their magazines and papers; two have also run stories on the publishing venture. Help, too, came from BBC Radio 4 and Newsnight on BBC 2.

Pricing the book is a nightmare. Trying to calculate how many copies you are going to sell is a hopeless gamble – but you have to base your selling price on that guess! Keeping *French Leave 3* to a practical pocket-size works **heavily** against me. It could be twice as bulky, not have an extra word in it, and, apart from the additional paper content, the production cost would be the same: it would, of course, then 'appear' to be better value – but not very practical in use. Paperbacks would have made more commercial sense – they fall apart quickly!

On average a publisher receives about 57 per cent of the cover price (bookshops get 35/37½ per cent; wholesalers 50 per cent; large chains 45 per cent). Book club editions (there wasn't one with *French Leave 3*) and US editions earn, on average, 23 to 28 per cent of the cover price. One caveat: in the UK bookshops and wholesalers can return unsold or out-of-date books – and get a full 100 per cent credit for them.

I would like to finish by saying that all those associated with the publishing venture – my family and others – consider these two pages are an unnecessary part of *Best of Britain*. I take full responsibility for ignoring their unanimous advice. Many readers will not be interested; others will appreciate knowing the problems. It's not the end of the story – just another challenge. I'll be fighting hard to sell the remaining stock of *FL3* – in as many different outlets as possible.

Sales – for 12 months from date of publication (Nov '83)

	£	£	£
UK Edition: 13,500 copies @ £5.95 x 57%		45,800	
US Edition: 7,500 copies @ $9.95 x 28%		14,200	60,000

Expenses
Book Costs

Printing	29,600		
Maps (built up on previous costs of £4,000 for first two editions)	2,000		
Typesetting	4,500		
Cover design, editing, rights	1,200		
Libel advice and insurance	1,500		
Trade advertising	2,000		
Retail advertising	1,100		
Promotion	1,400	43,300	

Other Costs

Research – over two years	10,000		
Distribution/Storage/Accounts	2,000		
Commission, Motor Expenses, Phone, Post, Stationery, Audit, Depreciation, other Expenses	6,700	18,700	62,000
Loss – before drawing Salaries (our only source of earned income)			2,000

Notes

1. 'Break-even' comes when some 14,000 copies of the 'Chiltern House' (UK) edition are sold.
2. The *Printing* cost was for 7,500 US texts and 27,500 UK texts (of the latter 20,000 were bound initially – a further charge of £3,000 is due when the remaining 7,500 UK texts are bound).
3. Production costs were high: a hardback laminated cover, two-colour printing, colour illustrations, full-colour cover, page marker ribbon and dozens of maps (the most expensive way to fill a page) all incurred additional charges.
4. All the other *Book Costs* remain the same – whether one copy is sold or all 35,000 copies.
5. Some of the *Other Costs* are variable and depend in part on how many copies are eventually sold.
6. Some 14,000 copies remain unsold. It is hoped that at least some of these will produce further income.
7. The *US Edition* was paid for by the American publisher on receipt of the books in the United States.
8. Cash flow: over £50,000 was spent before the first income was received from initial sales – offset by the £14,200 received within two weeks of the US edition arriving in North America. Thus nearly £40,000 was put at risk – much of it borrowed – before one 'Chiltern House' copy was sold in the UK.
9. The 'bottom line' makes it quite clear why our publishing venture – **in its present form** – may come to an end. Every copy sold beyond the 'break-even' point will help us to survive – subject to no problems with *Best of Britain*.
10. Analysis of UK bookshop sales – a publisher's dilemma:
    250 shops bought direct from CHP; av. sales 20 books per shop.
    Large groups (WH Smith/Boots/AA); av. sales 15 books per shop.
    2,750 shops bought from wholesalers; av. sales 1½ books per shop (it is likely the vast majority of these shops sold no books at all).

Introduction to Best of Britain

If I had published *Best of Britain* in France I may well have given it a different title altogether – one associated in an unusual way with the most important of my various French books, *French Leave*. A typical dictionary definition of 'to take French leave' is to 'depart without notice or permission'. Note you are not required 'to take French leave' in France; amusingly the French equivalent of the English expression would have provided the title – *filer à l'anglaise!*

Ever since I started my do-it-yourself publishing venture in 1980 I have been itching to write about Britain. As I saw more and more of France, its people, and its hotels and restaurants, I became more and more determined to persuade my readers to give some of their time to our magnificent British countryside. For many years now I have made a habit of asking as many people as possible if they knew some of the lesser-known areas of Britain – places like the Welsh Marches, the Derbyshire Dales, the Border Country and so on. Invariably I got blank looks or negative replies: I cannot say I was surprised.

So, whether you live here already, or whether you visit our islands from overseas, please don't make the mistake of only seeking out the most famous tourist towns.

I have made a **limited** start with this first edition. I have selected 15 areas that I love dearly – many of which are ignored completely by British and overseas visitors alike. It is a subjective, idiosyncratic choice; I would have liked to extend it, but, within the limits of cost I set for myself, I had to settle for just 15. In describing each area you will notice that, as in *French Leave*, I concentrate on persuading readers to get off the beaten track – the only real way of enjoying the best of our hidden countryside. Above all I implore you to get used to navigating Britain's numerous and uncrowded narrow lanes. What pleasures await you if you make a minimal effort; don't worry if you get lost – after all there's no language problem. And use your legs as often as you can; no other country is so richly endowed with so many signposted walks.

In each of the 15 areas I describe, in detail, a selection of personally recommended hotels and restaurants – ranging from simple inns to some of the finest country-house hotels in Britain. In addition, there is also a section in which I provide details of my favourite London restaurants (**in this first edition I make no London hotel recommendations**); highlight some of my other favourite hotels and restaurants elsewhere in the UK; and identify some of the better Chinese and Indian restaurants. There are over 160 entries; I visited every one during the ten months prior to the publication of *Best of Britain*. I also visited many restaurants and hotels – half of them in London – which I have **not included**; some of them – with guide book accolades – have reputations far exceeding actual performance (see page 14).

In the pages that follow I examine many aspects of the hotel and restaurant scene in Britain. To make those comments more telling – both complimentary and critical – I have compared much of what I saw on my travels with my wide experience of the French hotel and restaurant industry. I hope that my comments are accepted as constructive observations.

Included within the *Northern Dales* chapter is a two-page section by a close friend, Peter Harland. It is a personal, revealing insight into the Yorkshire Dales that Peter both loves, and knows, exceptionally well.

A suggestion: accept the advice Michelin gives. Let it be known your visit is on the recommendation of *Best of Britain.*

'French leave' or 'filer à l'anglaise'?

For over 30 years I have travelled extensively in all parts of Britain and France. Since I started my publishing venture five years ago I have visited over 1,000 hotels, inns and restaurants in both countries. As a result I feel reasonably qualified in drawing some conclusions about the many differences facing visitors to both countries. What are some of them?

The Countryside

Both nations have a wealth of superb countryside. France has the advantage of warmer weather – a great attraction for those seeking the sun. But, though I know France intimately, I cannot think of many scenic aspects there that match the majestic British landscapes, varying as they do from the most savage imaginable to the most peaceful on the face of this earth. Britain's weather may be frustratingly variable but it plays a priceless part in shaping her scenic glories.

The British make far more of their countryside – particularly when it comes to walking the tens of thousands of marked paths; some rights of way have existed for centuries and are stoutly protected. The French ignore most of Nature's best treats. Both nations have a wealth of man-made attractions: castles, cathedrals, churches, museums, mansions, old towns, villages and so on. I rate Britain's numerous gardens without equal anywhere: every reader should get the 'Yellow Book' – 1,600 private gardens open to the public – from the Nat. Garden Scheme, 57 Lower Belgrave St, London SW1 (£1.50).

Hotels and Restaurants

The importance of family-owned establishments

Perhaps the most welcome aspect of exploring Britain today is the steadily improving standards in its **provincial** hotels, restaurants and inns; the better establishments – like their counterparts in France – are run by their owners, usually husband and wife teams – sometimes helped by their families. But, alas, there are **too few of them** and, compared with their French equivalents, they win nothing like the support they deserve.

It is at the bottom end of the hotel and restaurant pyramid where the biggest changes must come. In Britain the lack of a huge base of family-owned establishments creates all sorts of problems which, in turn, influence the higher parts of the pyramid. France has a centuries-old tradition of family-owned hotels and restaurants, in some cases built up through many generations (alas, so rare in Britain); there is a vast number of hotels and restaurants – particularly at the **inexpensive** base of the pyramid. The lack of that tradition in Britain affects so much.

It may well prove impossible for Britain to match the sheer size of the cheap end of the hotel and restaurant base that exists in France. In Britain much of that foundation has been filled in the main by thousands of Chinese and Indian restaurants – only too willing to meet the huge demand for cheap eating out or take-away food. In France their equivalents are family-owned establishments serving French food – or *charcuteries* in the case of take-away produce – and it is they who give the initial training to numerous local teenagers, eager to become chefs or waiters. (Most of them have hotel facilities – offering clients value-for-money bedrooms.)

The myriad Chinese and Indian restaurants in the UK do nothing to help the development that is so needed at the bottom end of the market – indeed they positively **hinder** it. For a start not one of them provides low-cost bedroom accommodation – as so many places do in France. They are doing nothing to revitalise British cooking and they are doing nothing to train chefs other than in their own Eastern cuisine skills. Put my claims to the test: take any small British town that you know well – and then compare it with its equivalent in France.

Many pubs help to fill the gap at the bottom end of the eating-out scene in Britain but, alas, many are going out of business, and too many are owned by huge brewery groups whose only interests are to add steakhouses and 'theme' restaurants to their freehold properties. Fast food operations are seen more often these days in France – but not in the epidemic-like numbers you come across in Britain. They are a **major threat**; the explosive growth of the British fast food industry (£2.2 billion a year) could choke our fledgling culinary revolution to death.

Starting-up costs

Though it is becoming increasingly difficult in France for young couples to start off on their own, it is much tougher in Britain. The costs and problems here are terrifying. It's more likely than not that privately-run hotels in Britain are owned by couples who have made their initial money elsewhere and who can afford the high capital outlay involved in starting-up. Often they are newcomers to the trade and 'employ' young chefs and other staff. No wonder therefore that overheads are so high in the UK – in France all but a few owners are the chefs, waiters, receptionists and jacks of all trades. The same applies to many restaurants – particularly in London – where the 'owners' are happy to live with the tag 'restaurateur': they, too, 'employ' chefs, managers and waiters. Prices reflect this.

I should identify, in the defence of hoteliers and restaurateurs, what some of the high start-up costs are: local and national bureaucracy puts up hurdles everywhere – particularly in the planning area; and rates and heating bills are more onerous in the UK – as are building and furnishing costs.

Newly-built hotels in Britain are more likely than not to be owned by one of a large number of British hotel groups. (In France one sees more and more hotel groups but they represent a small percentage of the total number of establishments.) In the UK this type of hotel – usually frighteningly expensive – seems to depend entirely on the support of the business community.

Cost of bedrooms

The most serious complaint that I level at the British hotel industry is this: it should be greatly concerned at the painfully high prices of hotel bedrooms. At any provincial hotel in France – from simple to de luxe – you can expect to pay not much over half the price of the equivalent room in Britain: the high British prices put off many who would otherwise be happy to stay in Britain. ('Family' rooms are rare in the UK.) The comment I hear most often in defence of high bedroom prices is this: "It's the profit from rooms that makes good the losses from the meals we serve." Therein lies the problem; I'll try to analyse it.

It is a chicken and egg situation – but the exact opposite of the one that exists in France and which I explained in *French Leave*. In France the cost of a meal, or the cost of a hotel bedroom, represents a **great** deal less to the French when expressed as a percentage of their **take-home** pay than it does to their counterparts in Britain. Because of this - and a long established tradition of eating out – the whole French hotel and restaurant industry is supported far more extensively; thus it is able to provide quality meals and a greater number of bedrooms at lower cost. This attracts **more** support from clients - and tourists - and, in turn again, **more** business.

In their defence I should stress that British hotels offer more amenities – like lounges; have more staff, and must meet expensive bureaucratic 'rules' – fire regulations for example. Room prices usually include full cooked breakfasts; perhaps quoted prices should show the alternative cost if breakfast is not eaten. It would certainly bring prices down for those on tighter budgets. But the 'rot' starts with the large, multi-starred, group-owned hotels – looking for rich business clients and charging sky-high prices. (Numerous 'weekend-break' terms prove my point they are so rare in France, where tourists travelling midweek get a much fairer deal.) Each star level down the ladder then pegs prices as close as possible to the level above it; it's at the bottom end – with minimal costs – where prices are often most outrageous. Country-house hotels are depending too much on English-speaking guests from North America and the southern hemisphere. The problem will be licked when all our hotels are full of European tourists – like France!

Chefs

However much cooking has improved in the UK there are few chefs who can match the **consistently** high skills of the top 100 or so French *cuisiniers*. I cannot agree with the suggestion that a 'score of chefs have established themselves who could hold their own with the **best** in France' – words written by the editor of *The Good Food Guide*. Equally misleading was a report in *The Daily Telegraph* this year which ran these words: 'London now rivals Paris as one of the finest eating places in the world – according to Egon Ronay.' Really? Inconsistency is the frustrating and annoying London weakness, Mr Ronay.

Backing up those few top chefs in Britain is a great mass of excellent, second-rank chefs – many of whom are self-taught, gifted amateurs who do thoroughly commendable work; it is they who have done so much to improve the eating out scene in Britain. At the lowest level of the culinary ladder in Britain it is fair to say that any really competent cook, working at home, can emulate the efforts of the average 'employed' chef; yet there is no way those same home cooks could ever match the skills of the many thousands of professionally-trained chefs at the bottom end of the French culinary pyramid.

Training

Compared with France there are some vital differences that cost us dear in Britain. Consider first the attitude of young people embarking on the necessary training to become chefs or waiters (**particularly** the latter), when, in the UK, they are still too often looked upon as second-class citizens. Training itself is another aspect of the problem. In France there are hundreds of top-class restaurants where youngsters can get a thorough training; that's not possible yet in Britain. No wonder that many of Mosimann's and the Roux brothers' apprentices have made their mark in the UK; what's rare here is commonplace in France.

Attitudes

Attitudes to restaurants, chefs and waiters – and their suppliers – are still poles apart in the two nations. Everyone in France takes pride in the country's chefs – at all levels. Waiters are proud of the job they do. The French pay little attention to 'junk' food; they put cooking skills first in deciding where to eat – in Britain the decision frequently depends on the best place to be seen.

In Britain one still finds a guilt complex or, worse still, a hypocritical outlook towards good eating – let alone praising in public the talents of exceptional chefs. We need more Bernard Levins to enthuse and encourage us all – the habit may catch on and who knows where it will take us.

The culinary scene in Britain today

At every opportunity I will implore you to search out the glorious British countryside – the more remote it is, the more enjoyable it is. In your travels do not expect miracles when it comes to the cooking you will find at the simpler inns, restaurants and hotels *en route*. But it has been a revelation on my travels – particularly away from London – to discover just how dramatically cooking standards have improved.

In each of the 15 areas I provide a number of recommendations – ranging from the simplest inns to the homes of some of our best chefs. (Please note the important **differences** between categories 2 and 3 – see page 5.) In addition, I list my favourite London restaurants together with details of other favourite hotels and restaurants elsewhere in Britain and some of the better Chinese and Indian establishments. On the whole I continue to favour those restaurants where the chef is *in situ*, where there's an unfussy atmosphere and where attention to detail is paramount. The test I apply is simple: if I begrudge spending my own money at a restaurant then I am not likely to recommend you to do so. You would be surprised how many London restaurants – with fancy reputations – failed to pass that acid test during 1984.

Slowly but surely the great benefits of *cuisine moderne* – modern-day cooking – are being appreciated in Britain. *Cuisine moderne* is the marriage of the best of classical cuisine and the much abused (by some chefs) and much misunderstood (by many clients and writers) *nouvelle cuisine*. The ground rules were laid down decades ago – by Fernand Point in France before the Second World War and by Elizabeth David 30 years later here in Britain. Today, *cuisine moderne* means an imaginative, light style – where simplicity and a natural, spontaneous touch count most. The use of fresh produce is paramount - vast helpings, covered in rich, heavy sauces are out. The earlier stupidities that one came across in France some years ago are still encountered from time to time in the UK. But, thankfully, culinary good taste is taking root here in Britain at last. If ever a country needed the benefits of the modern ways to be applied more widely, then it's Britain. *Faites simple* – make it simple – is the **key** to the best modern cooking: that same advice applies to restaurant fixtures and to the basic art of service. Take note British chefs: many of you add far too many unnecessary 'trimmings' to your dishes.

In many ways food in Britain still lacks refinement. Vegetables, fish and meat are too often overcooked – and frequently are just not fresh enough. But, worst of all, far too much food is served – obscenely so at times. Waste is a scandal: I shudder when I think of the vegetables that are thrown away. No wonder, too, that obesity is such a problem here in the UK. Chefs say they would love to serve less. They should do so. Huge benefits would accrue: apart from the health aspects, there would be less waste - and costs would come down. At the lowest levels of establishments – ones not recommended in this book – you find far too many fast foods are served; rich in fat, salt, and all those colourings, preservatives, flavourings, thickeners and goodness knows what else that do one no good at all. No wonder heart disease is such a problem in the UK. Presentation of food is still often a disgrace - even in the 'best' restaurants, where food is heaped pile upon pile on plates which are far too small. And it would be nice to see more *menu dégustation* offerings.

Perhaps the greatest difficulty chefs have in Britain is obtaining top class, fresh produce – **consistently,** day in, day out. (Poor refrigerated transport is no help.) At times in inland Britain you conclude that the only fish in the world is the ubiquitous trout – usually of the 'farm' variety at that. It may be that British chefs are scared of fish – always the best test in sorting out the men from the boys. Though most chefs complain, quite rightly, that many clients only order meat - even when fish is on the menu! (That's crazy when you consider how good fish is for a healthy diet.) Even in areas like Scotland it is immensely difficult to get access to the freshest of locally-caught fish and shellfish – the best goes to Europe. Too many 'top' chefs in Britain depend, in part, on the great Rungis market near Paris for their produce: how utterly ludicrous that is. Many country restaurants here have developed invaluable contacts with local suppliers who provide them with fresh ingredients. These contacts should become the rule, not the exception, for **all** restaurants. You, their clients, can help by your attitude to chefs: **enquire, encourage, enthuse** and **enjoy.**

Take British cheeses as one example. More restaurateurs should follow the example of Patrick Rance (his shop in Streatley - see *Chilterns* map – sells over 150 cheeses, 50 of which are British); they should pester the farms that make 'real' cheese. Supply would soon increase to meet demand. Why don't we all clamour for varieties like Cloisters, Cotherstone, Shropshire Blue, Single Gloucester and Somerset Brie?

Until recently, regional cooking in restaurants was all but dead. Increasingly more restaurateurs are making a supreme effort to revitalise British cooking – though generally **not enough** is done to promote local cheeses and produce, pork products and traditional recipes.

On the whole the British restaurateur knows far more about wines than his French counterpart. At the simplest of places wine is often treated as a joke - it's badly handled and there's little choice; but that's true in France, too. What I am certain of is that the best French wines are much cheaper here than in France - where mark-ups are now quite horrendous. I have no complaints about short wine lists; work out for yourself what it takes to finance a cellar. Take note wine buffs.

It is also high time laws were passed in Britain to standardise the way in which hotel and restaurant prices are shown – VAT and service should **always** be included. (Many chefs are taking a lead in this area - others should follow.) We should outlaw the wretched 'cover charge'. And why are many restaurants in Britain so dimly lit? You need a torch in some places.

Tourists could be forgiven for thinking that the staple food of Britain is served by Chinese and Indian restaurants – judging by the number of them. Cheap, plentiful fare is their stock in trade. Some are classics – worthy champions of their countrys' cooking skills. But more often than not it's 'junk' – served with the simple objective of 'make it hot' or 'make it plenty'; I wonder how 'fresh' some of the food is at times.

On the credit side the tourist in Britain will more often than not relish marvellous breakfasts (after which they can forget lunch) and will savour, too, truly enterprising snacks served in many pubs at lunchtime. The 'Great British Breakfast' and 'pub grub' are two of our best culinary treats – the French don't know what they are missing. (French breakfasts these days are often a joke – my advice is to give them a miss: that also applies to French autoroute restaurants.)

I have selected all my recommendations with care. Many are simple places – don't expect miracles – and some are the homes of the best chefs in the land. The majority are category 2 establishments – read page 5 **again**. Put them all to the test.

Michelin I, for one, was delighted to see the Michelin Red Guide re-appear in Britain 12 years ago. It's a slimmer version than its French brother - it has some 4,000 entries compared with 10,000 in the France Guide. It's equally invaluable and, for me, it is by far the best of the British Guides.

The maps are superb and there's an immense amount of detailed help for the travelling motorist. The use of symbols works well for me – after using the shorthand for 30 years I find 'pictures' forming in my head as I read the text; but I know many readers find it hard to translate the symbols.

To their credit the British inspectors, unlike their French colleagues, have been cautious in awarding chefs the coveted Michelin stars – prized just as much in Britain as in France. A master stroke by the British guide editor was the incorporation of an **M** classification (**not** to be confused with the French **R** accolade) which is awarded to many dozens of restaurants supposedly just short of one-star standard.

I find Michelin's British accolades are far more reliable than other guides' awards though I do think a few chefs with **M** classifications -- **outside** London – deserve their first stars; in France they would have won them already. Inconsistency is the Achilles' heel of many of the capital's Michelin starred and **M** classified restaurants.

Note two important observations. If Michelin choose to omit an establishment from their guide, it probably means they have found it wanting in some way or other – they visit all newly-opened restaurants and hotels. Secondly, restaurants themselves set their own standards and adopt **whatever** culinary style they choose to; Michelin then assess those standards – they do **not** claim to have specified them in the first place. Take note Italian and British restaurateurs: if you want to win stars!

The Good Food Guide According to its talented young editor, Drew Smith, in a reply to a broadside from Nigel Buxton in *The Sunday Telegraph* who called it a 'fundamentally amateur publication', *The GFG* has 126 unpaid inspectors – 'doctors, vets and solicitors figure prominently'. Smith claims that '*The GFG* is more accurate than *other people* because opinions are the sum of many different views from many different nights, often from my experienced inspectors'; and the guide claims it is 'uniquely informed'. If the editor is saying that opinions on the 1,001 entries in *The GFG* are based partly on **readers'** letters, well, so what, all guide editors get thousands of them. If he means opinions are based only on several **inspectors'** inspections then I would guess that the total cost of all restaurant bills for *The GFG* (including those places that do not make the guide) must be about £100,000 a year; study pages 8 & 9 – it's unlikely that would make financial sense. Whatever the interpretation, it's clear the average *GFG* inspector eats between 20–40 'inspection' meals a year; compare that with the consistent, experienced handful of full-time Michelin inspectors. Bold claims indeed!

Some readers like its cutting comment; for others it's too clever by half – chef's offerings are often dissected as if forensic scientists are at work.

AA Hotels and Restaurants Guide Another good but bulky guide – though it does contain many thousands of recommendations. Its price is kept down by the inclusion of about 1,000 advertisements from establishments recommended within its pages. At least with the AA Guide you realise that they are 'adverts' – which cannot be said of **numerous** guides on the market where entries are paid for and there's no obvious sign that that is the policy. For someone who has turned his back on financial aid of any sort for his books, it will not surprise you to know that I am unhappy with this type of approach – though in the AA's case I know the editorial team is independent from the advertising department. No less than 200 restaurants are awarded AA 'rosettes'.

Egon Ronay's Lucas Guide It is often claimed that guides have done a great deal to improve standards in the UK. As I said earlier guides cannot directly influence standards; what they do is to identify good restaurants and hotels where standards are higher than others and then they publicise those establishments. In that way the owners of those better establishments are encouraged to go on to greater things – others, lower down the skill scale, have to work even harder to catch up; the overall result is that general standards improve tremendously. Ronay deserves the major credit in the UK for consistently identifying and promoting, over 27 years, the nation's best hotels and restaurants. To his credit, too, he has never held back from criticising, but only in **general** terms, those areas of performance in hotels and restaurants that needed improvement. Too many 'stars' are awarded in my opinion – particularly in London.

Ronay has a dozen or so inspectors. Knowing the arithmetic of book production only too well, and the likely cost of keeping an inspector on the road for a year, I am not surprised in the least that the guide needs a major sponsor – Lucas – and that it requires to be filled with pages of advertisements. The guide is beautifully designed and typeset – a tribute to the really clever work of Ronay's wife, Barbara.

Every year major criticism is levelled at targets such as ferry and airline catering, motorway cafés and the like. This always has the desired result of winning hundreds of inches of press coverage when the guide appears annually. (The '85 guide is likely to feature catering in the Services – 'publicity' started months before publication.) But, believe me, books need publicity. Without it there would be no publishing business. Ronay has had rough treatment in the publicity area from Nigel Buxton of *The Sunday Telegraph*. To judge from some of his observations about the Ronay and Michelin guides, NB is surprisingly naïve about the commercial costs of producing guide books and what it takes to sell them.

Who is 'Paul Spencer'? I would guess that 'Paul Spencer' is a 'pseudonym' – a critic who hides behind the protective cloak of anonymity. A year ago, PS made a blistering attack in a Fleet Street newspaper on the major guides. The article was laced with acid comment: 'the men who compile them lack expertise' (but not PS); (Michelin) 'provided you know it is obsessed with the idiocies of the nouvelle cuisine is reasonably good' (yet four of the six two and three-star UK restaurants use a cooking style which, in the main, is built up from a classical base – and many one-star places rely on Roux-style 'new classic cuisine'); 'The GFG cannot be taken seriously – it fails to mention Boulestin' (laughingly, a month later Michelin also dropped Boulestin from its 1984 edition: can we take them seriously PS?) and 'once, however eccentrically compiled, they were reasonably reliable guides to where to eat and why.' I agreed with just one of his head-thumping rebukes: the *GFG* proclamation that 'John Tovey may prove to be the most important English restaurateur of the '80s.' PS finally ended his spiky feature with this bit of Alice in Wonderland logic: 'These guides which seem to proliferate every year are in danger of doing more damage than good.'

Useful Addresses & Other Guides

My prime objective with *Best of Britain* is to open the door for readers on 15 favourite areas and to encourage them to explore them to the full. To get the best from each area use the local Tourist Boards; they will supply you with a wealth of tourist literature and they will provide you with lists of relatively inexpensive bed and breakfast accommodation at inns, guesthouses and farmhouses – useful if you have a tight budget. All 15 area maps identify towns with Tourist Information Offices – see page 5. First the addresses of the main Tourist Boards:

English Tourist Board 4 Grosvenor Gdns, London SW1 0DU.
Scottish Tourist Board 23 Ravelston Terr, Edinburgh EH4 3EU.
Wales Tourist Board 2 Fitzalan Rd, Cardiff CF2 1UY.
British Tourist Authority (BTA) offices in North America:
New York (NY 10019), 680 Fifth Ave.
Chicago (Illinois), 875 North Michigan Ave – Suite 3320.
Dallas (Texas 75201), 1712 Commerce St – Suite 2115.
Los Angeles (Cal. 90017), 612 South Flower St.
Toronto (M5S 1T3 Ont.), 151 Bloor St West – Suite 460.

For further detailed information on each of the 15 areas write to these local Tourist Boards (TB) – see page 3 for the key to the letters:
A   Dunoon & Cowal TB, Pier Esplanade, Dunoon, Argyll.
    Mid Argyll, Kintyre & Islay TB, The Pier, Campbeltown, Argyll.
    Oban, Mull & Dist TB, Boswell House, Argyll Sq, Oban, Argyll.
    Fort William & Lochaber TB, Travel Centre, Fort William.
B   Scottish Borders TB, Municipal Bldgs, High St, Selkirk.
    Northumbria TB, 9 Osborne Terr, Jesmond, Newcastle-upon-Tyne.
C   Thames & Chilterns TB, 8 Market Pl, Abingdon, Oxon.
D   Heart of England TB, PO Box 15, Worcester.
E   As above & East Midlands TB, Exchequergate, Lincoln.
    North West TB, Last Drop Village, Bromley Cross, Bolton.
F   West Country TB, Trinity Court, Southernhay East, Exeter.
    Southern TB, Town Hall Centre, Leigh Rd, Eastleigh, Hants.
G   Cumbria TB, Ashleigh, Holly Rd, Windermere.
H   West Country TB, Trinity Court, Southernhay East, Exeter.
I   Yorkshire & Humberside TB, 312 Tadcaster Rd, York.
J   As above & North West TB, Last Drop Village, Bromley Cross, Bolton.
    Northumbria TB, 9 Osborne Terr, Jesmond, Newcastle-upon-Tyne.
K   Perthshire TB, PO Box 33, George Inn Lane, Perth.
    St. Andrews & North East Fife TB, 2 Queen's Gdns, St. Andrews.
    Loch Lomond/Trossachs TB, Beechwood Hse, St. Ninians Rd, Stirling.
L   East Anglia TB, 14 Museum St, Ipswich.
M   Heart of England TB, PO Box 15, Worcester.
N   Wales TB, 2 Fitzalan Rd, Cardiff.
O   As above & Heart of England TB, PO Box 15, Worcester.
National Trust properties: 36 Queen Anne's Gate, London SW1.

I also recommend the following guides for low-cost accommodation:
The Best Bed & Breakfast in the World U.K.H.M. Publishing (In USA from The Eastwoods Press, 429 East Boul, Charlotte, NC 28203.)
Egon Ronay's Guinness Pub Guide Mitchell Beazley.
The Good Pub Guide Consumers' Association.
AA Guesthouses, Farmhouses & Inns – Britain Automobile Assoc.
Farmhouse holidays: details from NAC, Stoneleigh, Kenilworth, Warw

OS maps (see next page) are available in North America from:
Seattle (WA 98107), David Morgan, 1523 NW Ballard Way.
Skillman (NJ 08558), Ardic Book Dists Inc., Montgomery Center.
Houston (Texas 77005), British Market Inc., 2366 C Boul.
Washington (DC 2006), The Map Store Inc., 1636 Eye St NW.

Maps

Readers of all my French books will know well enough by now that I seize every chance I get to enthuse about maps and the special joys they offer to all those who use them. I do not expect readers to be *mapoholics* like me – probably only members of that masochist breed called 'rally navigators' will understand why I have such a passion about maps. *Best of Britain* gives me yet another opportunity to write about them and it provides me with the first chance I have had to promote some of the world's greatest maps – made by the Ordnance Survey. Their maps, alas, are expensive – but try to use as many as you can for each area you explore. I'll describe in some detail the maps you should be using in Britain.

The Ordnance Survey (OS) publish many maps. For route planning the Routemaster maps (1 inch to 4 miles) are useful – though I prefer the Michelin yellow '400' series for this purpose (1 in. to 6.3 m.). (Every hotel and restaurant entry, outside the large cities, indicates the '400' series map number and reference square on which the recommendation is located.) I suggest you use, as much as possible, the OS **large-scale** maps. For some of the well-known touring areas the OS print 1 in. to 1 m. maps; for walkers over two dozen maps are produced for popular areas and are called Outdoor Leisure maps (2.5 in. to 1 m.).

For the best general purpose maps – perfect for the motorist – use the Landranger series (1.25 in. to 1 m.). There are 200 or so covering the whole of Britain. At the end of each area introduction I list the Landranger maps you need; the map numbers specified for each recommended drive are also Landranger maps.

Getting the best from them

I was once admonished by a reader for suggesting that 'nothing could be nicer than a picnic lunch alongside a quiet *étang* in the Dombes area of France.' Where were those *étangs*? It transpired that the map the reader was using had a scale of 1 in. to 16 m.!

In Britain – and France – you are wasting your time if you use small-scale maps like that. In Britain the Landranger series highlight just about everything you'll find *en route*. Desert the main roads and head up as many of the 'yellow' and 'white' lanes that you can – particularly the 'dead-end' roads.

In *Best of Britain* I have used a new technique to identify some of the most enjoyable drives you can make in each area – using those 'yellow' and 'white' lanes. Each drive is illustrated by the use of a small sketch map – **not to scale** – and brief accompanying notes. You can thus locate precisely the roads I want you to use on the specified Landranger maps. (Unlike France our minor roads are not numbered – neither on maps nor on signposts.) I drove over **all** the routes during 1984.

Learn how to use map references. Landranger maps are divided into one km. squares. If I write 125–9122 I am asking you to locate a 1 km. square on map 125: 91 is the 'easting' reference (the numbers along the top and bottom edges); 22 is the 'northing' reference (the numbers along the left and right hand edges). A six-figure reference is shown as 125-914228. Locate square 91 again and a point four-tenths 'eastwards' (914); then square 22 with a point eight-tenths 'northwards' (228). Where the two lines cross locates a point lying in a 100 metre square. Easy? "No," Anne says.

In the UK, OS maps are available from bookshops. In the event of difficulty use Stanfords, 12–14 Long Acre, London WC2 or Geographia, 63 Fleet St, London EC4. For suppliers in the USA see the addresses listed on the opposite page.

ARGYLL

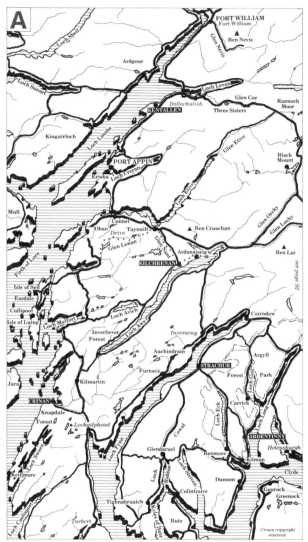

The west coast of Scotland is one of Europe's great glories –
perhaps even the greatest. Here in Argyll it is at its best – a
spellbinding marriage of sea and land: a jagged coastline, long,
lonely lochs, desolate glens, bubbling burns, rugged peaks,
extensive natural woods and vast conifer forests. Nature leaves
you reeling; relish this romantic landscape when it is at its best in
late spring. On top of all this natural splendour there's fishing,
walking, mountaineering and golf second to none. And who said
the Scots were dour, taciturn folk? Nonsense – visitors are
welcomed royally.

Start at **Dunoon** and give some time to the **Cowal** Peninsula; it's the mass of land between **Loch Fyne** and **Loch Long**. The **Argyll Forest Park** covers 100 square miles north of Dunoon. Your first port of call should be the Younger Botanic Garden at **Benmore** (56–144855); huge Wellingtonias, some 150 ft high, azaleas and rhododendrons make it a special delight. Nearby at 147841 is Puck's Glen Forest Walk and at 160825 the hillside **Kilmun** Arboretum – with every imaginable variety of conifer. **Loch Eck**, north of Benmore, should be renamed Bluebell Loch. All the nearby forests have numerous marked forest trails.

Strike west from Benmore and drive down either side of **Loch Riddon**: at **Colintraive** you can cross by ferry to the Island of **Bute**; my preference would be to use the western shore – with its eagle-eye views of the **Kyles of Bute**, some four miles south of **Glendaruel** as you head towards **Tighnabruaich**. In late spring Argyll is a wonderland: deserted roads, captivating deciduous woods, burning gorse, dazzling rhododendrons and blankets of bluebells. The primrose-strewn drive up the eastern side of Loch Fyne is the best way to **Strachur**. Near the head of the loch use the B839 and B828 to detour to the legendary pass called Rest and Be Thankful. Back to Loch Fyne and the Stone Gardens at **Cairndow** (56–1710) – see Strachur entry.

At **Inveraray** there's the handsome castle home of the Duke and Duchess of Argyll and The Bell Tower (Scotland's finest bells). Two miles south of the town is a Wild Fowl Park and at **Auchindrain** visit the Museum of Country Life – it tells the story of the sort of life Highlanders used to live years ago in remote parts of Scotland. Beyond **Furnace** (55–9897) is the Crarae Woodland Garden – an informal gem at Crarae Burn.

At **Lochgilphead** you can continue south to **Tarbert** and Kintyre – my suggestion is to head north towards your first real contact with the sea. Linking Lochgilphead with the small port of **Crinan** on the coast is an 18th-century canal – still much used today. Use your legs and enjoy **Knapdale Forest**, south of Crinan; there are several lochs within the woods. Many roads in Argyll are dead ends; get used to driving up them. One example is the B8025 from Crinan to **Keillmore** – views of **Jura.**

Kilmartin is renowned for prehistoric remains: see the stone circle at 55–827979 and the Bronze Age Burial Cairn at 826972 – a short walk from 'yellow' road; the church, too, is famous for its 14th-century sculptured gravestones. A mile or two to the north is the ruined Carnassarie Castle. Below the castle is the start of the B840 which takes you inland again to glorious Loch Awe – put aside time to expore *both* shores. On the western side is **Inverliever Forest**, the oldest in Argyll; there are many trails, enchanting views, burns and glens.

The Hebridean **Isle of Seil** has an odd claim to fame: it is linked to the mainland by the only single span bridge to cross the Atlantic! Explore the island: use the ferry to tiny **Easdale** Island and another to the larger **Isle of Luing.**

The heart and soul of **Oban** is its harbour – it's the mainland port serving the Inner and Outer Hebrides. Enjoy some sea trips; **Mull** is a must – you may be lucky and see basking seals. Then head inland to **Taynuilt**; but why not do the recommended drive that follows – full of interesting pleasures.

From **Connel** northwards there's a succession of scenic sights: the Island of **Eriska**, whitewashed **Port Appin**, the first sight of Loch Linnhe and the mountains beyond, the ferry crossing to **Ardgour** – at the narrowest point of the loch – and finally **Fort William**. **Ben Nevis**, Britain's highest mountain, towers above you; if you are not up to climbing it then enjoy it by making use of the narrow road up **Glen Nevis** to the south.

My suggested clockwise tour now takes you inland again through the ghostly **Glen Coe** – famous for the 1692 massacre; the brooding **Three Sisters** peaks remain silent witnesses to that atrocity. At Glencoe village, before you head up the glen, stop and visit the Glencoe and North Lorn Folk Museum.

Beyond Glencoe the road crosses one of the wildest, most desolate parts of Britain – the peat bog of **Rannoch Moor**; it's an eerie, forbidding place, quite frightening in the depths of winter. A ring of high peaks encloses the chilling marshy plateau. If time allows there are several worthwhile diversions from the main A82. The first is the long, desolate, dead-end road through **Glen Etive** to the head of **Loch Etive**; this diversion starts just before you reach Rannoch Moor and is an ornithologist's dream – the return trip is even better! Beyond **Black Mount** two other alternatives are to the west of the A82: the **Glen Orchy** run down the B8074 and the **Glen Lochy** drive using the main A85 that heads west to Oban. As you head south you can look forward to even more scenic and man-made treasures – see *Scottish Lochs*.

OS Landranger maps: 41.49.50.55.56.62.63
OS Routemaster map 4. Michelin map 401
Airports: Glasgow. Prestwick – near Ayr
Distance from London – Dunoon 431 miles.

Recommended Drive

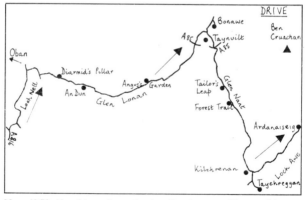

Maps 49/50. *Absorbing, alternative Argyll and a taste of Lorn prehistory: Diarmid's Pillar, a neighbouring stone circle and Iron Age 'duns' – in Glen Lonan; two gardens; Bonawe Iron Furnace – charcoal fired, built in 1753; Glen Nant – a Nature Reserve; and Loch Awe.*

Start 49–877254 on A816. N thru 8826; note cairns – one 'chambered' where Neolithic people deposited remains of their dead. W thru 8929. At 907289 (cattle grid) Diarmid's Pillar (standing stone) and nearby stone circle – both dating to about 1,500 BC. In Glen Lonan note 'duns' – Celtic Iron Age hill forts. Standing stone at 925285. 200 yds An Dun – knoll on right. 944275 view of twin peaks of Ben Cruachan. At 980289 Angus's Garden – a living memorial to a son; a memorable spot indeed. NE thru 9929. Bonawe Furnace at 50–010318. S thru 0129. At 015282 use bridge over Tailor's Leap. At 020273 walk Glen Nant Forest Trail – oak woods, once Bonawe's charcoal supply. Detour Taychreggan at 047215 – views. Finish 088248 – glorious gardens and woods. Approx. dist. 25 m.

Hotel and Restaurant Recommendations

This space should have been filled by an entry for a hotel – recommended by *FL3* readers and many guides. On my arrival I was met by 'new' owners; the meal they served was an insult to all those hardworking, enterprising chefs who are striving like Trojans to find and use local, fresh produce in their personally-prepared fare. Instead, the pretentious 'à la carte' menu proved to be a succession of 'out-of-the-bag' products, prepared in a 'factory' far away from the hotel's kitchen.

It seems appropriate to use this space, at the start of my British hotel and restaurant recommendations, to suggest that the Government should pass legislation, under the Trade Descriptions Act, to ensure that any restaurant offering food prepared elsewhere should say so on its menu. Regrettably, The Dept. of Trade and Ind. appear not to be interested.

Let 'cheating', 'conning' chefs have the freedom to serve such food – it's probably better than their own efforts anyway; but at least they should be honest about it.

ARDENTINNY
Ardentinny

Simple hotel(S)
Quiet Gardens

New, friendly owners – John and Thyrza Horn, together with her sister, Hazel – took over the Ardentinny in 1984. Much the most attractive aspect of this 18th-century hostelry is its tranquil, waterside setting – on the western shore of Loch Long. Walkers are particularly spoilt with endless trails and paths in the numerous forests nearby; for the energetic the most exhilarating is the long walk to Carrick and its ruined castle. Cooking is utterly conventional and straightforward.

menu **B** (din) Bar lun *rooms* 11 **C-D** *cards* A AE DC Visa
closed Nov-Feb.
post Ardentinny, Dunoon, Argyll PA23 8TR.
phone (036 981) 209 *Mich* 401 (F15) Dunoon 13 m.

CRINAN
Crinan/Lock 16

Comfortable hotel
Gardens/Lift
®

Nick Ryan, so enthusiastic in everything he does, and Frances, his auburn-haired, artistic wife, have perfected the difficult art of creating a relaxed atmosphere but backed by behind-the-scenes hard work. Enjoy a variety of seafood, literally plucked from the sea at their doorstep – clams, prawns, lobsters, mussels; what's offered depends on the day's catch – do ring ahead as bad weather can affect things. In the event of the latter Nick can still please with gravlax, Loch Fyne kipper pâté, Scottish beef and lots more. Admire his 'Arab' *bain-marie*! Light, airy bedrooms fitted out with stylish care by Frances. Lock 16 is the more expensive seafood restaurant on the third floor with spectacular views of Jura; book ahead.

menus **B-D** *rooms* 22 **D-D2** *cards* A AE DC Visa
closed Nov-mid Mar.
post Crinan, Lochgilphead, Argyll PA31 8SR.
phone (054 683) 235 *Mich* 401 (D15) Dunoon 69 m.

Several chefs spoke highly of the award-winning Longhouse Buttery at Cullipool on the **Isle of Luing**; the Allens visit it regularly – high praise for Audrey Stone and Edna Whyte. Lunch only on Mon-Sat, Easter-Sept; *phone* (085 24) 209.

FORT WILLIAM

Inverlochy Castle

Luxury hotel/Michelin ★
Secluded/Gardens/Tennis/Fishing ⓡ

Superlatives dry up when one describes Inverlochy and its setting: priceless is the only word that does justice to the grounds and the castle's interior treasures. People appeal, too: delightful Greta Hobbs, the owner – 'involvement' to her means, as one example, rearing dozens of Canadian geese; and the chef, François Huguet, who each year has the unenviable task of training a new team (like Guérard) – as friends reported, you may encounter some rough edges at the start of the season. Our visit was exemplary. François, a keen ornithologist, is renowned for his skill with game – particularly birds. His style is light and creative. If nothing else enjoy a good-value lunch – at one of Britain's greatest hotels.

menus C (lun) D (din) *rooms* 14 D3-D5 *cards* A Visa
closed Nov-Mar.
post Inverlochy, Fort William, Inverness PH33 6SN.
phone (0397) 2177 *Mich* 401 (E13) Dunoon 118 m.

KENTALLEN

Ardsheal House

Comfortable hotel (S)
Secluded/Gardens/Tennis ⓡ

Overnight rain and winds leave the northern air crystal clear – highlighting to great advantage the idyllic surroundings of Ardsheal (watchtower): it's a mile from the nearest road; has a backdrop of lovely trees; overlooks Loch Linnhe – with its own beach alongside the sea loch; to the west the Ardgour peaks; and to the north the huge hump of Ben Nevis. Cooking is of average standard; the chef is a young, local man, Robert Gardiner, partly self-taught and guided also by the friendly owners, Robert and Jane Taylor. Get to know 'Dilly' and 'Alice' – real characters! Marvellous full-size snooker table.

menus C (din) Bar lun *rooms* 12 D-D3
closed Mid Oct-Easter.
post Kentallen, Argyll PA38 4BX.
phone (063 174) 227 *Mich* 401 (E14) Dunoon 98 m.

KILCHRENAN

Ardanaiseig

Very comfortable hotel
Secluded/Gardens/Tennis/Fishing

Anne and I visited the 150-year-old Ardanaiseig on a 'Mediterranean' day in May. The setting is majestic: mixed woodlands and gardens with flaming rhododendrons and blazing azaleas (numerous perfumed 'yellows') – all of it in utter seclusion alongside Loch Awe with snow-capped Ben Lui to the north. Cuisine is mainly classical *(Châteaubriand and tournedos Argyll* as examples) – of the sort you would be ordering at the Savoy; the chef, David Merriman, did his training there before moving north five years ago. Tight budget? Try 'Victorian' afternoon teas – at modest cost in cosseting luxury.

menus B (lun) C-D (din) *rooms* 15 D-D4 *cards* A AE DC Visa
closed Mid Oct-Easter.
post Kilchrenan, Taynuilt, Argyll.
phone (086 63) 333 *Mich* 401 (E14) Dunoon 79 m.

KILCHRENAN   Taychreggan

Comfortable hotel
Secluded/Gardens/Fishing/Good value (meals)   Ⓡ

Long before I set eyes on Taychreggan I received the most
glowing of recommendations from *FL3* readers. Once a coaching
inn, today it's a modernised hotel of great charm, blending
perfectly into its lochside setting. Protected by trees, the view
south down Loch Awe is magnificent. The owners, John and Tove
Taylor, are the epitome of what all hotelkeepers should be:
informed about their locality and personally involved in every
aspect of their guests' well-being. Good cooking: prawns as fresh
as daisies, superb River Awe salmon and, at breakfast, delicious
smoked haddock. Danish cold table at lunch.

menus **A** (lun) **B** (din) *rooms* 17 **C-D2** *cards* A AE DC Visa
closed Mid Oct-mid Apl.
post Lochaweside, Kilchrenan, Taynuilt, Argyll PA35 1HQ.
phone (086 63) 211 *Mich* 401 (E14) Dunoon 75 m.

PORT APPIN   Airds

Comfortable hotel
Quiet/Good value (dinner)   Ⓡ

It's no hardship to be 'on time' for dinner. You can continue to
soak up the views of Loch Linnhe and the peaks beyond from the
lounges and main dining room. Being punctual is your
contribution to ensuring that Betty Allen, a self-taught, talented
cuisinière, husband Eric, so proudly Scots, and their small team
of Scottish lasses get the preparation of a wide choice of
excellent specialities just right. A category three entry is truly
deserved for many mouthwatering Scottish recipes and masterly
desserts. Even if you don't stay be sure to relish a really good-
value dinner and some fantastic bargains from Eric's list of 200
wines. Bibendum: why not 'light' a star overhead?

menus **B** (din) Bar lun *rooms* 15 **D-D2**
closed Nov-Mar.
post Port Appin, Argyll PA 38 4DF.
phone (063 173) 236 *Mich* 401 (D14) Dunoon 90 m.

STRACHUR   Creggans Inn

Comfortable hotel
Gardens/Good value (meals)   Ⓡ

Be sure to enjoy a meal here. The pride in the day-to-day running
of this ancient, lochside inn starts with the owners, Sir Fitzroy
and Lady Maclean – it's then complemented by the enthusiasm of
Laura, Nan, Meg, Jimmy and all their staff. How rewarding it is to
see so much 'local' produce being presented in such *faites
simple* ways: huge, sweet *langoustines* and sea trout from Loch
Fyne; Creggans' smoked salmon and spiced beef; mouthwatering
beef and venison patties; smoked trout, oysters and much else
besides from John Noble at Ardkinglas (56–1710); and home-
made sorbets and other delights. If only all this marvellous
initiative could become nationally infectious!

alc **A-B** *rooms* 22 **D-D2** *cards* A AE Visa
closed Open all the year.
post Strachur, Cairndow, Argyll PA27 8BX.
phone (036 986) 279 *Mich* 401 (E15) Dunoon 19 m.

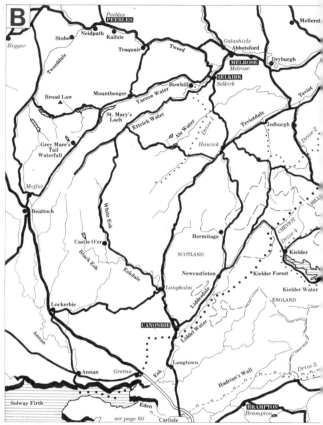

I would guess that for every hundred British visitors to France, perhaps just one or two could say that they knew something of this magnificent part of their homeland. Border Country is the perfect name; the border between England and Scotland cuts diagonally across the area – from the left-hand corner to the right-hand side. I'll start with the English 'triangle'.

The deserted terrain within that triangle is Northumberland – the most unspoilt, least populated county in England. It is utterly unnerving how alone you can be on the moors and in the vast forests of the high **Cheviot Hills –** whether you are in your car or enjoying some of the best walking country in Britain. The **Northumberland National Park** runs from **Wooler** in the north to **Hadrian's Wall** in the **Tyne** Valley. Huge forests fill the gap between the Park and the Scottish border – **Kielder, Wark** and **Redesdale**.

Hadrian's Wall is a must – the greatest Roman military landmark in northern Europe. The wall runs a total distance of 73 miles from **Carlisle** to **Newcastle**; it's at its best when it snakes over the high crags of the Great Whin Sill (*sill* – basalt). For specific sites worth visiting see drive 5.

Now head north to several villages: **Simonburn, Wark,**

see page 82 Crown copyright reserved

Bellingham and **Elsdon**. Explore the huge forests mentioned earlier. Marked forest trails in Wark Forest begin at **Stonehaugh** – west of Wark. Complete the long drive through the **Kielder Forest** – starting at **Falstone**, passing through the newly-completed **Kielder Water** (reservoir) to **Kielder** and then, heading eastwards, on a toll road to the A68. (See drive 4.) All this country is well known to rallyists. At Kielder there's a little-used road across to Scotland's **Liddesdale** – note the dismantled railway.

One of the best dead-end roads in England is the one you'll find in glorious **Coquetdale** – the upper reaches of the river valley are the most intoxicating. Don't be faint-hearted about it – follow it right up to its end on map 80-8009. Downstream are many man-made pleasures: **Alwinton, Harbottle, Holystone** (nearby are walks, an Iron-Age fort and the 'Lady Well') and **Rothbury**. Near the latter is the unique **Cragside** House and Country Park – 900 acres of sheer enchantment; the Victorian mansion was the first house in the world to be lit by electricity generated by water power. My visit was one of the highlights of 1984 – a three-star wonder. (See drive 3.)

Not the least of Northumberland's treasures is the wonderful coast. There's **Amble** and **Warkworth** – a castle first built in the 11th-century gives the latter extra appeal; another fine castle at **Alnwick; Howick** Gardens; the small port of **Craster** – famous for its kippers; the ruined **Dunstanburgh** Castle, sitting on top of the last but one outcrop of the Whin Sill; **Bamburgh** with its formidable, restored red sandstone castle; and, finally, the romantic site of Lindisfarne Castle on **Holy Island** – restored by Lutyens in 1902 – and its walled garden. The **Farne Islands** are the eastern end of the Whin Sill; the most famous of Britain's sea-bird sanctuaries, you'll see puffins, scores of other birds and grey seals – the islands are easily accessible from **Seahouses**.

Across the Cheviots is the other 'triangle' – a Scottish one with **Peebles** at the right-angle in the north-west corner. Part of the Scottish Lowlands, the 'Borders' is one of my favourite British areas. What variety there is to entice you: incomparable river country; green, gently-rolling hills; moorlands; vast forests and, on top of all those natural delights, many man-made wonders. Yet it's bypassed by most tourists.

Consider first the architectural treasures – each a page from Scottish history. In **Tweeddale** you'll find **Traquair**, the oldest inhabited house in Scotland – 27 kings have visited it; **Abbotsford** – the home built and lived in by Sir Walter Scott; the medieval tower of **Neidpath** Castle, near Peebles; at **Kelso** the ruins of a 12th-century abbey and the vast 'pepperpot' Floors Castle, west of the town; at **Dryburgh** there's an isolated abbey; and at **Melrose** a historic Cistercian abbey. There are some gardens to visit: the Dawyck Forest Garden near **Stobo**, upstream on the **Tweed** from Peebles; the **Kailzie** Gardens, just downstream from Peebles on the southern bank; and the Priorwood Garden, newly-created and beside Melrose Abbey.

Other man-made sights lie away from the River Tweed; near **Selkirk** is **Bowhill** – a Georgian mansion in attractive woodlands; there's another great Georgian house at **Mellerstain**, north-west of Kelso; far to the south, north of **Newcastleton**, is **Hermitage** Castle – in a wild, secluded border setting; and at **Jedburgh**, the ruins of another 12th-century abbey and also Mary Queen of Scots' House – now a museum.

As much as I find all those places interesting, it's to the deserted hills that I would prefer to head – get out your large-scale maps and drive up the numerous dead-end roads. From the Tweed head south up **Yarrow Water** to **St Mary's Loch** – an unspoilt stretch of water; continue on for a few miles to the **Grey Mare's Tail Waterfall** – a 200 ft drop and worth the climb from the A708. Double back to **Mountbenger** and then, using the B709, cross to **Ettrick Water**; follow the stream to a point near its source – a dead-end road in romantic country.

South now from Ettrick to **Eskdale** (B709 again) – and more invigorating, lonely hills, woods and streams. Have your fill of remote Eskdale, particularly the west bank of the **White Esk**, through **Castle O'er**; then head north to **Hawick**. But not by the obvious A7; I would follow the **Esk** to **Langholm**, head north on the A7 and, on an exhilarating road east to Hermitage Castle. I would then use the B6357 up Liddesdale and on to Hawick. From there you can absorb the gentler charms of **Teviotdale** – or if solitude is your desire, drive up the dead-ends of Kale Water and Bowmont Water, in the shadow of the Cheviots.

OS Landranger maps: 72.73.74.75.78.79.80.81.85.86.87
OS Routemaster map 4. Michelin map 402
Airports: Edinburgh. Newcastle-upon-Tyne
Distance from London – Newcastle-upon-Tyne 283 miles

Recommended Drives

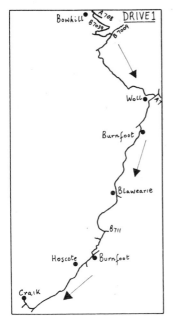

Drive 1 maps 73/79

A deserted paradise, heaven for nature lovers: unbelievably I saw no other cars on this drive during a blazing June day!

Start 73-433281 – entrance to Bowhill; loved by Sir Walter Scott, this fine Georgian house is set in wooded grounds and has some magnificent art treasures. SE on B7039. SW thru 4325. SE thru 4324 – gasp at the view north. 472224 – then SW thru 4621. Map 79. SW thru 4418. Note 'stells'; circular stone wall enclosures for sheep, designed to make snow blow clear. SW thru 4316 – views of Cheviots. SW thru 4012 and 3608. Finish at 347080; marked walk to Wolfcleuch Waterfall – 1½ m. Picnic 200 yards from carpark. You will have noticed how important sheep are in the Borders – renowned for its woollen industry. Visit Hawick – you can see tweeds being woven at Teviotex Ltd. Plenty of shops, too! Approx. dist. 21 m.

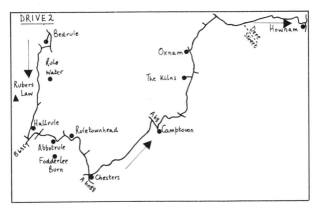

Drive 2 map 80 *Perfect for those who need a 'tonic' of fresh air.*
Start Bedrule Church – 599180. Bewitching view of wooded Rule Water and Rubers Law peak beyond. 'Rule' country – see plaque in church, flick thru visitors' book, study map. S thru 5916. 1st 4 m. road runs thru fine trees. SW thru 6013. Fodderlee Burn to S where legend says Robert the Bruce saved by kinsman who 'turned' attacking bull aside – the hero then given the name 'Turnbull'. E thru 6411 – views of Cheviot 'wall'. N thru 6914. At 700168 visit Peter Fishley-Holland, a 7th-generation potter, at The Kilns. SW thru 7219. 740190 (grid) stop; panoramic view *par excellence* – The Cheviot to E. Note Dere St – old Roman road. Finish Hownam. Approx. dist. 22 m.

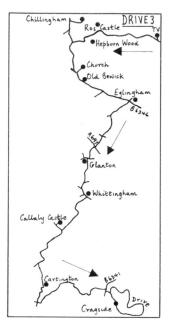

Drive 3 maps 75/81
*Revel in this majestic drive –
full of happy surprises.*
Start 75-109244 (road to TV
mast). At 079249 climb to Ros
(or Ross) Castle – a 3,000-yr-old
hill fort. Fantastic views of
Cheviots and 7 castles on the
coast. 074248; walks in Hepburn
Wood – worth the effort. Detour
063261 – Chillingham Wild Cattle Park; a unique herd of 50. S
thru 0622. Detour 067221 –
church, a 12th-cent. gem. SE
thru 0820. Map 81. S thru 0917 –
lovely view W. Glanton. Pretty
Whittingham. SW thru 0610.
050097 – Callaly Castle and Gardens. S thru 0304. Use white
thru 050042 – roughish but rewarding. 067034 (B6341) ent.
Cragside. It's a three-star marvel of unique home, forests,
park, lakes and Visitor Centre –
the latter one of the best of its
kind. At rhododendron time it's
a dazzling sea of colour. Approx. dist. 33 m. (inc' 6 m. drive
at Cragside).

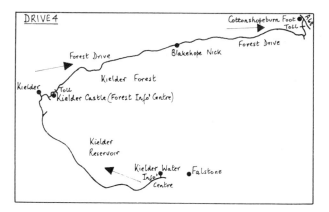

Drive 4 map 80 *A dramatic example of how man can dominate a remote
landscape; for some not too well – for me, a truly successful marriage!*
Start 699867 – Kielder Water Info Centre. Interesting exhib showing how
Kielder Resr. was constructed and how it's used today. Boat trips, sailing,
fishing, walks, picnics – the visitor can use the site in many ways. N thru
6588 to Kielder. E to Kielder Castle (632935), fascinating Kielder Forest
Info Centre. Kielder Forest covers 200 sq. miles – some motor rally stages
are 40 miles long! Leaflets explain the many interesting diversions that
await the walker and the ornithologist. Do 12 m. Forest Drive thru 7198
(Blakehope Nick – 1500 ft) to A68. Approx. dist. 21 m.

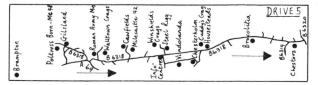

Drive 5 maps 86/87 *Hadrian's Wall.*
Start Gilsland (86-6366): park Stat. Hotel; 200 yds Poltross Burn Milecastle
48 – fine example, wooded site. E B6318. 666657 – Roman Army Mus.; good
intro' to Wall (WC/refreshments); walk E to Walltown Crags. 713666 –
Cawfields; walk E to Milecastle 42 and one of steepest bits of wall (WC).
751677 – Steel Rigg: fine walk/views E; Winshields Crags to W highest point
wall – 1230 ft (WC). 766664 – Vindolanda; fort. Ignore 'Access Only' sign. E
to 774664 – Chesterholm; house, gardens, museum (WC/refresh). N thru
7867. 794684 – Housesteads; infantry fort, walk W Cuddy's Crag (no WC).
Map 87. 860713 – Brocolitia; remains Temple to Mithras (no WC). 911705 –
Chesters; cavalry fort, museum (WC/refresh). Approx. dist. 20 m.

Hotel and Restaurant Recommendations

BRAMPTON

Crosby Lodge

Comfortable restaurant with rooms
Quiet/Gardens/Good value (meals)   ®

Follow my advice to the letter: leave the M6 at its terminus (junc.
44), follow signs for Brampton and, five miles before the town,
put the value-for-money cooking skills of Michael Sedgwick to
the test. 20 starters – matching Sharrow Bay – and delicious
sweets (supervised by the experienced eye of Patricia Sedgwick)
are the highlights of both lunch and dinner. Fresh produce,
particularly fish and shellfish, dominates; it takes enthusiastic
persistence to mastermind menus as varied as these. Bravo
Michael, Patricia and son James, now working alongside dad.
The lodge is a listed 18th-cent. building, with a fine walled garden,
some four-posters and useful family rooms.
menus A (lun) B (din) *rooms* 11 **D-D2** *cards* AE DC
closed Xmas-3rd wk Jan. Rest: Sun evg.
post Crosby-on-Eden, Carlisle, Cumbria CA6 4QZ. (B6264)
phone (0228 73) 618 *Mich* 402 (L19) Newcastle 55 m.

BRAMPTON

Farlam Hall

Comfortable hotel
Quiet/Gardens/Good value (meals)   ®

A picturesque garden - the 'Boggy' Beck plays a part in its natural
appeal – more than compensates for the austere exterior of the
house. The interior is richly furnished and the Quinion family add
that important ingredient of friendly personalities. Mum, Dad
and Helen do the serving; son Barry is the chef. His menus show
off his cordon bleu training: hot fish terrine, *piccata Milanaise*,
good vegetables, a dozen English cheeses and a selection of
'tuck-in' sweets; all of it enjoyable. A good choice of half-bottles
of wine. Be sure to meet Arnold, the 14-year-old with a gammy
leg. Who could that be?
menus B (din/Sun lun) *rooms* 11 **D-D2** *cards* A AE Visa
closed Feb. 1st 2 wks Nov. Mon/Tues (Nov-Jan). Lun (Mon/Sat).
post Brampton, Cumbria CA8 2NG. (3 m. SE on A689)
phone (069 76) 234 *Mich* 402 (L19) Newcastle 47 m.

CANONBIE
Riverside Inn

Simple inn with rooms (S)
Good value (meals) '

The River Esk – a few yards away across the road and beside a tree-lined playing field – is renowned for its sea trout and salmon. Robert and Susan Phillips are renowned, too – no wonder they have won many guide book accolades. Their quiet, good taste reflects in their personalities, cooking and the furnishings. Book ahead: raw materials are fresh and every dish is home cooked; the dining room is small and has few tables. You are offered three or four starters and sweets and a couple of main courses – perhaps pink trout or roast sirloin of beef which looks a picture if ordered rare. Tremendous breakfasts – with a huge choice. The A7 now bypasses the village.
menus **B** (din only) Bar lun *rooms* 6 **D** *cards* Visa
closed 2 wks Jan. Sun.
post Canonbie, Dumfries DG14 0UX.
phone (054 15) 295 *Mich* 402 (L18) Newcastle 74 m.

MELROSE
Hoebridge Inn

Comfortable restaurant (S)

Locals claim Carlo and Joy Campari run the best restaurant in the Scottish Borders. One thing is certain: the Hoebridge is one hundred times better than the 'disaster' I had 24 hours earlier in a nearby town – where the menu, as long as your arm, was no more than a succession of commercially-made products. Here you can go 'Italian' or 'Scottish': a typical choice could be Parma ham and melon or salmon; breast of chicken Sophia Loren or charcoal grills; *coppa Amaretto* or sherry trifle. Stay at the basic Burts Hotel, Melrose – *phone* (089 682) 2285: if you want to get up an appetite you can walk to Gattonside, using a footbridge across the Tweed – allow 15 minutes.
alc **B-C** (dinner only served) *cards* Visa
closed 2 wks Apl and Oct. Xmas. Jan 1. Mon (Oct-April).
post Gattonside, Melrose, Borders. (N bank of River Tweed)
phone (089 682) 3082 *Mich* 402 (L17) Newcastle 70 m.

OTTERBURN
Percy Arms

Comfortable hotel (S)
Gardens/Fishing/Good value (meals)

Carl and Jean Shirley, the new owners, are slowly but surely injecting much needed new life into this long-established hotel. After 30 years in the hotel business (including a spell with Holiday Inns) Carl has returned to the place where he was a kitchen lad! He and his chef are committed to using fresh produce as much as they can, whether it be a Redesdale broth, a *matelote* of salmon and turbot, medallions of local lamb, or in desserts like fresh cherry cake and home-made ice creams. Some bedrooms have been improved tremendously these overlook the garden and the River Rede at the rear. Visit Otterburn Mill – fine tweeds and woollen goods.
menus **B** (din/Sun lun) Bar lun *rooms* 30 **D-D2** *cards* A AE DC Visa
closed Probably Jan.
post Otterburn, Northumberland NE19 1NR.
phone (0830) 20261 *Mich* 402 (N18) Newcastle 31 m.

PEEBLES
Cringletie House

Comfortable hotel (S)
Secluded/Gardens/Tennis/Lift/Good value (meals)   Ⓡ
The small, red sandstone, turreted mansion is renowned locally
for its attractive grounds and walled garden; so, too, are Áileen
Maguire's well-balanced menus. An example could be a choice,
from several alternatives, of melon with an elderflower sorbet –
fresh and cold; a small bowl of consommé; then scallops with
leeks – or sea trout; and finally a selection of enterprising sweets
– one of which may be a Scottish variety. It takes an experienced
hand to have the confidence to keep things simple and not serve
vast portions. The lounge is a fascinating room – with panelled
walls and a painted ceiling.
menus **A** (Sun lun) **B** (din) Bar lun *rooms* 16 **D-D2**
closed Xmas-early Mar.
post Peebles, Borders EH45 8PL. (3 m. N on A703)
phone (072 13) 233 *Mich* 402 (K17) Newcastle 85 m

SEAHOUSES
Olde Ship

Simple inn with rooms (S)
Gardens/Good value (meals)   Ⓡ
Owned by the same family for 75 years, Alan Glen is the third-
generation licensee of this super inn. It's more like a nautical
museum – packed full of unusual exhibits; even the stained-glass
windows are sensibly explained (see ground floor lounge). If you
cannot make the Farne Islands you can still see sea-birds in the
inn – of the stuffed variety! Book ahead as the home-cooking is
popular: you may be able to try 'beef stovies', a 'clootie dumpling'
or a 'Brown Betty'; or alternatively fresh fish, a roast and always a
selection of desserts like bramble tart, plum sponge or
gooseberry crumble – try a glass of Lindisfarne mead with them.
Be sure to explore all the passages, lounges and bars. Craster
kippers, too.
menus **A** (din/Sun lun) Bar lun *rooms* 10 **C-D**
closed Mid Oct-mid Mar.
post Seahouses, Northumberland NE68 7RD.
phone (0665) 720200 *Mich* 402 (P17) Newcastle 46 m.

SELKIRK
Philipburn House

Comfortable hotel (S)
Quiet/Gardens/Swimming pool/Good value (meals)   Ⓡ
How I wish all hoteliers enjoyed their work just half as much as
Jim and Anne Hall, the owners of this happy hotel. Children will
adore the heated pool, the covered trampoline and the gardens;
adults will love the nearby rivers, fishing, golf and numerous
walks (try to win the 'Plodders' Tie'). Much of the cosy feeling
comes from the extensive, Austrian-style use of wood – at its best
in the poolside restaurant. Jim, an ex-architect, is a self-taught
chef: he uses Scottish produce well – smoked salmon and oysters
from John Noble, salmon and trout from the Ettrick and Mull
giant prawns are examples.
menus **A-B** *rooms* 16 **D-D2** *cards* A AE DC Visa
closed Jan.
post Selkirk, Borders TD7 5LS. (W of town – junc. A707/A708)
phone (0750) 20747 *Mich* 402 (L17) Newcastle 63 m.

CHILTERNS

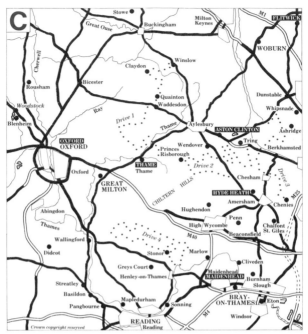

My favourite woods are near my home – the beech woods of the
Chiltern Hills. Each autumn, for perhaps no more than a week,
the heart beats faster as they put on their glittering display; how
sad that it comes just once a year. Every few years the spectacle
is breathtaking. So it was at the end of October 1983 when, during
a few days of brilliant sunshine, all of us who live in the Chilterns
were able to feast our eyes on a palette of glowing golds, coppers,
reds and browns.

But the Chiltern Hills deserve your time and attention during
all the seasons of the year. There are many good reasons why you
should seek them out: the glorious wooded hills; along their
southern and western borders is arguably some of the finest river
country in England; a rich heritage of historic man-made
treasures; many fine gardens; and, as a bonus, some of Britain's
best restaurants are concentrated in the area.

Consider Nature's treats first. The most renowned of the beech
woods is **Burnham** Beeches – easily reached, they lie between
the **M4** and **M40**, north of **Slough**. But I would head for the higher
ground on the northern escarpment of the Chilterns; to the
countryside behind Coombe Hill and Whiteleaf Hill – between
Wendover and **Princes Risborough**. Enjoy the extensive views
from the heights but then explore the mass of lanes that lead
southwards into the beech woods. The same advice applies to the
terrain east of Wendover; Aston Hill is another fine viewpoint
and explore the adjacent Wendover Woods, a Forestry
Commission property with marked trails. Beyond **Tring** is
Ashridge – another extensive area of attractive woodland. Much
of the best country lying along the escarpment can be enjoyed by
both serious and less-dedicated walkers who use the Ridgeway –

considered the oldest path in Britain. It starts its 85 mile journey west of Marlborough in Wiltshire and finishes at **Ivinghoe** Beacon, just north of Ashridge (Beacon Hill on OS maps).

The **Thames** provides an enchanting contrast to the gentle hills on its northern banks. From **Windsor** to **Oxford** every mile of the way is full of interest – whether you hire one of the hundreds of craft that ply its waters, walk its banks, or use a car to take you along the riverside roads. Windsor is a must – the castle and park have entertained my family on many occasions; **Eton**, too, is famous enough; Dorney Court, a Tudor manor house and gardens, is to the west of Eton; and **Cliveden** House, in a commanding position high above the Thames, is renowned for its gardens (it will soon be a hotel). Beyond Cliveden and upstream to **Henley** the river is at its most alluring. **Marlow** and its weir is a treat – but head up the many lanes to the north into superb wooded hills. In those hills is the magnificent **Stonor** House and Deer Park – and to the west of Henley is **Greys Court** with its own renowned gardens.

Sonning comes next – an idyllic setting; further upstream, beyond **Reading**, is **Mapledurham** House, Country Park and 15th-century flour mill; at **Pangbourne** there's a lock, weir and toll bridge; and **Basildon** House is a Georgian estate surrounded by a park and woodland. A few miles north – at **Streatley** – is the Goring Gap, where the Thames separates the Chilterns from the Berkshire Downs. At **Wallingford** there's a 900-ft-long bridge spanning the river and, at **Abingdon**, there's much to interest visitors in the riverside town. Finally, you reach **Oxford** – a treasure-chest of pleasures: the colleges will appeal, of course – but be sure to see the Ashmolean Museum; the Bodleian Library; and the Botanical Gardens – alongside the River **Cherwell**.

American visitors will want to search out 'Penn' country: the parish church at **Penn**; Old Jordans, to the south-east, the 17th-century farm where William Penn and the Quakers held meetings; the Mayflower Barn; and the Meeting House. Detour to Milton's Cottage at **Chalfont St. Giles** and to old **Amersham** with its ancient High St houses – No.49 will soon be a museum.

Lovers of great houses are thoroughly spoilt: to the north of Oxford is the huge **Blenheim** Palace with fine gardens and a vast park; north of **High Wycombe** is **Hughendon** Manor – once the home of Disraeli; north-west of **Aylesbury** is **Waddesdon** Manor and its superb interior – a personal favourite; to the north of the latter is the 17th-century **Claydon** House and, nearby, **Winslow** Hall and gardens; near the **M1** is the famous **Woburn** Abbey with a huge deer park; and, finally, small **Chenies** Manor – not so famous and east of Amersham, above the pretty Chess Valley.

Children will be enthralled by **Whipsnade** Park Zoo, near Dunstable, and the model village at Bekonscot in **Beaconsfield**. Garden lovers will head for the incomparable Saville/Valley Gardens in Windsor Great Park; Ashridge House Gardens at Ashridge; the gardens and caves at West Wycombe Park, High Wycombe; **Stowe** School Gardens, north of **Buckingham**; and **Rousham** Garden, north of Blenheim. Museum fans must not bypass the Wycombe Chair Museum; and railway buffs should detour to both **Didcot** and **Quainton** – the homes of so many preserved steam engines. Bird lovers should not miss the National Nature Reserve at the Tring reservoirs.

OS Landranger maps: 164.165.175.176
OS Routemaster map 9. Michelin map 404
Airport: London Heathrow
Distance from London – High Wycombe 34 miles.

Recommended Drives

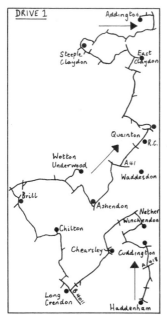

Drive 1 map 165

North Bucks: villages and many unexpected views in the largely ignored Vale of Aylesbury.

Start at Haddenham Church (742080). N to Cuddington. Nether Winchendon from SW. At 731120 walk to River Thame. S thru 7111 to Chearsley. Long Crendon – use B4011. Chilton. Brill from SE. Windmill & views at 653143. Detour to Wotton Underwood Church (688159). Ashendon from NW. Westcott. A41. Detour to Waddesdon Manor if time allows. Steam buffs will enjoy Quainton Railway Centre (737190). Quainton Windmill (746202). East Claydon. Middle Claydon – Claydon House & Park. Steeple Claydon. Loop via North End & Verney Junction to Addington. Detour at 748287 to Addington Church. Approx. dist. 40 m. Attractions nearby are Winslow Hall in Winslow to the east (on A413) and Stowe School Gardens (N of Buckingham).

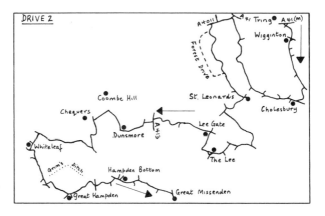

Drive 2 map 165

Bucks at its best: beech woods, hills and many pubs to tempt you! Try it in the autumn.

Start at 936110. Wigginton. Past Champneys Health Resort. 944070. Cholesbury. N thru 9008. A4011. S at 887108. Within 300 yards turn right off 'yellow' road into Wendover Woods – nature trails, views. Exit from woods at 898084. S to St. Leonards. SE thru 9105. The Lee (900043). Lee Gate. Cross A413. Dunsmore. At 852063 use your legs – Coombe Hill views. S thru 8405. Chequers on your right – country home of our prime ministers. W thru 8304. SE thru 8203. Great Hampden. At 852022 walk NW to Grim's Ditch. Hampden Bottom. Gt. Missenden. Approx. dist. 31 m.

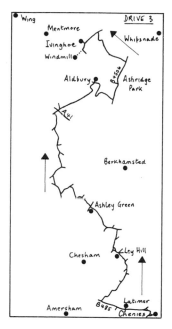

Drive 3 map 165

Valleys and woods in commuter land – and a chance to use your legs, too.

Start at 979996. At bluebell time walk SW up hill, under railway, into woods. Detour SE along B485 to Latimer and Chenies with its fine Manor House and gardens. Back to start! Past Blackwell Hall to Ley Hill. B4505. At 983035 take care – new junction. Ashley Green. 960065. 954070. N thru 9508. Fine views. Aldbury. Thru woods to 977117. B4506 N and then NW thru 9714. More views– use your legs to climb Ivinghoe Beacon (Beacon Hill). Finish at Windmill (945157). Approx. dist. 25 m. Children? You will have seen the famous White Lion to the east from Ivinghoe Beacon – take the family to Whipsnade Park Zoo (east edge map). Adults will want to see famous Mentmore – NW of Ivinghoe; and Ascott House at Wing.

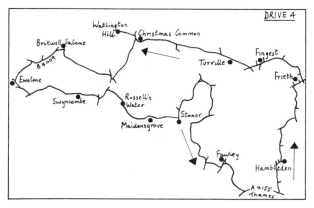

Drive 4 map 175

Start and finish in the loveliest stretch of the Thames: in between enjoy the Chilterns – woods, views, churches, splendid pubs, many walks, attractive 'brick and flint' cottages and a surprise 11th-cent. church.

Start at 785850 – but first explore mill and weir (park ¼ m. to N). Hambleden Church. 784880. Parmoor. 800904 from W. Fingest. Turville. Christmas Common. Detour Watlington Hill – views (use car park). SW thru 7091. NW to Britwell Salome. Ewelme Church. Walks and views at 666914. 11th-cent. St. Botolph's Church at 683903. Maidensgrove. Stonor Ho. N thru 7490. S thru 7487. Fawley Church. Finish A4155 (7685). Approx. dist. 32 m.

Hotel and Restaurant Recommendations

ASTON CLINTON
Bell Inn

Very comfortable hotel
Gardens
®

I would guess Anne and I have visited the Bell 20 times since 1970; then it was the only restaurant in the area that came close to matching the best French standards. It's a sign of changing times in culinary Britain that it now takes second place to other brighter stars in the Chilterns. Nevertheless, there remain many reasons for visiting Michael and Patsy Harris at their old family coaching inn: a sense of occasion – in a stylish English dining room; unchanging classic and international cooking; a superb cellar – over 500 wines; alluring, rose-perfumed gardens; splendid bedrooms off the flower-bedecked courtyard; and Hugo – for me Britain's best *maître d'hôtel*.

alc **C-D** *rooms* 21 **D2-D4** *cards* A Visa
closed Sun evg (Oct-Mar) and Mon to non-residents.
post Aston Clinton, Aylesbury, Bucks HP22 5HP.
phone (0296) 630252 *Mich* 404 (R28) High Wycombe 16 m.

BRAY-ON-THAMES
Waterside Inn

Luxury restaurant/Michelin ★★

Michel Roux: you either love him or hate him! That seems to sum up the views of my readers and leading guides. *The GFG* is not exactly kind; Ronay puts him on the same pedestal as Girardet and Wynants; as usual, Michelin, for me, gets it just right. Like them I raise my hat to skill – whether it be the kitchen *équipe* or the professional care of the dining room staff. Of the main courses on the *menu exceptionnel* I enjoyed *canon d'agneau Germain* (created by Christian – see *FL3*, page 229), a sorbet served in a pastry 'shuttlecock' and a *tarte au citron et délice cassis* with its sugar 'buttonhole'. The best time to enjoy the Waterside, shaded by the umbrella of a massive willow tree, is at lunch. Not surprisingly – considering my record with 'famous' chefs – Michel was absent on my '84 visit.

menus **D** *alc* **D** *cards* A AE DC Visa
closed Xmas-Jan. Mon. Tues lun. Sun din (Nov-Easter). Bk hols.
post Ferry Rd, Bray-on-Thames, Bucks SL6 2AT.
phone (0628) 20691 *Mich* 404 (R29) High Wycombe 7 m.

FLITWICK
Flitwick Manor

Very comfortable restaurant with rooms
Quiet/Gardens/Tennis/Good value (meals)
®

July 1984 saw Somerset and Hélène Moore fulfil a life-long ambition – they made the move from the well-established White Hart at Flitton to their own newly-purchased Queen Anne mansion, set in gorgeous grounds amid some of the finest trees in Bedfordshire. Anne and I visited during their opening week. You should seek out Somerset, the chef, for another reason; his magnificent offerings of fish and shellfish – particularly the latter. To find such fresh produce in the middle of England is amazing – his loyal fish suppliers give him fantastic support.

menus **B** *rooms* 6 **D2-D4** *cards* A AE DC Visa
closed Sun evg to non-residents
post Flitwick, Bedfordshire MK45 1AE. (S ent. to village)
phone (0525) 712242 *Mich* 404 (S27) High Wycombe 37 m.

GREAT MILTON
Le Manoir aux Quat'Saisons
Luxury hotel/Michelin ★★
Quiet/Gardens/Swimming pool/Tennis
BEST MEAL IN 84 Ⓡ

In my opinion the most talented UK-based chef is found here at Gt. Milton – French-born Raymond Blanc, a 35-year-old, pencil-thin, effervescent genius of a cook who I believe could become one of the great chefs of our time.

Anne and I first had the privilege of meeting Raymond and Jenny Blanc a year or two after they opened their minuscule 'bistro' in Oxford's Summertown in July 1977 (see next page – Le Petit Blanc). We have thrilled at Raymond's prodigious progress: self-taught, he has developed, polished, honed and re-polished a unique personal style – the epitome of *cuisine moderne*.

1984 – ten years after they were married – saw them jump the mind-blowing financial hurdle of opening a newly-purchased, completely refitted-out, 15th-century manor house. Unlike Wynants, Girardet and Robuchon – who have relatively simple restaurants – they have chosen to go along the luxury hotel road of three-star French couples like the Guérards, Boyers, Vergés, Meneaus and Georges and Jacqueline Blanc – described by one *FL3* reader as 'the culinary counterparts of *Gucci e tutti quanti.*'

With the help of a £95,000 Government grant and awesome Mont Blanc-sized borrowings it is already a flourishing, foreign currency-earning business; with over 50 employees at Le Manoir that £2,000 per head grant was a real taxpayers' bargain. I utterly deplore the sour 'digs' made throughout '84 by the right-wing national press about the grant – fed to them I would guess by a short-sighted journalist mole based in Oxford.

Like Frédy Girardet – whom he may possibly one day join on the dizzy summit of culinary supremacy – Raymond has the essential mixture of talents needed for greatness: an eagle's eye for detail; good taste; explosive, creative skill; and unquenchable ambition – an essential prerequisite Jenny shares with him. Unlike Frédy, youthful exuberance very occasionally leads to over-elaboration. Years ago, before he won his second star, I wrote that Raymond would become a three-star chef before he was 40 – a club that has few members; with five years to go he'll make it easily. Painfully expensive it all is – but then it should be. If the pennies count why not try a weekday lunch (band **C**)?

menus **C-D** (lun) *alc* **D** *rooms* 10 **D3-D6** *cards* A AE DC Visa
closed Xmas-Jan. Sun evg and Mon to non-residents.
post Great Milton, Oxon OX9 7PD. (M40-junc. 7; W-2nd turn rt)
phone (084 46) 8881 or 230 *Mich* 404 (Q28) High Wycombe 19 m.

HYDE HEATH
Plough

Very simple inn (S)
Good value Ⓡ

One of the best examples I know in Britain of just what 'pub grub' means – in this case conjured up by the talented Sandra Willcocks and her team. Consider these: three dozen snacks and main dishes – including prawns, whitebait, beef, venison, swordfish, fish and chips and goodness knows what else; ten 'dips'; 15 salads and vegetables; and three breads.

alc **£1-£5** (No restaurant – bar meals only)
closed Sun evg. Christmas Day.
post Hyde Heath, Amersham, Bucks. (2 m. NW – 165-930003)
phone (0494) 783163 *Mich* 404 (S28) High Wycombe 9 m.

MAIDENHEAD
Fredrick's

Very comfortable restaurant-hotel
Gardens

If you're a businessman faced with the wretched prospect of an overnight stay near Heathrow then stop fretting; here's the ideal place for you. On a midweek evening visit three-quarters of the clients were expense-account diners, enjoying the enterprising formula shaped by the owner, Fredrik Lösel, and 35-year-old chef, Chris Cleveland – both ex-Sheraton employees. Attention to detail, skilled service, extensive choice, good appetisers and bread are highlights. Average sweets and some courses where meat and fish are combined are less successful.

menus C (lun) D (din) *rooms* 30 D2-D4 *cards* A AE DC Visa
closed Rest: Sat lunch.
post Shoppenhangers Rd, Maidenhead SL6 2PZ. (Nr Stat. & A423)
phone (0628) 35934 or 24737 *Mich* 404 (R29) High Wycombe 8 m.

OXFORD
Elizabeth

Comfortable restaurant/Michelin ⋆
Good value (lunch – Tues-Sat)

This is where 'Paul Spencer' should head for (see p.17): a typical Michelin one-star French restaurant of two decades ago; then there were hundreds of them in France – serving classical dishes of the *quenelles de saumon sauce Nantua, escargots à la Bourguignonne, Châteaubriand* variety. PS would feel at home here – there's even an 'Alice in Wonderland' lounge. Give credit where it's due: I respect traditional skills applied to old-fashioned classics, served in an old-fashioned dining room – it seems so appropriate in Oxford. But thank heavens the culinary clock has not stood still – see below.

menus B (lun: Tues-Sat) *alc* C-D cards A AE DC Visa
closed Good Friday. 1 wk Xmas. Mon.
post 84 St. Aldates, Oxford OX1 1RA.
phone (0865) 242230 *Mich* 404 (Q28) High Wycombe 26 m.

OXFORD
Le Petit Blanc
BEST
MEAL,
Comfortable restaurant
Good value (lunch)
IN 84 Ⓡ

Tourists, using a 1983 guide book, could visit 272 Banbury Rd quite certain it was the home of the great Raymond Blanc. They would not be disappointed. The Blancs have moved on to their 15th-century manor at Gt. Milton (see previous page); they still own Le Petit Blanc and have left it in the capable hands of chef John Burton-Race and his wife Christine – from the Touraine in France – who looks after the small dining room with quiet, unassuming grace. A Gt. Milton visit may well be well beyond the means of most readers; but, shed no tears, the young *équipe* here will seduce you just as much – for **half** the price. John, now 26, has learned well from his mentor, Raymond – and from his sojourn at Chewton Glen. Yes, it's category 3 – and I'll bet now that a Michelin **M** accolade is not far away.

menus B (lun) C (din) *cards* A Visa (Rooms? Speak to Christine)
closed Last wk Aug. 1st wk Sept. 2 wks Jan. Dec 25. Sun. Mon lun.
post 272 Banbury Rd, Summertown, Oxford OX2 7DY. (A4165)
phone (0865) 53540 *Mich* 404 (Q28) High Wycombe 26 m.

READING

Milton Sandford

Very comfortable restaurant/Michelin ★
Gardens/Good value (lunch)   ℝ

Richard Sandford learns fast. In his early thirties, he opened his restaurant just five years ago – it was the Victorian vicarage at Shinfield, 4½ m. south of Reading on the A327 (off the main road, by the church). Yet in that time he has put to effective use more good taste than most chefs do in a lifetime. You see it at every stage of a meal: the appetisers; the personalised, light specialities – which follow no particular style; and the *petits fours* are a few examples. His wines are a good-value choice – ask to see his special Burgundy list. The food looks as good as it tastes: quail eggs, roast sucking pig – with a crisp 'scratchings-like' crust – and marinaded duck are delicious.
menus **B** (lun) **C** (din) *cards* A AE DC Visa (Rooms? Ask rest.)
closed Xmas-Jan 1. 2 wks July-Aug. Sat (lun). Sun. Bank hols.
post Church Lane, Shinfield, Reading, Berks RG2 9BY.
phone (0734) 883783 *Mich* 404 (Q29) High Wycombe 21 m.

THAME

Thatchers

Simple restaurant with rooms
Good value (meals – Tues-Fri)   ℝ

Jeremy O'Connor is living proof of how a chef can dramatically change his culinary outlook practically overnight. Three years ago, at 28, Jeremy had had enough of dishing up 'veal cordon bleu, frozen veg and the like.' He resigned his job, sold his house and off he went to France – prepared to work for nothing alongside talented, skilled cooks. Today he's both a different man and chef: enthusiasm, long hours of hard work, a library of notes and books, endless experiments, annual return trips to work with other French *cuisiniers* and a new, friendly boss – it's a combination of sparkling facets. Seek out the young man – still busy polishing his newly-found passion in life. But Thatchers, put better lighting in the dining room, please.
menus **B** (not Sat) *alc* **B-C** *rooms* 6 **D-D2** *cards* A Visa
closed Sun. Mon and Sat (lunch).
post Lower High St, Thame, Oxon OX9 2AA.
phone (084 421) 2146 *Mich* 404 (R28) High Wycombe 19 m.

WOBURN

Paris House

Comfortable restaurant/Michelin ★

Take care as you enter Woburn Park: you're likely to encounter numerous deer as you drive to the reproduction 'folly', built in 1878 and now the expensive restaurant home of 31-year-old Peter Chandler – the first Englishman to be 'sponsored' by the Roux brothers. His style is Roux-dominated – but perhaps not so rich: a *feuilleté de langues d'agneau et champignons sauvages* and a *hure de saumon* are masterly. Peter: drop the all-French menu (with its spelling errors); forget the addictive Roux 'tomato' rose (it appears with everything); throw the artificial flowers away; and install more lighting.
menus **D** *alc* **D** *cards* A AE DC Visa (Rooms? Bedford Arms, Woburn)
closed Feb. Mon. Sun evg (Oct-Mar).
post Woburn Park, Woburn, Beds MK17 9QP. (B528 – S Woburn)
phone (052 525) 692 *Mich* 404 (S28) High Wycombe 36 m.

COTSWOLDS

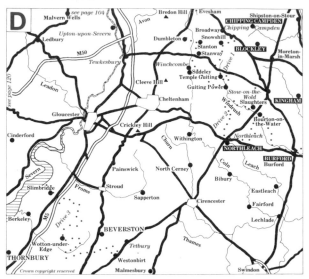

My family fell in love with the gentle, green hills of the Cotswolds long ago. So it came as no surprise to us, during recent years, when two sets of friends decided to make their retirement homes in the area. Both couples are active folk and have travelled widely throughout the world. For them, and for many of us who adore the area, the Cotswolds is an unspoilt corner of England. Why does it have such a special charm?

It's a combination of factors. One is the exclusive use in all building work of the honey-coloured limestone that lies under the ground; the stone has a mellow, soothing appearance and blends perfectly with the pastoral background. The architectural heritage that tourists admire today was created centuries ago when Cotswolds wool made the area amazingly prosperous. That wealth was shown off by the merchants of the day in the hundreds of fine houses and glorious 'wool' churches that grace so many villages and towns. The word 'Cotswolds' is derived from 'cot' – a Saxon word for sheepfolds – and 'wolds' – meaning high ground. Nature's handiwork and man's skills have blended together more alluringly in these hills than perhaps anywhere else in the British Isles. It's a contented marriage.

To demonstrate what I mean seek out the tranquil valley of the River **Windrush**. Near its source is Ford, a minute hamlet; further downstream are the villages of **Temple Guiting** and **Guiting Power**; then the **Slaughters** – Upper and Lower – in the valley of the Eye, a tiny tributary of the Windrush; next comes famous **Bourton-on-the-Water** – it sits astride the gentle waters of the river; and finally **Burford** – a handsome town. Has the Cotswolds magic started to work?

Other streams match the allure of the Windrush. Consider the River **Churn**: the village of **North Cerney** is one of many – its small church a gem; further downstream is **Cirencester**, one of my favourite market towns – it was Britain's second Roman city and the Corinium Museum has one of England's best collections of Roman remains. The River **Coln** is another example: the villages of **Withington** and **Bibury** are both delightful; and further downstream there's a splendid example of a 'wool' church at **Fairford**. Or it may be the River **Leach** that will capture your heart most: one of the most famous 'wool' churches is at **Northleach**, near the river's source; downstream, at **Eastleach**, a clapper bridge over the stream joins together the two hamlets that combine to form the village.

The many dozens of beguiling villages and towns in the Cotswolds have always held a great attraction for me; no more so than the twin villages of **Stanway** and **Stanton** – nestling under the western edge of the hills and looking across to the rounded, wooded **Dumbleton** Hill. More famous ones include picture-postcard pretty **Broadway** – a 'honeypot' tourist trap; **Chipping Campden** – once a prosperous 'wool' town; and **Moreton-in-Marsh** and **Stow-on-the-Wold** – both on the Roman Fosse Way. Near these six villages and towns are several fine man-made diversions: **Sudeley** Castle and Gardens is perhaps the most remarkable – a Tudor house with Elizabethan gardens; the ruins of Hailes Abbey, also near **Winchcombe; Snowshill** Manor – a 17th-century house three miles south of Broadway in a flower-filled hamlet; and the early 17th-century Chastleton House, south-east of Moreton-in-Marsh.

The western escarpment of the Cotswolds provides many fine viewpoints – views that stretch across the Vale of Severn: **Bredon Hill** requires you to walk to the top if you want to enjoy the 360 degree panorama from its summit; from Broadway Hill there's the magnificent sight of the Vale of Evesham to the north; Salter's Hill and **Cleeve Hill** sit astride Winchombe; Leckhampton Hill, **Crickley Hill** – a Neolithic hill fort and the site, in '84, of archaeology's most exciting new finds; Birdlip Hill and Haresfield Beacon are to the east and south of **Gloucester**.

Towards the southern end of the escarpment is a small ring of unusual terrain. Encircling **Wotton-under-Edge**, it's known as The Bottoms – a mixture of hills and valleys bypassed by all the rushing motorists on the M5 and A38 to the west (see drive 3). Further north, Stroud dominates the valley of the **Frome**; head upstream into Golden Valley and then north-east to the wooded landscape surrounding the village of **Sapperton** and the Duntisbournes – all reflect the Cotswolds charm.

There are many other diversions: the quite exceptional Wildfowl Trust at **Slimbridge** on the River **Severn** – a thrill for all bird lovers; the incomparable **Westonbirt** Arboretum, south-west of **Tetbury** – try to go in October; **Berkeley** Castle – where Edward II is said to have met his death; ancient Gloucester and its breathtaking cathedral; **Cheltenham** – an elegant, Georgian spa and a captivating garden town; Batsford Park Arboretum, north-west of Moreton; nearby Sezincote Gardens; two magnificent houses and gardens near Chipping Campden – Hidcote Manor and Kiftsgate Court; Chedworth Roman Villa in Chedworth Woods, south-west of Northleach; the Whitcombe Roman Villa at Brockworth – at the foot of Crickley Hill, outside Gloucester; the Cotswold Farm Park – near Guiting Power; and, finally, the Wild Life Park – two miles south of Burford.

Further afield, off the bottom edge of the map, is Bath – which, together with Edinburgh and York, is one of my favourite British cities. It has many treasures to entice you – and, as a bonus, several fine restaurants (see pages 135/136).

OS Landranger maps: 150.151.162.163
OS Routemaster map 7. Michelin map 404
Airports: Birmingham. London.
Distance from London – Gloucester 105 miles.

Recommended Drives

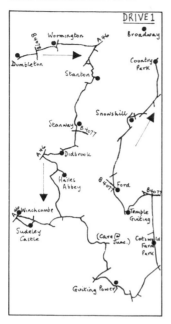

Drive 1 maps 150/163
Honey-coloured stone villages and extensive views.
Start 150-0135; Dumbleton Church – fine walk SW to 0035. E thru Wormington. Explore Stanton (0634) and Stanway – visit House (open Wed/Sun summer). SE thru 0430 to ruined Hailes Abbey and adjoining museum. S thru 0428 – views. Map 163. Detour Sudeley Castle (ent. in Winchcombe on A46). Return E thru 0527. At 062278 ignore 'Unsuitable' sign. SE to 084258. Guiting Power – note mem. to Sally Cochrane and her connection with Amersham. N thru 115266; ent. Cotswold Farm Park (rare farm animals); ideal for children and parents alike! Temple Guiting. Map 150. Picture postcard attractive Snowshill – and its Manor (0933); visit latter – owned by Nat. Trust. Finish 113360 – Country Park. Visit Broadway later. Approx. dist. 32 m.

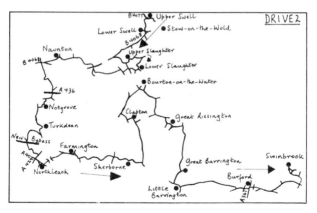

Drive 2 map 163 *The Swells, The Slaughters, The Rissingtons, The Barringtons – the most evocative of English village names.*
Start Upper Swell (1726). S thru Lower Swell. B4068. In 1423 SE to Upper Slaughter. E & S thru 1623 to Lower Slaughter – so pretty. 152226 from NE. W thru 1322. 120235 to Naunton – see church. Notgrove. Turkdean. At 097163 over new bypass. Hampnett. X-rds A40/A429 Mus. of Rural Life. Northleach – see church. Farmington. Sherborne (1714). N to Bourton-on-the-Water – a 'honeypot'; if you find space among the human 'swarms' visit Model Village and Bird Garden. Great Rissington. Little Barrington. E thru 2213. Burford. E thru 2711. Finish Swinbrook – Nancy and Unity Mitford buried in churchyard (see other tombs in church) Approx. dist. 40 m.

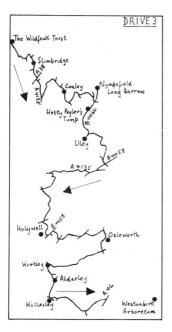

Drive 3 map 162
*Man and Nature combine well.
Enjoy 'big-dipper' Bottoms!*
Start at The Wildfowl Trust,
Slimbridge – ornithologist or
not it is a must for every reader;
also the home of Sir Peter Scott,
its founder. SE to A38. A4135.
NE thru 7502. SE thru Coaley. E
thru 7801. At 795014 (B4066):
extensive views of Severn
Valley and Wales; Nature
Reserve; and Nympsfield Long
Barrow (chambered tomb from
4,500 years ago) – see
explanation at N end of car park
near toilets. S on B4066. At
793000; Uley Tumulus (Hetty
Pegler's Tump – a covered
version of ancient Cotswold
tombs). SE thru 7998. B4058. W
on A4135. Care turn at 767967
(no signpost). S thru 7695.
Holywell. E thru 7793. S thru
7993. W thru 7791. SE thru 7889.
Finish A46. Approx. dist. 28 m.
Now detour to For. Comm's
Westonbirt Arboretum (8489) –
another must.

Hotel and Restaurant Recommendations
BEVERSTON
Calcot Manor

Very comfortable hotel
Quiet/Gardens/Swimming pool/Good value (lunch)   Ⓡ
Brian and Barbara Ball, and their son Richard, opened the doors
of Calcot Manor in August '84 – just ten months after taking the
mind-numbing decision to sell their Amersham home to create,
from scratch, their own country house hotel. Brian had run BP's
catering services; Richard was a college-trained hotelier. But like
all their friends, we were apprehensive initially; our fears were
groundless – their efforts in converting an old farmhouse have
succeeded magnificently. Barbara, helped by daughter Alison
and son-in-law Peter, an architect, have worked wonders in
complementing the old character of the house with eye-catching,
tasteful furnishings and the most modern of fittings.
Redmond Hayward, the talented 30-year-old chef, has also
deserted London and with the rejuvenating tonic of fresh country
air has made an impressive start – our meal was much the best
we had in the Cotswolds. Light, modern pleasures like a calves'
liver mousse quiche, marinated scallops with lime and ginger,
succulent local lamb, coffee parfait with a hazelnut sauce and
perfect soufflés – passion fruit is one example – are likely to win
many friends. Even if you have the most limited of budgets,
ensure you don't miss a real value-for-money lunch.
menus A (lun) C (din) *rooms* 7 **D-D4** *cards* A AE DC Visa
closed Open all the year. (Junc. A46/A4135 – 3½ m. W Tetbury)
post Calcot Manor, Beverston, Tetbury, Glos GL8 8YJ.
phone (066 689) 355 or 227 *Mich* 404 (N29) Gloucester 16 m.

BLOCKLEY
Lower Brook House

Comfortable restaurant with rooms (S)
Quiet/Gardens/Good value (meals)

Blockley appeals; in a quiet valley setting, the centuries-old village was once famous for its silk trade. Lower Brook House has an equally quiet appeal; 300 years old with a small, terraced garden – its toes in the infant Blockley Brook, always gurgling no matter how dry the weather. Once there were 12 mills in the village depending on that reliable power source; walk the High St and find Russell Spring. Ewan Wright's kitchen team tread a safe, competent path: baked eggs and quiche are the sort of things on the simple lunch menu; lamb with thyme, guinea fowl with lovage and pork with apricots and brandy is the type of fare available at dinner. Tasty home-made desserts.

menus A (lun) B (din) *rooms* 8 D-D2 *cards* A
closed Mid-end Jan.
post Lower St, Blockley, Moreton-in-Marsh, Glos GL56 9DS.
phone (0386) 700286 *Mich* 404 (O27) Gloucester 29 m.

BURFORD
The Lamb Inn

Comfortable hotel (S)
Gardens

Burford is one of my favourite small English towns – for me it's the most endearing in the Cotswolds. Some of its charm comes from the broad High St, fortunate in having a steepish slope as it falls northwards to cross the Windrush; the meandering stream is at its best near the town. Many flower-bedecked lanes and alleys lead off the High St – you'll find the 14th-century Lamb up one of them. Its walled garden is a rewarding, eye-pleasing bonus – so cool on a warm summer evening and complementing perfectly the timeless style of the ancient English inn. Cooking is adequate and entirely straightforward – no more.

menus A-B Bar lun *rooms* 14 C-D2
closed Open all the year.
post Sheep St, Burford, Oxon OX8 4LR.
phone (099 382) 3155 *Mich* 404 (P28) Gloucester 32 m.

CHIPPING CAMPDEN
Kings Arms

Simple hotel (S)
Gardens/Good value (meals)

Chipping Campden has always been a family favourite; it's not such a 'honeypot' as Broadway. It has character and a working, bustling feel about it. So it is with this old inn – between the 'island houses' in the main street. Rosemary Willmott looks all over the globe for inspiration: examples are spicy *samosas* (much too crispy), *taramosalata*, frog's legs with parsley butter, garlic and prawns and enterprising *crudités*. Most dishes are personal interpretations of English classics: beef Wellington, Dover sole, lamb and duckling are among many on the wide-choice menu. Cherry and cherry brandy ice cream was home-made; 'French sorbets', alas, were not.

menus B (din-Sun lun) Bar lun *rooms* 14 C-D2 *cards* A AE DC Visa
closed Jan-Feb (except weekends).
post The Square, Chipping Campden, Glos GL55 6AW.
phone (0386) 840256 *Mich* 404 (O27) Gloucester 30 m.

KINGHAM   The Mill

Comfortable hotel (S)
Quiet/Gardens/Good value (meals)   ®

What a success John and Valerie Barnett have made of The Mill's metamorphosis during the last six years. Dating from Norman times, the present building has been skilfully extended and modernised yet retains much old world charm. It's an exceptionally attractive hotel – off the beaten track but close to all the tourist sites. No wonder satisfied clients return – the formula is near perfect: ideal hosts, assisted by old friends Frank and Betty; a capable chef, John Beach, who uses first-rate, fresh produce; young, helpful staff; and Charlie – who says 'Merry Christmas' 14 times over! Who can that be?
menus A *rooms* 20 D *cards* A AE DC Visa
closed Open all year.
post Kingham, Oxfordshire OX7 6UH.
phone (060 871) 8188 *Mich* 404 (P28) Gloucester 32 m.

NORTHLEACH   Country Friends

Simple restaurant (S)
Good value

How Northleach changed for the better in August '84: a welcome bypass was opened. Peter and Beryl Mardon are the new, friendly owners at this homely restaurant with its tiny, flower-filled patio and stone-wall dining room. Beryl, a self-taught chef, cooks simply but with her heart; like Anne, she's a fan of Marika Hanbury Tenison, that gifted cookery writer who, alas, passed away a year or so ago at the peak of her talented short life. Home-made fare at modest cost – ideal for those with small budgets and simple tastes. Don't miss the church.
menus A (Sun lun) *alc* A-B (din) (Rooms? Speak to the Mardons)
closed Sun evg. Mon. Lunch-except Sun.
post Market Place, Northleach, Glos.
phone (045 16) 421 *Mich* 404 (O28) Gloucester 22 m.

THORNBURY   Thornbury Castle

Very comfortable hotel
Quiet/Gardens   ®

The first seeds of what is now a flourishing, rapidly-growing British culinary 'tree' were sown 30 years or so ago by a handful of chefs: Kenneth Bell was one of them. I first enjoyed his skills in the early 60s at the Elizabeth in Oxford. Today he's the justifiably proud owner of one of England's most appealing hotels – a 16th-century Tudor castle. The 11 magnificent bedrooms have been available to clients for only three years; and since the start of 1984 Kenneth has handed over the kitchen to Timothy Cheevers, an Army-trained chef, who wins a category 3 rating by a hair's-breadth – with Kenneth's help he'll improve further. Varied specialities are complemented by a formidable wine list: there are scores of half-bottles; over 50 bottles priced under £10; and a home-produced Mueller Thurgau!
menus C (lun) *alc* C-D *rooms* 11 D2-D5 *cards* A AE DC Visa
closed Christmas. (By parish church of St. Mary the Virgin)
post Castle St, Thornbury, Bristol, Avon BS12 1HH.
phone (0454) 412647 *Mich* 404 (M29) Gloucester 23 m.

DERBYSHIRE DALES

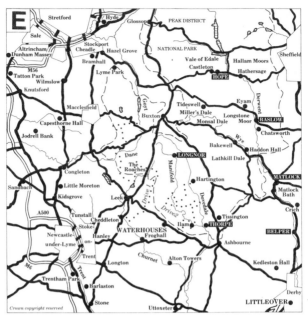

Crown copyright reserved

Why do so many folk turn their backs on this pleasing part of inland Britain? I have called it the Derbyshire Dales; though I have extended the boundaries to the west and south to include corners of Cheshire and Staffordshire. But the heart of the area is the limestone hills and the river valleys that give the landscape such a special character; much of it is named the 'White Peak' – at its best in spring and autumn.

Much of the area is part of the **Peak District National Park** – the first of its kind when it was founded in 1951. The highest and wildest moors rise to just over 2000 ft above sea-level; dozens of roads bisect the windswept moorlands – nearly all of them lined with drystone walls. In the depths of the night – in midwinter's fog and rain – rally navigating is always difficult when trying to find turns in those dark limestone walls.

The dales themselves are among England's finest. Some are famous: **Dovedale**, north of **Ashbourne**, is surely the most appealing; **Miller's Dale** and **Monsal Dale** – both part of the River **Wye** – are east of **Buxton** (views from 119-1871); the **Manifold** Valley – it joins the Dove near **Ilam**; the **Goyt** Valley, north-west of Buxton; and **Lathkill Dale**, south of **Bakewell**. Use your legs to see them at their best. Other dales have a wilder aspect: seek out the **Hope** Valley with its caves and, to the north, the **Vale of Edale** – where hedges largely replace walls.

Combine your walking with drives across the best of the moorlands: the circuit of **The Roaches** – a battlement-shaped gritstone ridge of rocks north of **Leek**; and **Longstone Moor** – east of Miller's Dale (fine views from 119-2073) are two examples. Sometimes the change in scene in just a few yards is amazing – the **Derwent** Valley is one example; from high, lonely **Hallam Moors** (north-east of **Hathersage** – use 'yellows' on 110-2383/2580) you descend to green, wooded terrain.

Spare time for one of Staffordshire's delights – the River **Churnet** as it heads south-east from Leek. The ruins of **Alton Towers**, the hundreds of acres of parkland and the fantastic, Disneyworld-styled 'Theme Park' will interest both adults and children alike (the pleasure park cost £40m.) Enjoy horse-drawn, narrow-boat trips on the Caldon Canal (**Froghall** – 119-0247).

What of other man-made sights? Buxton and **Matlock** are spa towns; the former is one of the highest towns in England (see Poole's Cavern) – the latter, together with **Matlock Bath**, is in the Derwent Valley. Bakewell, famous for its tart (and pork pies), is a favourite; so are Ashbourne, to the south, and **Uttoxeter** in Staffs – both towns played a part in Samuel Johnson's life.

There are many captivating villages. **Castleton** and Hope are perfect bases to explore the Derwent Valley reservoirs, Peveril Castle, the limestone caverns and the bleak 'Dark Peak' to the north. See Hathersage – the church (useful leaflets), Little John's grave in the churchyard and the medieval tower of North Lees Hall (you can visit), reputed to be Thornfield Hall in Charlotte Brontë's *Jane Eyre*. You're likely to meet 85-year-old Sam Wilson at the churchyard; have a 'natter' – he's a living Hathersage history book. A few miles south is **Eyam** – the 'Plague Village' of 1665; see the 800-year-old church and the amusing cricketing gravestone of Harry Bagshaw. Other favourites are **Tideswell** – its church is called the 'Cathedral of the Peak'; **Hartington** with its duck pond and home of a village-made Stilton cheese; and **Tissington** – famous for its Ascension Day 'well-dressing' ceremony (magnificent, laborious mosaics of floral art – seen at many villages during the summer).

On the eastern and western borders of the Dales are some of Britain's finest 'Great Houses' and parks. **Chatsworth** House, home of the Duke of Devonshire, graces the Derwent Valley and is surrounded by idyllic parkland; it's an absolute must (hot feet? – paddle in the cascade). Nearby **Haddon Hall** is a perfect example of a medieval manor house. North-west of Derby is **Kedleston Hall**. In the far west are: **Tatton Park**, the epitome of the magic that man can create in both parkland and mansion – a stately house, a 1,000 acre deer park, a mere, gardens, a farm and an old hall make it another must; Quarry Bank Mill, at Styal, north of Wilmslow – the 1984 'Museum of the Year'; and **Dunham Massey** – a huge deer park and the home of the Earls of Stamford. **Lyme Park, Capesthorne Hall, Little Moreton** and **Trentham Park** are additional attractions in the west.

Of equal interest are the many museums in the south-west. The vast dish of the radio telescope at **Jodrell Bank** is space-age stuff – and don't miss the exhibition building. At **Tunstall** seek out the Chatterley Whitfield Mining Museum – you can visit underground coal-face workings. The Gladstone Pottery Museum at **Longton**, south-east of **Stoke**, is a working pottery; see, too, the nearby Wedgwood Visitor Centre at **Barlaston**.

North-east of Stoke is **Cheddleton** Flint Mill – used in the past to prepare clays and glazes. At Leek there's a restored James Brindley corn mill. Matlock Bath has two attractions: The Heights of Abraham – a wooded hill, intriguing lead mine and an Alpine-style cable car system; and Gulliver's Kingdom and Royal Cave – a children's delight. Take them also to the National Tramway Museum at **Crich**, south-east of Matlock.

OS Landranger maps: 109.110.118.119.127.128
OS Routemaster map 7. Michelin map 403
Airports: Birmingham. Manchester. East Midlands (SE Derby)
Distance from London – Derby 132 miles

Recommended Drives

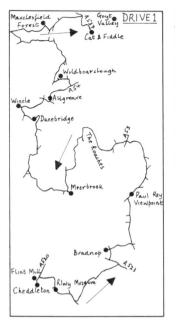

Drive 1 maps 118/119

Staffordshire Moorlands – and a quiet corner of Cheshire; full of eye-pleasing attractions and isolated pubs to distract you!
Start 118-972526 – Cheddleton Flint Mill (open Sat/Sun p.m.). See local 12th-cent. church. 982521 – North Staffs Rlwy; on Sun try 11 m. train trip down Churnet Valley. NE thru 9952. Map 119. N thru 0256. Paul Rey viewpoint at 028595 – vast panoramic views inc' Jodrell Bank. W thru 0263. At 006634 climb The Roaches – heather-covered gritstone ridge. Map 118. S thru 995640 – super views. W thru 9760 – more views S. N thru 9664 – Dane Valley is a superb delight. NE thru 9666 and 9867. Wildboarclough. N thru 9870 – lovely wooded valley. W thru 9671, then E to Macclesfield Forest and 9872. A537. Finish 119-001719 – Cat & Fiddle pub and fine views to W. Approx. dist. 35 m. Fine walks in nearby Goyt Valley.

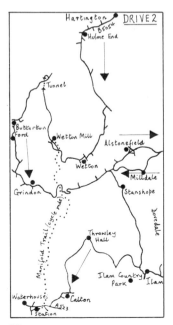

Drive 2 map 119

Staffordshire Surprise: roads except first ½ m. in Staffs. Drive, walk and later – cycle!
Start 1260 Hartington – buy village-made Stilton at shop by duckpond. SW thru 1159. S thru 1156. Wetton. At 100552 note Thor's Cave to S. Wetton Mill (WC/refreshments) – 100 yds S, in dry weather, Manifold disappears in 'swallow hole'. N thru 090570. SW thru 0857. E thru 0854 – then Grindon Hairpins. NE thru 1154. Alstonefield (explore village). At 139547 – Milldale; walk 2½ m. S down Dovedale. S thru 1253. At 132506 – see Manifold re-appear again ('boil hole'). Detour to southern end Dovedale in 1450 (WC) – walk N along dale; steep-sided wooded valley where water is main appeal – be sure to walk this one. S thru 1051. Finish 085501 – ent. Waterhouses Station. Approx. dist. 27 m. Now do cycle ride (dots on map – see next page).

CYCLE RIDES

Parsley Hay
Wetton Mill
Manifold Trail
Ilam
Tissington
Thorpe
Waterhouses
Ashbourne

Cycle Rides map 119
Have fun – use your legs!
The Peak National Park hire out cycles at various centres (summer); the marked trails use tracks laid down on old dismantled railway lines – with the advantage of no hills to climb and no cars either. The 'Manifold Track' (mostly along the dry River Hamps) is specially recommended – but not beyond Wetton Mill; ideal for wheelchairs. Hire centres: Manifold Track (5 m.) – Waterhouses (085501); Tissington Trail (12 m.) – Ashbourne (175469) and Parsley Hay (146637).

Hotel and Restaurant Recommendations

BASLOW
Cavendish

Comfortable hotel
Gardens/Fishing ®

Britain needs more hoteliers like Eric Marsh. He has worked like a Trojan to establish his splendid hotel and success has come for several reasons: a fortuitous setting – on the Chatsworth Estate and near super country; comfortable furnishings – improved year by year as profits allow; friendly staff; and because chef Nick Buckingham, who started alongside Eric when he took over the hotel in 1975, is now showing all the signs of an increasingly confident, capable *cuisinier*. His efforts in obtaining fresh produce are exemplary: super shellfish from the Island of Mull are just one example. His light, imaginative style is a whisker away from category 3.

alc **C** (lun/din) Bar lun also *rooms* 23 **D2** *cards* AE Visa
*closed*Open all the year.
post Baslow, Bakewell, Derbyshire DE4 1SP.
phone (024 688) 2311 *Mich* 403 (P24) Derby 27 m.

BELPER
Rémy's

Comfortable restaurant
Good value ®

With a 'disaster' under my belt the previous evening (further upstream in the Derwent Valley and it's not in this guide) it was a refreshing tonic to visit this tiny, modern, first-floor restaurant. Rémy Bopp, who hails from Mittelwihr in Alsace (near Kaysersberg), now performs his culinary tricks in Belper: a hot, tasty, 'disappear-fast' appetiser; light-as-air sea trout terrine; and, as a *pièce de résistance* (to be expected from any Alsace chef), an apple and almond tart with pistachio ice cream. Produce is fresh and everything is home-made. Try a midday visit – but be sure to book ahead for lunchtime meals.

menus **B** *cards* AE DC (Rooms? See Thorpe hotels)
closed Last wk July. 1st 2 wks Aug. Sun. Mon.
post 84 Bridge St, Belper, Derbs. DE1 3LA. (Nr junc. A6/A517)
phone (077 382) 2246 *Mich* 403 (P24) Derby 8 m.

HOPE   Poachers Arms

Comfortable inn with rooms (S)
Good value (meals)

July 1984 saw Tony and Barbara Singleton change the name of
their modern inn – previously called 'The House of Anton'. It was
a sensible choice and it does justice to Tony's great interests –
shooting and fishing; but not as a 'poacher' you understand. The
couple are involved, happy hosts. Tony's lively imagination
combines well with his outside interests in the entertainingly
described specialities: 'Poachers Warning' (guinea fowl) and
'Lord of the Manor Pie' (game) are examples; pigeon, wild rabbit,
salmon and beef also feature on the menus.

menus **A-C** *rooms* 7 **D** *cards* A AE DC Visa
closed Jan 1.
post Castleton Rd, Hope, Sheffield, South Yorks S30 2RD.
phone (0433) 20380 *Mich* 403 (023) Derby 36 m.

LITTLEOVER   Restaurant 524

Comfortable restaurant   **BEST**
                                              MEAL
Good value   **IN 84**   ®

By the end of the decade Craig Dent will be nationally
acknowledged as one of Britain's best chefs. Anne and I are so
grateful to Jeremy O'Connor at Thame (see *Chilterns*) who gave
us the tip. We made a return trip of 240 miles on a blazing August
Saturday to marvel at one of the most perfect meals we ate in
1984. Wherever you live – Los Angeles, New York, Glasgow,
London or Derby – be sure to seek out Craig and Freda's recently-
opened restaurant. Craig, just 40, spent 20 years away from
kitchens, but his natural talent is intuitive and the spells he has
recently spent working, for nothing, at the French homes of
Robin, Troisgros and Haeberlin have sharpened his culinary
good taste no end. There's no space to list his talents: he's so
clever with herbs; conjures up Girardet-perfect sorbets; and is a
magician with everything he touches. Take my advice: just go!

menus **B** (lun: Tues-Fri) *alc* **B-C** *cards* A AE DC Visa
closed Sun. Mon. (Rooms? Crest nearby – or speak to Dents)
post 524 Burton Road, Littleover, Derby, DE3 6FN.   (Nr. junc
phone (0332) 371524 *Mich* 403 (P25) Derby 2 m.   A5250/A5111)

LONGNOR   Ye Olde Cheshire Cheese

Simple inn with rooms (S)
Good value (meals)

Recommended for those of you with tight budgets – both meal
and bedroom prices are unlikely to break the bank. A small, very
popular inn with a typical British 'pub' dining room: friendly
waitresses, piped music, dark wooden furniture, plenty of brass
and copper, red candles and red paper napkins. The Rowleys
make a big effort to use fresh produce whenever possible and
cook all their offerings on site. Graham Rowley was a butcher
and is proud of his Scottish beef: roast duckling, local lamb and,
thank heavens, a 'home-made' Black Forest gâteau.

menus **A-B** *rooms* 5 **B-D** *cards* A AE DC Visa
closed Rest: Sun evg. Mon.
post Longnor, Buxton, Derbyshire SK17 0NS.
phone (029 883) 218 *Mich* 403 (024) Derby 29 m.

MATLOCK   Riber Hall

Comfortable hotel
Secluded/Gardens/Good value (lunch)   ®

At the end of a scorching July day there's nothing in the world
more pleasing than the evening stillness of an English walled
garden – when the perfume of old-fashioned and climbing roses,
honeysuckle, delphiniums and clematis is so seductive . . . or
perhaps more so in the early morning when the sun is already
warm, the bees are buzzing and the scented air is even headier.
Riber Hall is not a place to be on your own – share the romantic
allure of the Elizabethan manor house and its timeless garden
with a loved one. Enjoy, too, the remarkably competent cooking
of Howard Moseley; fresh produce predominates – the Kyle of
Lochalsh scallops I tried were superb. Bedrooms with four-
poster beds are magnificent, too. Simple, good-value lunches.
menus **A** (lun) *alc* **B-C** (din) *rooms* 10 D2-D3 *cards* A AE DC Visa
closed Open all the year.
post Riber, Matlock, Derbs DE4 5JU. (SE, off A615 at Tansley)
phone (0629) 2795 *Mich* 403 (P24) Derby 20 m.

THORPE   Peveril of the Peak
                                                  Izaak Walton
Comfortable hotels (S)
Quiet/Gardens/Tennis (P of the P)/**Fishing** (IW)

I tried both these famous hotels but I can only recommend them
as 'bases': visit the marvellous restaurants at nearby
Waterhouses or at Littleover. If you eat in it's basic fare you'll be
offered. Both hotels open all the year.
Peveril *menus* **A** (din) Bar lun *rooms* 41 **D-D2** *cards* A AE DC Visa
post Dovedale, Thorpe, Ashbourne, Derbyshire DE6 2AW.
phone (033 529) 333 *Mich* 403 (024) Derby 16 m.
Izaak *menus* **A-B** *rooms* 27 **D-D2** *cards* A AE DC Visa
post Dovedale, Thorpe, Ashbourne, Derbyshire DE6 2AY.
phone (033 529) 261 *Mich* 403 (024) Derby 17 m.

WATERHOUSES   Old Beams

Comfortable restaurant
Gardens/Good value   ®

At last Staffordshire has a restaurant that is really worth getting
excited about. Midlands readers should ensure that they beat a
path to the happy, talented couple who became their own bosses
five years ago when they moved north from Essex; holiday
visitors should consider this a must – for dinner, or for lunch
when the fixed-price menu represents just about the best value in
Britain (£6.50 in '84). Ann Wallis is a sparkling hostess – and
husband Nigel is a skilled chef. Savoy-trained, his style is a
splendid example of how classical cooking can be transformed
into a modern-day lighter interpretation with eye-catching
presentation. The couple pay a lot of attention to details; you see
it in her immaculate dining room – you taste it in his specialities.
Rooms? Speak to Ann about local, inexpensive B&B; or use the
two hotels at Thorpe (see above). Don't miss Old Beams.
menus **A** (lun) *alc* **B** (din) *cards* AE DC Visa
closed 2 wks Jan. Sun evg. Mon.
post Waterhouses, Stoke-on-Trent, Staffs ST10 3HW.
phone (053 86) 254 *Mich* 403 (024) Derby 23 m.

DORSET & THE NEW FOREST

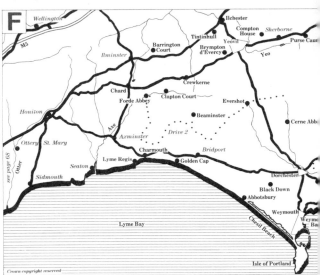

Dorset seems to have a magnetic hold on all those who ever live there. During the last 15 years no less than three friends of mine – promoted to jobs elsewhere in Britain – chose to keep their family base in this captivating county. Why?

Well for a start Dorset is perhaps the most unspoiled county in the south of England: a mixture of hills and downs, heaths, streams, thatched cottages and an entrancing coast – one of the most varied and attractive in the British Isles. For many it's better known as 'Hardy's Wessex'; Thomas Hardy was born at Higher Bockhampton in 1840 and died there 88 years later. Much of the appeal of Hardy's Wessex is that it has changed so little – it is possible to visit many of the places he immortalised in his novels and recognise the scenes he described.

Dorchester (Casterbridge) is the most important; the County Museum is a must and in the town you can identify sites featured in *The Mayor of Casterbridge* and *Far From the Madding Crowd*. Higher Bockhampton (Upper Mellstock) is the site of Hardy's Cottage. He went to school at Lower Bockhampton. Though his ashes are at Westminster Abbey, his heart is buried in Stinsford (Mellstock) churchyard. **Puddletown** (Weatherbury) and **Bere Regis** (Kingsbere) featured in *Far From the Madding Crowd* and *Tess of the d'Urbervilles* (see drive 1).

But perhaps it is the coast that bewitches visitors the most. **Bournemouth** is famous enough though the real surprises start at the vast sheet of still water called **Poole Harbour**. Brownsea Island, in the middle of it, is a tranquil, isolated oasis of woodland, heaths and beaches. It's a nature reserve – like its neighbour the Arne Reserve, on the western shore of Poole Harbour. The Purbeck Hills lie to the south; **Corfe** Castle sits on a commanding hill in the middle of them and nearby, in 195-9383, is the world-famous Blue Pool – a colourful sight.

It's Nature that weaves the magic hereabouts. **Studland** Heath, at the southern entrance to Poole Harbour, is a nature reserve – acres of sand dunes and masses of heather and gorse heathland. Then, with a bang, the Dorset hills start their

54

westwards sweep – at **Ballard Down**, north of **Swanage**. South of the town is **Durlston Head**; geologically it's quite different – here you see for the first time the great cliffs of Portland stone, curving westwards to the 350 ft high **St. Alban's Head**. Beyond is **Kimmeridge Bay** (195-9078) – renowned for its fossils and marine life; the sea has cut away at the cliffs and the shore is lined with smooth limestone ledges. **Worbarrow Bay** comes next – part of the Purbeck Marine Wildlife Reserve; see the **Tyneham** Exhibition at the village church (194-8880).

Serious walkers will relish the prospect of using the Dorset Coast Path that runs from Studland Bay westwards along the 72 mile length of the county's coastline. But even less-dedicated walkers can enjoy small sections of the path – an example is the five mile section from **Lulworth Cove** to **Ringstead Bay**. The small, naturally-formed harbour of Lulworth Cove is an amazing sight; so, too, are the limestone arches of **Durdle Door** and Stair Hole. From the hill above Ringstead Bay (194-7582) there are fine views of **Weymouth Bay** and the **Isle of Portland**. At the start of that southern sweep chalk cliffs dominate the scene; at the end of the curve the solid limestone walls of the Bill of Portland rise from the sea – stone used to build St. Paul's Cathedral. **Weymouth** is a busy port and resort.

The eye-catching variety of Dorset's coast continues relentlessly on westwards. First comes the astonishing **Chesil Beach** – 16 miles of pebbles that form a vast sea wall. At its end is **Abbotsbury**, once the home of a Benedictine abbey, today famous for its Tithe Barn (276 ft long), sub-tropical gardens and Swannery, a sanctuary for hundreds of Mute Swans. High above Abbotsbury is **Black Down** where, at 777 ft above sea-level, is a monument to Vice-Admiral Thomas Hardy, Nelson's flag-captain at Trafalgar. Nearby, to the east, is Maiden Castle – a huge Iron Age hill-fort.

Four miles before **Lyme Regis** comes the last great natural wonder of Dorset's coast – the 625 ft high **Golden Cap**, the highest on England's southern coastline. It's so named because

55

the cliff is capped by an orange-coloured sandstone bluff. A National Trust property, it's famed for its fossils. Then, beyond it, is Lyme Regis – its unassuming Georgian character and elegant charm is admired by all who visit this seaside town.

Lyme Regis would be a good starting point to enjoy the best of inland Dorset. You get a taste of it immediately – in the north of **Charmouth**. Narrow lanes, high hedges and a tumbling rim of hills encircling Marshwood Vale all combine in an alluring way (see drive 2; there's much to interest you).

Garden lovers are spoiled hereabouts. There are several fine examples in the neighbourhood – most just over the border in Somerset: the ten acres of **Clapton Court** Gardens, three miles south-west of **Crewkerne** on the B3165; the **Forde Abbey** Gardens near **Chard**; the grounds and vineyard of **Brympton d'Evercy**, two miles west of **Yeovil**; the formal gardens of **Tintinhull**, north-west of Yeovil – surrounding an old manor house and maintained by The National Trust; **Barrington Court** – an Elizabethan house and gardens north-east of **Ilminster**; and Lytes Cary Manor, a 15th-century manor house near **Ilchester**.

Back in Dorset, **Sherborne** has much to attract visitors: an abbey church and its famous bell, Great Tom; Sherborne Castle, south-east of the town, was once associated with Raleigh – other attractions are the park and lake; and east of the town, the 16th-century **Purse Caundle** Manor. Due south of Sherborne, and in the heart of the North Dorset Downs, is the village of **Cerne Abbas**. Outlined in the chalk above the village is the Cerne Abbas 'giant' – 180 ft high and 'drawn' by a trench dug into the hill. West of Sherborne is **Compton House** – famous for its worldwide butterflies and Lullingstone Silk Farm.

Shaftesbury is an old market town – its hill-top site rewards visitors with extensive views over Blackmoor Vale. Another hill-top diversion, 700 ft high, is the village of **Ashmore** with its circular duck pond, 80 ft wide and 16 ft deep; use the B3081 from Shaftesbury – hairpins and fine views. To the south is **Cranborne Chase** – an extensive forest, said by Hardy to be the oldest wood in England. Further north still is the remarkable church of **Wimborne Minster** – full of treasures.

Beyond the eastern boundary of Dorset is the superb **New Forest**. Created by William the Conqueror it remains Crown Land – 145 square miles of heathland, marshes and stunning mixed woods, Nature's free pick-me-up for drooping spirits. Lying in an arc south-west of **Lyndhurst** is the best of the forest. Use the Bolderwood and Rhinefield Ornamental Drives to take you to the many marked forest walks. Maps 195/196 are musts – drive carefully, watch the horses, stop often (many car parks) and use your legs. Visit **Beaulieu** with its palace, abbey ruins and huge motor museum. **Buckler's Hard** is an 18th-century restored riverside village; the Maritime Museum is a fascinating place, telling the story of the massive oak ships built there from 1745 to 1822. Less crowded will be the eight acres of the informal Furzey Gardens, near **Minstead** (195-2711); like the forest itself, the gardens are at their best at rhododendron time.

Beyond the New Forest boundaries seek out **Romsey** Abbey and the pretty **Test** Valley; nearby Broadlands – the 18th-century home of the late Lord Mountbatten; and in the **Avon** Valley, north of **Fordingbridge**, the 16th-century **Breamore House**.

OS Landranger maps: 183.184.193.194.195.196
OS Routemaster maps: 8.9. Michelin map 403
Airports: Bournemouth. Southampton
Distance from London – Bournemouth 107 miles.

Recommended Drives

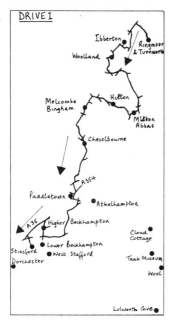

Drive 1 map 194

A taste of Hardy's Wessex.
Start 816085: NT's Ringmoor &
Turnworth Down; fine walk
west – views, woods. Drive N –
views 8109 Stour Valley. S thru
7908. S thru 7706. Views from
78058. SE thru 8003. Milton
Abbas – a planned village. 15th-
cent. Milton Abbey – the setting
for TV's *To Serve Them All My
Days.* Hilton. Melcombe
Bingham. Thru Cheselbourne.
Puddletown. S thru 7492 – a
rhododendron road. 7292;
Hardy's birthplace and also
walks in deciduous woods. SW
thru 7192 (A35). Stinsford
Church at 712910 – Hardy's
grave just inside entrance to
churchyard. Approx. dist. 27 m.
More Hardy associations –
Dorchester, Lwr Bockhampton,
West Stafford, Wool, Lulworth
Cove. Athelhampton (with its
Great Hall). Other sites:
Lawrence's Cloud Cottage at
824909; Tank Mus. at Bovington
Camp (828884).

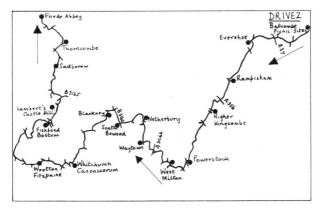

Drive 2 maps 193/194 *The timeless peace of the lush green Dorset Hills;
narrow, deserted lanes with high hedges, filled with blackberry bushes.*
Start Batcombe Picnic Site (194-635040); newly-completed viewing table –
vast views, walks. W to Evershot. SW to Rampisham (note thatched cott).
SW thru 5499 (radio masts – BBC World Service). Powerstock. West
Milton. W thru 4997 (care – maps overlap). Waytown. Netherbury. W to
B3162. N thru 4499. Blackney. S thru 4197. 12th-cent. church at Whitchurch
(3995). Forest walk 355970. Fishpond Bottom – what hideous pylons!
370983 – Lambert's Castle Hill (Iron Age hill fort). N thru 3701/3703. Forde
Abbey; Cromwellian house created from 12th-cent. Cistercian monastery
(Wed/Sun-May/Sept). Approx. dist. 37 m.

Hotel and Restaurant Recommendations

BOURNEMOUTH
Lansdowne
Courtyard

Comfortable restaurants (S)
Good value

No, I'm not crazy! These two restaurants are part of The Dept. of Catering at Bournemouth & Poole Coll. of Further Educ. Like other schools elsewhere in the UK you should see for yourselves the marvellous work many chefs/tutors are doing in training the next generation of British cooks. What makes this school special is the splendid job Peter Taylor has done persuading over 20 top French chefs to take 40+ college students each year for months of on-the-job training. That know-how is put to good use in the evenings when *menu dégustation* meals are available – copies of those served by the students' French hosts. Book ahead.
menus £4 (lun) **A** (dinner-served Tues, Wed, Thurs)
closed School hols. Sat. Sun. All evgs-except above.
post Gervis Rd, Bournemouth, Dorset. (Corner of Meyrick Rd)
phone (0202) 295511 (ring 9.00-9.30 am) *Mich* 403 (O31)

BOURNEMOUTH
Provence

Comfortable restaurant
Good value   ®

Those of you who have visited La Riboto de Taven at Les Baux in France will be thrilled to know that a talented son of Provence has come to Bournemouth in the shape of 30-year-old Jean Pierre Novi. Seek him out and his gracious wife, Claire; the hardworking couple have started down the long, tough road to culinary fame and fortune – help them on their way. Value-for-money, light classical cooking with many a delight: *le boudin de loup de mer, pot au feu de la mer au vin rouge, gâteau de fromage blanc* and *crêpe chaude aux poires* are representative examples. Attention to detail will ensure success: you see it in Jean Pierre's work; in the wine list; and in the table settings. Rooms? Use the Waterford Lodge Hotel, Christchurch – *phone* (042 52) 72948; special rates for visitors to 'Provence' (**C-D**).
menus **A** (lunch) *alc* **B-C**
closed Feb. Sun. Mon.
post 91 Belle Vue Road, Southbourne, Bournemouth, Dorset.
phone (0202) 424421 *Mich* 403 (O31)

EAST STOKE
Kemps

Comfortable restaurant with rooms (S)
Gardens/Good value (meals)

An extremely useful find – my thanks to Peter Taylor (see first entry above). Mike and Valerie Kemp met at the Bournemouth College – Mike went on to complete his training at the Savoy. That stint shows in his much above average cooking: classics like poached egg Benedictine, *poussin Americaine*, vol au vent of seafood Thermidor and beef *Bordelaise* appear on his good-value menu. Sweets are a particular highlight. The couple have two youngsters – and in the four years since they opened they have worked like Trojans to establish themselves.
menus **B** (din/Sun lun) *alc* **B** *rooms* 8 **C-D** *cards* A AE DC Visa
closed Open all the year.
post East Stoke, Wareham, Dorset. (3 m. W Wareham; on A352)
phone (0929) 462563 *Mich* 403 (N31) Bournemouth 16 m.

NEW MILTON   Chewton Glen

Luxury hotel/Michelin ★   Ⓡ
Secluded/Gardens/Swimming pool/Tennis/Good value (lunch)

A stunning hotel where the Skan family's experienced, sure touch comes close to achieving perfection. There's a Riviera atmosphere about the colourful gardens and the sunny terraces – matched in an eye-catching way by the light, airy feel of the superb bedrooms, lounges and dining room. All the staff seem to be influenced by the sparkling character of the place – professional and skilled, of course, but relaxed and friendly, too.

If all that is not enough then there's another good reason for visiting Chewton Glen. The 26-year-old chef, Pierre Chevillard, from Le Coteau, across the Loire from Roanne, is a master of *cuisine moderne*; innovative specialities, perfectly presented and served in such sensible proportions. Light, flour-free sauces and a magician's touch with *pâtisserie* are the highlights of Pierre's repertoire. Consider these. a mousse of mushrooms in a port wine sauce; a *marinière de turbot au pistou*; *noisette d'agneau* stuffed with spinach in a light garlic sauce; and a mouthwatering *millefeuille de fraises*. Ask to see the newly-installed cooling systems for the cheeses and wines.

The quite staggering low-cost lunch menu means that even readers with the tightest of budgets can relish a flavour of this supreme British hotel. Don't miss it.

menus **A** (lun) **D** (din) *rooms* 48 **D2-D5** *cards* A AE DC Visa
closed Open all yr. (2½ m. E A35/A337 junc; L Walkford sign, 1st R)
post Christchurch Rd, New Milton, Hants BH25 6QS.
phone (042 52) 5341 *Mich* 403 (P31) Bournemouth 11 m.

STURMINSTER NEWTON   Plumber Manor

Very comfortable restaurant with rooms
Secluded/Gardens/Tennis

Many *French Leave* readers sent me glowing reports of this 18th-century manor house restaurant when I asked dozens of them for their British favourites. In the same family's hands for centuries, it's in a tranquil setting with extensive lush lawns, handsome trees and bordered by the young River Divelish. Three-course dinners with a wide choice – 10 starters, 10 main courses and a dozen good-looking sweets; competent cooking with mainly classical-based specialities such as *paupiettes* of smoked salmon, sirloin steak *chasseur*, beef Wellington and so on. Some niggles: salad for one comes in a tiny bowl which makes mixing in the salad dressing wellnigh impossible; no appetisers with drinks; commercial mints as *petits fours*; and only 40 minutes spent in the dining room is much too fast a turnaround.

menus **C** *rooms* 12 **C-D2**
closed 2 wks Nov and Feb. Mon. Sun (Nov-Mar) to 'non-res'.
post Hazelbury Bryan Rd, Sturminster Newton, Dorset. (SW 2 m.)
phone (0258) 72507 *Mich* 403 (N31) Bournemouth 30 m.
FL readers have recommended:
Summer Lodge Hotel at **Evershot**; quiet, attractive grounds, pool, cordon bleu cooking, dinner only – *phone* (093 583) 424.
Gulliver's at **Lilliput** (east of Poole); low cost dinners and Sun lunch only. Richard Pearce's initial training at Bournemouth Coll. Some dishes have Malayan touch (Josephine, his wife, is from Malaya) – *phone* (0202) 708810.
And don't forget the excellent Castle at **Taunton** (p.139).

ENGLISH LAKES

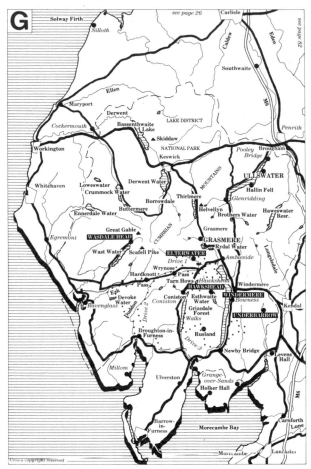

The 'Lake District' is described by the Cumbria Tourist Board as 'the most beautiful corner of England'; it requires little help from me in publicising its unique beauty. Much the most famous tourist area in Britain it's also the most popular National Park. Like millions of others all my family have been bewitched over many decades by the magnetic appeal of its peaks, woods (England's best?), closely-cropped fells (many bracken covered), myriad footpaths, ever-changing moods of light and shade, and by the varying pleasures of its 16 lovely lakes.

During the last 30 years I must have driven down every lane there is in the area – many of them on wet, foggy nights when rallyists are out and about. The spectacular **Hardknott Pass** takes on a quite different perspective when you are challenged to cross it in the dark from one end to the other in five minutes flat. Don't try that – please!

My objective in these introductory notes is to make reference to the more famous sites and sights – but I will also try to entice you to the lesser-known corners which the vast majority of visitors totally ignore. The English Lakes are a delight at all seasons of the year – but particularly so in the winter, spring and autumn (oh those breathtaking woodland and bracken colours) when they are relatively uncrowded.

The largest and most popular of the lakes is **Windermere** – a 10½ mile long sheet of water. The smallest is **Brothers Water**, under one-half mile and at the northern foot of the Kirkstone Pass as you head towards the 7½ mile long, twisting **Ullswater** – most artists consider the latter the most beautiful of the lakes. **Coniston** is the third largest – its wooded, eastern shore is ignored by most visitors; **Rydal Water, Grasmere** and **Elterwater** are three small jewels between Windermere and the long, thin strip of **Thirlmere**, in the shadow of **Helvellyn**. **Derwent Water** is an oval lake with several islands dotted in its 3½ mile length; **Bassenthwaite Lake** is to the north of Keswick and, because of its calm breezes, is popular with sailors. **Wast Water** is the deepest lake in England and is dominated by Scafell; **Buttermere** is the only valley in the Lake District that can claim three lakes – **Loweswater, Crummock Water** and the dramatic **Buttermere** itself. **Ennerdale Water** is the westernmost lake; and, finally, **Esthwaite Water** sits just below **Hawkshead** – with the vast, interesting **Grizedale Forest** to the south (**don't** miss the 'Theatre in the Forest').

In addition to the 16 main lakes there are scores of small tarns, pools, rivers and streams: perhaps the most stunning is **Tarn Hows**, near Hawkshead. Water plays a vital part in the visual seduction that leaves you gasping; magnificent trees and green pastures play their part, too; and mountains, moulded into every permutation of shape and size, complete the idyllic landscape. Of the many peaks that dominate the terrain some soar to over 3000 feet: **Scafell Pike** (3206 ft) is the summit of England; Helvellyn (3116 ft) is climbed reasonably easily (my family have all done the ascent at various times of their lives); and **Skiddaw** (3054 ft) – which dominates Bassenthwaite.

There are many tourist-infested drives: the A592 along the eastern shore of **Windermere** is the most popular – you are left in no doubt how busy the lake is with boats everywhere; the A591 threading north through **Ambleside** is always crowded; so, too, is the B5289 that heads south from **Keswick** past Derwent Water, through wooded **Borrowdale**, and over the Honister Pass to Buttermere; and the Kirkstone Pass can be a crawl.

But there are many minor 'yellow' roads that will give you some relative freedom from traffic. One example is the climb from Braithwaite (90-2323) that heads south over the Newlands Pass to Buttermere; another is the climb over the **Wrynose Pass** and the demanding Hardknott Pass; a third is the dead-end road that leads you to **Wasdale Head** – the views from Wast Water of Scafell Pike and **Great Gable** are richly rewarding. A deserted drive is the lovely **Duddon** Valley road that starts at 90-2401; so is the dead-end road up **Longsledale**, north of **Kendal**. Not so deserted these days are the 'brown' and 'yellow' roads that form a circle west from Elterwater (90-3204); do it clockwise for the best views of the Langdale Pikes.

For the walker there's no more rewarding terrain anywhere in Britain. Armed with the superb books created by Alfred Wainwright, a genius with pen and ink, you can choose any one of hundreds of alternatives. Two easy, not-so-crowded walks are in the south-west corner of the Lake District: the splendid climb up Stanley Ghyll – your reward is the sight of Stanley Force cascade

(96-1799); another is the easy trek to **Devoke Water** – reached from the minor road at 96-1797. Other walks are the ones up Stonethwaite Beck in Borrowdale (90-2613); the paths through the mixed woodlands of Holme Wood on the southern side of Loweswater; the easy climb to Aira Force, a 90 ft high waterfall – you can park at the junction of the A592 and A5091 on Ullswater; and the ascent of **Hallin Fell**, on the eastern side of Ullswater – delightful vistas of the lake and fells.

There are many man-made sites worth a visit; but first visit one of The National Trust Information Centres – Ambleside and **Grasmere** are just two – for details of their properties. There's the 17th-century Hill Top farmhouse at Near Sawrey – at the southern end of Esthwaite Water; it was here that Beatrix Potter wrote her children's books. Several houses have associations with Wordsworth: Dove Cottage and its new museum at Grasmere, where he lived from 1799 to 1808 – he is buried in the village churchyard; Rydal Mount in Rydal, north of Ambleside, with a captivating garden; Wordsworth's House in Cockermouth – his birthplace; and the Hawkshead Grammar School where he was a student. The terrain between Coniston Water and **Underbarrow** has many connections with Arthur Ransome of *Swallows and Amazons* fame: Peel Island at the southern end of Coniston Water is 'Wild Cat Island'; he lived his last years near **Rusland** and is buried there (see drive 3 and walks). On the east bank of Coniston Water, at the northern end, is Brantwood where John Ruskin lived the last 28 years of his life.

Seek out the Abbot Hall Art Gallery and Museum of Lakeland Life and Industry at Kendal – and its branch, the Courthouse at Hawkshead; both are full of fascinating displays – the former has some of Arthur Ransome's possessions. Windermere has a splendid Steamboat Museum and at Brockdale, just north of the town, is the Lake District National Park Centre with attractive gardens and a lakeside setting. **Levens Hall** is a 16th-century house, famous for its topiary garden and collection of steam models. **Holker Hall**, too, is a 16th-century house in a grand Victorian park and it has all sorts of interesting exhibits – a motor museum and model railway among them. If you are brave enough to try the steep Hardknott Pass, spare time for the vast, impressive remains of a Roman fort.

You will have many opportunities to use pleasure craft on Windermere – but perhaps even more appealing would be a trip on The National Trust's marvellous steam yacht 'Gondola', which sails on Coniston Water. Adults and children will love the miniature Ravenglass and Eskdale Railway – it runs from **Ravenglass** on the coast to Dalegarth in Eskdale (90-1700).

Of the many attractive gardens in the Lake District – some have been mentioned already – spare time for Lingholm Gardens on the west bank of Derwent Water; apart from the woodland and formal gardens you also win exceptional views of Borrowdale and Skiddaw. Holehird, just north of Windermere, provides a walk through unusual trees, shrubs and plants (run by the Lakeland Horticultural Society). Be sure to visit, too, Sizergh Castle at Kendal – a handsome building and lovely grounds with a series of lakes, pools and waterfalls. Muncaster Castle at Ravenglass is famous for its rhododendrons and azaleas as is Stagshaw Garden, near Ambleside.

OS Landranger maps: 85.89.90.96.97

OS Routemaster map 5. Michelin map 402

Airport: Manchester

Distance from London – Kendal 270 miles

Recommended Drives – and Walks!

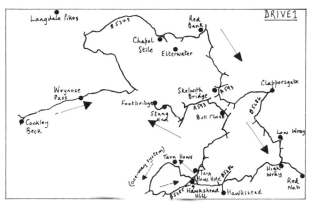

Drive 1 maps 90/96 *An eye-catching magical show – Mother Nature at her most extrovert. Walks galore – take stout shoes.*
Start 90-2401; Cockley Beck (foot of Hardknott). Fine views E Wrynose Pass summit. N thru 290051 – superb view Langdale Pikes. B5343. E thru 325056 – eye-catching views S. At 340055 walk E to Loughrigg Terr – what a pretty aspect N! S thru 3404. Skelwith Bridge (walk to Skelwith Force waterfall). 352030. B5286. S thru 3700. Map 96. Detour Red Nab (3899). W thru 3599. 327996 from E – Tarn Hows; wow! SW thru 3299. B5285. N thru 3499. Map 90. N thru 3401. A 593. Use 'white' rd, finish 316029; wooded, riverside picnic spot – usually deserted. Use footbridge to cross river. Approx. dist. 31 m.

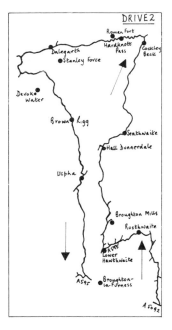

Drive 2 maps 89/96
Breathtaking roads, views, fells & streams – most of it largely ignored.
Start 96-262849 (A5092). N thru 2587. W thru 2389. A593. N thru 2291 & 2195. Wordsworth called the River Duddon 'Child of the Clouds'; it's a glorious valley. Map 89. W over Hardknott Pass – an amazing, drunken-like, meandering path (note Roman fort). 1700–try the R&E Light Railway. Detour 172003 – car park; walk S to Stanley Force waterfall. Map 96-1499. (If the mood suits head N on map 89 to Wasdale Head – 1808 – at the heart of England's best mountain country.) Otherwise S thru 1797 (views) & 2090 to finish at A595. This last section optional. Approx. dist. 33 m. Note: not a lake on this drive – and you'll see few cars; if Hardknott too daunting start drive 1 at Cockley Beck. But, don't under any circumstances miss the superb Duddon Valley.

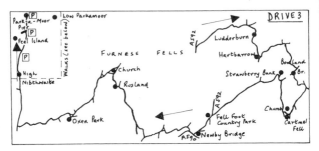

Drive 3 map 96 *Superb Arthur Ransome Country.*
Born in 1884, he spent much of his life in the Lakes – the inspiration for his universally-loved *Swallows and Amazons*. Written in 1930, I 'discovered' the book in the 1940s – my son did the same over 20 years later. (The series is published by Penguin.) As an intro' visit the Abbot Hall Mus. in Kendal – it has some of his possessions. Start 386907 (A592). NE. S thru 405913 (Low Ludderburn cottage on left was his first Lakes home – he started the series here, based on childhood holidays at 'Swainson's Farm', High Nibthwaite.) S thru 4190. Cartmel Fell from NE. Detour church (417880) – escaped Cromwell's wrath. Strawberry Bank. SW to A592 (Fell Foot Country Park). In 3686 ride L&H 'steamer' Rlwy – Cumbria's most popular attraction. Furness Fells – loved by Wordsworth and Ransome. N thru 3487 to Rusland. Visit Hall (int. exhib). Ransome lived his last years in valley. Died 1967 – buried in churchyard (SE corner) at 338896. W thru 3187. N thru 2988 to High Nibthwaite. N via Park-a-Moor Pier (298923) to 299927 (car park). See walks below. Approx. dist. 23 m.

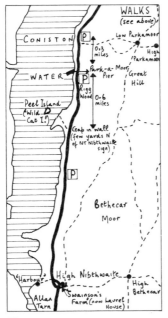

Walks map 96
Lakeland's seductive appeal – the inspiration for Swallows and Amazons.
(Even if you haven't read series be sure to see this area.) As alternative to using car parks why not enjoy 'Gondola' run (125-yr-old steam yacht) from Coniston to Park-a-Moor Pier. (Ransome took the wheel as boy in 1892.) From 299927 climb to Great Hill (via Low Parkamoor) on Bethecar Moor – views of Peel Island ('Wild Cat I.'), lake &, in 2797, The Old Man of Coniston ('Kanchenjunga'). To see Peel I. thru gap in wall 0.6 m. S of Park-a-Moor Pier (gap is few yds N of NT Nibthwaite sign). High Nibthwaite: walk 'Harbour' (use small black swing gate); 'Swainson's Farm' (now Laurel House); use track thru 300909 to reach Bethecar Moor. See map for High Nibthwaite locations. From Pier southwards you can walk in woods alongside road.

ELTERWATER   Britannia Inn

Very simple inn with rooms (S)
Quiet/Good value (dinner)

A 400-year-old whitewashed inn, overlooking a small green and
at the heart of so much marvellous country. David (a computer
buff) and Margaret Fry and their sons Paul and Richard (both
rally driver addicts) are involved, interested hosts. Simple
dinners (7.00 p.m.) with a choice of dishes like cream of leek and
potato soup, rump steak and home-made damson ice cream.
menus **B** (dinner) Bar lun *rooms* 10 **C-D**
closed Xmas. Rest: Nov-Easter (except Fri/Sat-Feb/Mar).
post Elterwater, Ambleside, Cumbria LA22 9HP.
phone (096 67) 210 *Mich* 402 (L20) Kendal 19 m.

GRASMERE   Michaels Nook

Comfortable hotel
Secluded/Gardens   Ⓡ

'Michael' was the shepherd immortalised by Wordsworth: Reg
and Elizabeth Gifford's 'Nook' is in a pretty setting – full of
Georgian and Victorian treasures. Add to that the best cooking in
the Lakes – and the only restaurant going down the *cuisine
moderne* road. That's no surprise when you realise that the
young chefs, Philip Vickery and Paul Viduc, were trained by Nigel
Marriage, previously at the 'Nook' and now head chef under
Blanc (p. 39). The hotel is open 365 days a year – for lunch and
dinner – and you get a choice. Five-course meals: a warm salad of
calves' liver and a breast of duck with a peach *coulis* and green
peppercorns were outstanding. Staying or not, don't miss a meal
here – and don't trip over Seb! (The Giffords own the
Wordsworth Hotel, too – use its heated indoor pool.)
menus **C** (lun) **D** (din) *rooms* 10 **D2-D5** (din incl.) Book ahead
closed Open all the year. (E side A591 – map 90-340086)
post Grasmere, Cumbria LA22 9RP.
phone (096 65) 496 *Mich* 402 (K20) Kendal 18 m.

GRASMERE   White Moss House

Comfortable hotel
Gardens   Ⓡ

Nature and man combine harmoniously at White Moss but, like
all hotels and restaurants that really please, it's the human side
that matters most. It's a real family enterprise here: Arthur
Butterworth and his daughter Susan welcome guests and do all
the serving (for about 20); Jean and her son-in-law Peter are the
culinary wizards. Good taste dominates – not least in the
cooking. Dinner is at 7.30 for 8.00 – five courses with a choice of
sweets only; primarily English delights with the odd trip overseas
– like delicious *crémets*. The Butterworths' touch is light and
they serve sensible, balanced portions. I hope they develop those
talents; it **can** be done with English cooking – and they do it as
well as anyone in the UK. Superb British cheeses – including
many unknown varieties.
menus **C** *rooms* 6 **D2-D4** (din incl.) Book ahead
closed Mid Nov-mid Mar.
post Rydal Water, Grasmere, Cumbria LA22 9SE. (On A591)
phone (096 65) 295 *Mich* 402 (K20) Kendal 16 m.

HAWKSHEAD   Tarn Hows

Comfortable hotel
Secluded/Gardens/Swimming pool/Good value (dinner)

What an alluring setting for a Lakeland hotel – over 600 ft above
sea-level, in 25 acres of grounds, a super view and a heated pool!
New owners Derek and Marie Lilley are going to put it back on
the Lakeland hotel map – I'm certain of it. I think, too, that their
son John is going to please guests with his competent cooking –
such good value and a choice at every course: specialities like
local lamb and venison, English veal, salmon trout and tasty
home-made puddings.

menus **B** (din) Bar lun *rooms* 20 **D-D2** *cards* A AE DC Visa
closed Jan ('86). (See drive 1 for exact location)
post Hawkshead, Ambleside, Cumbria LA22 OPR.
phone (096 66) 330 or 382 or 254 *Mich* 402 (L20) Kendal 20 m.

ULLSWATER   Sharrow Bay

Very comfortable hotel
Secluded/Gardens   Ⓡ

I realise many of you may not be able to afford an overnight stay
here; but that should not stop you making the not-so-big financial
sacrifice to enjoy a lunch at this appealing hotel. Francis Coulson
and Brian Sack's Sharrow Bay has the most bewitching of
settings: on a dead-end road alongside Ullswater, the view across
the placid lake to woods and fells, rising to the crags of Helvellyn,
is a rejuvenating tonic for flagging spirits. They are great
supporters of English produce – Morecambe Bay shrimps,
Cumberland ham, Eden salmon and local lamb are just a few
examples. Wholesome, old-fashioned fare and vast portions – the
choice is amazing (that's the reason for the category three entry,
won by a whisker); 20 starters alone! Unbelievably, 80 half-
bottles on the wine list.

menus **C** (lun) **D** (din) *rooms* 29 **D2-D3** (dinner incl.)
closed Dec-1st week Mar.
post Pooley Bridge, Ullswater, Cumbria CA10 2LZ. (See map)
phone (085 36) 301 or 483 *Mich* 402 (L20) Kendal 32 m.

UNDERBARROW   Tullythwaite House

Comfortable restaurant   Ⓡ

The 'restaurant' is in fact the front rooms of the Johnsons'
farmhouse; 300 years old, it's a 'home' bubbling with character –
part of a small dairy farm. You are one of just 20 or so guests – all
of whom are welcomed by the ever-smiling, so gracious and
courageous Mary, now 88 years young. Her daughter-in-law
Barbara (herself a grandmother) is the unseen cook in the
kitchen, where she conjures up English dinners of the sort any
wife or mother would be truly proud – home cooking at its very
best: a choice from six starters, soup, duckling (or lamb) with all
the trimmings and fresh vegetables, two sweets and finishing
with fruit and English cheeses. Book ahead – dinner is at 7.00.
Take your own wine – the restaurant is unlicensed.

menus **C** (din only) (B&B? Speak to the Johnsons)
closed Dec-Mar. Sun. Mon. Bk hols (except Good Fri).
post Underbarrow, Nr Kendal, Cumbria LA8 8BB. (Map 97-472915)
phone (044 88) 397 *Mich* 402 (L21) Kendal 4 m.

WASDALE HEAD   Wasdale Head Inn

Simple inn with rooms (S)
Secluded/Gardens/Good value (dinner)

The Hammond family's mountain inn is ideal for those of you who want to get down to some really serious fell walking; on hand are Scafell, Great Gable and a host of less-demanding climbs. Ritson's Bar (the first landlord) is a popular haven for climbers; thankfully it's separated from the cosy 'hotel' part of the inn. Simple, copious, home-cooked dinners.
menus **A** (din) Bar lun *rooms* 10 **C-D2** *cards* A Visa
closed Nov-28 Dec.
post Wasdale Head, Gosforth, Cumbria CA20 1EX.
phone (094 06) 229 *Mich* 402 (J20) Kendal 65 m.

WINDERMERE   Miller Howe

Comfortable hotel
Gardens

Chefs face a dilemma: how do they tell the world at large of their endeavours? John Tovey has cracked the problem with globe-trotting public relations jaunts – putting his theatrical background to profitable use (study the scrapbooks on the landing). Like Bocuse and Vergé, Tovey's a 'media' chef; he's usually away in the 'closed' season – though there was no sign of him on my visit. (Why do I never seem to *see* 'media' chefs?) Typical no-choice dinner (apart from 'puds') is served at 8.30 'prompt' in a tightly-packed room: 'Utter Bliss' (melon with a punch!); French onion soup; scallops in cream sauce; multi-flavoured seven 'veg' (too many elaborate tastes fighting each other) accompanied by roast turkey and trimmings; and one of six puds or cheese 'platter'. Some readers may like Tovey's extrovert taste – it's not my style; oh for a touch of *faites simple*. It's dear: dinner, B&B, ½-bottle cheap wine cost me nearly £80. View is highlight; relish it for free 100 yds north of hotel.
menus **D** (din only served) *rooms* 13 **D2-D4** *cards* A AE DC Visa
closed Dec-mid Mar. (On A592 north of Bowness)
post Rayrigg Rd, Windermere, Cumbria LA23 1EY.
phone (096 62) 2536 *Mich* 402 (L20) Kendal 10 m.

WINDERMERE   Ravensworth

Simple hotel (S)
Good value (dinner)   ®

It's no surprise to me that clients return regularly to this small, immaculate, simple hotel. For those of you with modest budgets it offers a host of benefits: a warm welcome from the owners Bob and Ilse Eyre – they've been here 13 years; all bedrooms have bathrooms; there's a sheltered sun terrace; guests have the use of the Eyres' Mirror 16 for sailing – Bob will also take you out in his bigger craft; and Ilse's dinners are straightforward, enjoyable affairs – served at 7.00 pm. Ilse hails from Vienna; you see an Austrian touch in her cooking – particularly soups. No wonder 'regulars' are known by their first names.
menus **A** (din only served) *rooms* 13 **B-D** *cards* A Visa
closed Open all the year. (On A591 – 200 yards from station)
post Ambleside Rd, Windermere, Cumbria LA23 1BA.
phone (096 62) 3747 *Mich* 402 (L20) Kendal 9 m.

EXMOOR & DARTMOOR

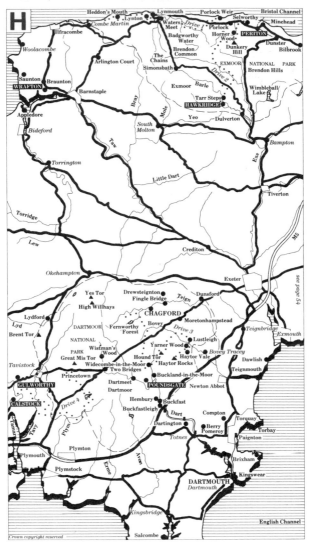

Like the Lake District, this is a part of England that requires little help from me in singing its praises. In the high season it's so crowded – though armed with large-scale maps you can bypass many of the 'honeypot' beauty spots. Out of season, in the spring and lovely autumn months, it's a paradise – with a never-ending display of Mother Nature's most masterly skills: two superb coastlines; wild, desolate moors; cool, green woods; quiet streams – and some wild, angry torrents, too.

For me the most fascinating aspect of the area's geography is the river valleys. The **Exe** rises in **The Chains**, a high, marshy moor in **Exmoor**, just miles from the **Bristol Channel** – it flows south to its mouth in the **English Channel**. The **Taw** on the other hand rises from an even higher source in **Dartmoor** and then proceeds to flow north to the Bristol Channel. Scores of streams are everywhere – many of them with superb wooded banks; they dominate much of what you will enjoy most.

Exmoor is my favourite – though, alas, it's a culinary desert. One of England's few national parks, its 265 square miles covers part of West Somerset and extends westwards into North Devon. A major attraction of the park is that its northern boundary is a 29 mile stretch of truly magnificent coastline – a series of hogs-back cliffs and huge bluffs are spectacular sights. Between **Minehead** and **Porlock Weir** is **Selworthy** Beacon – gasp at the vast panorama of the coast, the Bristol Channel, Wales and green woods and high moors to the south. Further west, near **Combe Martin**, are two huge bluffs – Little Hangman (716 ft) and Great Hangman (1043 ft); amazing views of the coast and distant Wales far to the north.

Just a handful of streams fall sharply northwards off Exmoor into the Bristol Channel – not one of them more than a few miles long. But in times of very heavy rain their waters become ferocious killers. Hoaroak Water, Farley Water and the East Lyn rise in the hills behind **Lynmouth**. On the night of August 15, 1952 the power of those combined streams and the West Lyn devastated the town. The point at which the first three become one is called **Waters Meet** – a famous beauty spot. Further west the River Heddon, too, has a short, spectacular life; it enters the sea at **Heddon's Mouth** – a 700 ft deep ravine.

Before you leave the coast seek out two exceptional sites: Culbone Coombe is just west of Porlock Weir – a 1¼ mile walk from Worthy leads you to Culbone Church, the smallest in England; **Dunster**, near Minehead, is well known for its handsome castle and interesting old buildings. Enjoy Minehead, Porlock Weir, Lynmouth, **Lynton**, Combe Martin and **Ilfracombe**. But if you want to miss the crowds head inland – to **Dunkery Hill** for the best views of the **Exmoor National Park**.

Now explore that marvellous terrain. See Selworthy. Then enjoy **Horner Wood** just north of the hill – the streams here give it extra appeal. Then head west to **Badgworthy Water** – where the Doone family was supposed to have lived. John Ridd of *Lorna Doone* fame went to Blundell's School, **Tiverton** – just as the author, R. D. Blackmore, did in real life. On the way to **Simonsbath** you'll cross **Brendon Common** – typical of the Exmoor moorlands and famous for red deer and Exmoor ponies.

The wooded Exe and **Barle** valleys repay handsomely the time you give them. **Tarr Steps**, on the Barle, is a unique stone bridge; who built it, and when, remains a mystery. **Dulverton**, too, should not be bypassed. Ornithologists will enjoy **Wimbleball Lake** – a man-made reservoir in the **Brendon Hills**.

Beyond the western boundary of the National Park are many pleasures: bird lovers will head for the huge expanse of sand-dunes called **Braunton** Burrows in the Taw Estuary; others will enjoy the market town of **Barnstaple** and the old ship-building town of **Appledore** at the mouth of the **Torridge**; garden lovers and fans of horse-drawn vehicles will head for **Arlington Court**, to the north-east of Barnstaple. Children will adore **Saunton** and **Woolacombe** sands – magnificent beaches.

Dartmoor is described in most tourist literature as the 'last wilderness in southern Britain'. It is – though in the high season it's literally overrun by tourists. If ever an area begged to be explored out of season it is the **Dartmoor National Park** – and the coast that lies to both east and south.

The moor is at its bleakest in the mass of terrain south of **Okehampton**. The highest points are **High Willhays** and **Yes Tor** (both just over 2000 ft high) – near the source of the River Taw. The granite 'tors' of Dartmoor are the most unusual features of the rock-strewn moorlands; they crown every hill-top like huge bare knuckles. The best known are **Haytor Rocks, Hound Tor, Great Mis Tor**, Yes Tor and **Brent Tor** with a chapel perched on its summit; all provide fine views.

Many streams spring to life in the desolate hills. As they fall towards the sea they take on a different character – and much of South Devon's enticing appeal owes a great deal to them. Among them are the **Teign, Bovey** and **Dart** – the most attractive examples on the eastern side of the National Park. As they descend from the high tors they pass through many beautiful woods – one example is the stretch alongside the Teign from **Fingle Bridge** to Bridford Wood, near **Dunsford. Yarner Wood** Nature Reserve, just west of **Bovey Tracey** is a gem; so, too, is Shaptor Wood – to the north-east of Yarner Wood. Try to see two woods in the hills: **Wistman's Wood**, a nature reserve and epitomising the haunting feel of Dartmoor, is north of **Two Bridges** – a good walk; **Fernworthy Forest** is further north-east and adjacent to Fernworthy Reservoir.

There's one spot where the dramatic differences between the high moors and the more sheltered lower wooded terrain is most clearly seen – **Dartmeet**, where the East and West Dart rivers join. It's fine walking country; enjoy the refreshing green woods downstream to **Buckfastleigh**, particularly **Hembury** Woods – a National Trust property. The villages of **Widecombe-in-the-Moor, Buckland-in-the-Moor** and **Lustleigh** are all renowned and are very popular with tourists.

Torquay, Torbay and **Paignton** are famous enough – loved by adults and children alike. What is certain is that all generations will enjoy the privately-owned Dart Valley Railways: one runs from Buckfastleigh to **Totnes** and the other from Paignton to **Kingswear**. Both are super 'steam' lines.

Of man-made sites seek out Castle Drogo, near **Drewsteignton** – a granite, fortress-like castle built this century; the 14th-century ruins of Okehampton Castle; **Dartington** Hall and Gardens – a working estate, centred on a 14th-century hall; Totnes Castle and the 13th century ruins of the nearby **Berry Pomeroy** Castle; **Compton** Castle, west of Torquay – a fortified manor house; **Buckfast** Abbey; and **Dartmouth** with its castle at the mouth of the Dart Estuary – the latter is so attractive.

On the western edges of Dartmoor are several essential ports of call. The most rewarding – and most popular – is **Lydford** Gorge; it's a 1½ mile long ravine, 60-70 ft deep, and the site of a 100 ft high waterfall, Dartmoor's finest. Double Waters is an alluring wooded area on the River **Tavy**, four miles south of **Tavistock** (201-4770); what a rewarding walk it is from 490710. If all that is not enough there remains, to the south, the captivating coast near **Salcombe** – with a Mediterranean-like climate it's a yachtman's paradise.

Above all do the four drives – or parts of them; they take you through the best of both Exmoor and Dartmoor.

OS Landranger maps: 180.181.191.192.201.202
OS Routemaster map 8. Michelin map 403
Airport: Plymouth-Roborough
Distance from London – Exeter 201 miles.

Recommended Drives

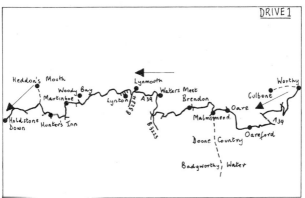

Drive 1 maps 180/181 Lorna Doone *Country. Take your walking shoes and some binoculars, too. Splendid coast and river terrain.*
Start 181-858482 (toll gate). Why not first enjoy marvellous wooded walk – 1¼ m. – to Culbone Church (8448), smallest in England? Room to park. W thru 8347 and 8246. Oare – Lorna married John Ridd at church. Map 180. At Malmsmead (7947) start of walk S to Doone Country in Badgworthy Water. Brendon. W thru 7547 to A39. Park at 741478 or further N on A39 – but do see Waters Meet. A39 to Lynmouth. Thru 7049 – Valley of Rocks. W thru 6748. Park at Hunter's Inn (6548) – relish 1 m. walk N to Heddon's Mouth. Finish 624475 (car park); many fine walks and rewarding, vast views. Approx. dist. 23 m.

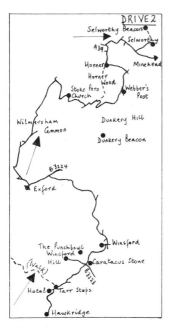

Drive 2 map 181
Superb Somerset: heather hills, wonderful woods, sparkling streams, peerless panoramas.
Start Hawkridge (8630). N to Tarr Steps (medieval or Bronze Age?). (If heavy rain start E bank of Barle.) Detour 876343; Wambarrows, walk to edge of Punchbowl. See Bronze Age Caratacus Stone – 890335. Pretty Winsford. N thru 8936 & 8643. Stoke Pero Church. 892430 – view, woods, wow! Same at 903436; walks galore. Horner (8945) – walk S to Horner Wood. A39. Finish Selworthy – the 'perfect' English village. Approx. dist. 24 m. Now why not walk from village N to Selworthy Beacon? Or, if you are not up to that, drive from Minehead thru 9447. Either way enjoy the fantastic views; in late summer, early autumn, it's a purple heather, golden gorse wonderland. Take a container – plenty of blackberries.

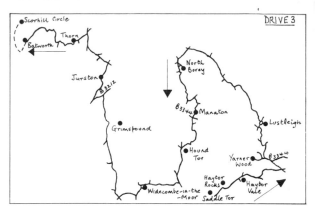

Drive 3 map 191 *The contrasting faces of Dartmoor: Bronze & Iron Age remains;* The Hound of the Baskervilles *country; dense woods.*
Start Haytor Rocks (7576) – vast views E to Lyme Bay. E thru 7777. NW thru 7978. At 785789 (off B3344) Nature Trail & Woodland Walk in Yarner Wood. NW thru 7881 & 7783. S thru North Bovey. S thru 7581. W thru 7479. Hound Tor – of the Baskervilles legend. Widecombe – a 'honeypot'. N thru 6980. At 697808 – E to Grimspound – prehistoric settlement (where Holmes hid seeking the 'hound'). Note purple blankets of heather. View north. N thru 6984. W thru 6886. Finish 664867: park and walk to Scorhill Circle (6587) using 'clapper bridge' at 654870. Approx. dist. 30 m.

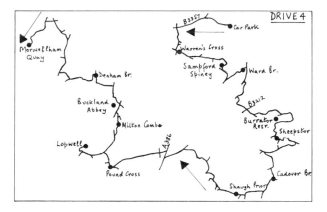

Drive 4 maps 201/202 *Quiet, largely-ignored wooded river valleys.*
Start 201-532752 (car park on B3357); ext. views Cornwall. SE thru 5173. Sampford Spiney Church. S thru 5470. Map 202 at 550693. Circuit of Burrator Resr. – fine walks 5669. Sheepstor. 560670 from E – lovely view. S thru 5564 to Cadover Br. Note numbers of stone crosses, hut circles, cairns and settlements in area – prehistoric remains. Map 201 at 550653. Shaugh Prior. NW thru 5264 – watch the ponies. W thru 4964. NW to Lopwell. Milton Combe village – pub 'Who'd have thought it'. 4866 – Buckland Abbey – Drake associations. W thru 4767. N thru 4668. Finish Morwellham Quay (4469); copper mine, museums, walks – absorbing. Approx. dist. 30 m.

Hotel and Restaurant Recommendations

CALSTOCK
Danescombe Valley

Simple hotel (S)
Secluded ®

FL3 readers will recognise Calstock as a category 1 entry – a *sans restaurant* 'base'. An enticing, south-facing site overlooking a bend of the River Tamar. 1985 will see the Wintles offering non-compulsory evening meals.
rooms 6 **C-D** *closed* Open all the year.
post Calstock, Cornwall PL18 9RY. (W of village – by river)
phone (0822) 832414 *Mich* 403 (H32) Exeter 41 m.

CHAGFORD
Gidleigh Park

Very comfortable hotel/Michelin ★
Secluded/Gardens/Tennis/Good value (lunch) ®

No British hotel has a more isolated setting – no British hotel has a more seductive approach road. Readers will know of my passion for dead-end lanes; well here's one that has the most rewarding goal of all – a superb hotel. Paul and Kay Henderson are dedicated hoteliers – they've worked wonders in their seven years here. I have seen the annual P&L A/cs for the hotel: no wonder our best country house hotels are dear when you see what is spent annually on fittings, repairs, wages, interest and heating as examples. And the mortgage, too. Truly hair-raising! The American couple have a splendid young British team: Kay and John Webber, a Mosimann protégé, mastermind the kitchen's work; Ian Neilson and Kate Grant lead a friendly, front-of-house group. The attractions are many: high-standard cooking; a fantastic list of 400 wines – with marvellous Californian varieties and French bargains; and a gorgeous, wooded setting, alongside the infant North Teign River. **Every** visitor to Devon should seek it out – even if it's only to relish a good-value lunch or afternoon tea costing £2 or so.
menus **B** (lun) **D** (din) *rooms* 12 **D2-D4** *cards* AE
closed Open all the year. (Book ahead for dinner)
post Chagford, Devon TQ13 8HH. (App. via 191 6887)
phone (064 73) 2367 & 2225 *Mich* 403 (I31) Exeter 17 m.
Dartmouth: see next page please.

GULWORTHY
Horn of Plenty

Comfortable restaurant with rooms
Quiet/Gardens/Good value (lunch)

Sonia and Patrick Stevenson opened the Horn of Plenty in 1967. Sonia had been a professional violinist before she turned her light, precise touch to the new skills of being a professional *cuisinière*. She's an expert with sauces – they appear in myriad ways with fish and meat specialities: cream, *beurre blanc*, *béarnaise*, madeira, hollandaise, sorrel, pine kernel, mustard – to name just a few. A typical menu could include a terrine of stuffed quails, her renowned *quenelles de saumon à la crème* and some rather conventional sweets like lemon cream crumble and Devonshire junket. Bedrooms available Easter '85.
menus **B** (lun) **D** (din) *rooms* (Easter '85)
closed Christmas Day. Thurs. Fri (lunch).
post Gulworthy, Tavistock, Devon PL19 8JD. (3 m. W – N of A390)
phone (0822) 832528 *Mich* 403 (H32) Exeter 41 m.

DARTMOUTH

The Carved Angel

Comfortable restaurant/Michelin ★
Good value (lunch)   Ⓡ

The British culinary 'sapling' has put down firm roots: a modern,
spontaneous and natural style, using 'fresh-as-daisies' and much
local produce in dishes based primarily on daily purchases. If any
British chef – experienced, newcomer or college student –
pressed me to give one example of a restaurant that epitomises
my thoughts set down in the introductory chapters, then this is
one of many that I would direct them to.

No praise is high enough for Handsworth-born Joyce
Molyneux (with that name and with me a Wolves fan for 37 years
my guess that she was a 'Brummie' proved to be right – one of
Birmingham's best); she's as talented as any *cuisinière* there is
in either Britain or France. And I know most of them.

Each day 24 or so delights grace her menu – each one of them a
perfect example of what will make British-style cooking great
again. Fresh produce from numerous local suppliers means that
offerings change at short notice – just a few examples of her
polished talents follow: a fish soup served with the right-sized
garlic *croûtons* and an eye-dazzling sun orange *rouille* – no
Mediterranean fish in this one but just as tasty; some brill, turbot
and sole lightly marinaded and served with two sweet tomatoes –
one red, one yellow; and breast of chicken with three spices and a
cream sauce over a slice of mango.

Tom and Sally Jaine have moved on and it's to be hoped that
George Perry-Smith and Heather Crosbie – Joyce's partners (see
Helford – page 137) – will soon have a capable front-of-house
hostess to emulate the efficient Sally.

If the 'sapling' is to become a sturdy 'tree', then the British
cooking scene needs 500 or more chefs like Joyce. Help her and
the others to flourish – exercise the 4 Es here and at all
enterprising, 'honest' British restaurants.
menus **B** (lun) **C** (din) *cards* A AE DC Visa
closed Jan. Mon. Sun (dinner). Tues (lunch).
post 2 South Embankment, Dartmouth, Devon TQ6 9BB.
phone (080 43) 2465 *Mich* 403 (J32) Exeter 36 m.

HAWKRIDGE

Tarr Steps

Comfortable hotel (S)
Secluded/Gardens/Fishing/Good value (meals)   Ⓡ

Set in the heart of the Barle Valley this is seductive Somerset at
its best – a wooded landscape of deciduous trees blanketing the
steep hillsides that climb up from the banks of the meandering
rocky stream. The rich purple of the clematis-covered porch is a
welcoming guard of honour – matched in warmth by the friendly
care of Desmond Keane, the owner of this former Georgian
rectory. Walkers and fishermen will be in their element here.
Cooking is country-house fare with alternatives like avocado
mousse with crispy bacon, guinea fowl in a cider wine sauce and
crème brûlée. Hurrah – a hotel with no TV!
menus **A** (din-Sun lun) Bar lun *rooms* 15 **C-D** *cards* AE Visa
closed Mid Nov-mid Mar (except Xmas).
post Hawkridge, Dulverton, Somerset TA22 9PY. (N of village)
phone (064 385) 293 *Mich* 403 (J30) Exeter 33 m.
For those with tight budgets – Rock Inn at **Haytor Vale:** simple,
modest fare (**A**); some rooms (**B-D**); *phone* (036 46) 305.

PERITON
Periton Park

Very comfortable hotel (S)
Secluded/Gardens/Fishing/Riding   ®

Valerie and Tony Wright made a great success of establishing the
Dragon House Hotel at nearby Bilbrook. November 1984 sees
them moving to their new pride and joy – a Victorian country
house set in a 30 acre estate near Minehead; they open in March
'85. In reality guests will be sharing their home and, in the
process, relishing some super benefits: cosseting rooms; gardens
and parkland so large that there's room for an intermediate class
cross-country course (the couple's horses and stables will be
available to experienced riders); a magnificent Victorian billiards
room; numerous walks in woodlands to the south; the scenic
beauty of the coast and adjacent Exmoor; and Valerie's
personally prepared dinners – fresh produce cooked with style.
rooms 4 **D2-D3** (din/wine incl.) (Also self-cont. flat)
closed Dec. Meals for res. only. (Periton Park opens Mar '85)
post Periton, Minehead, Somerset. (W of town – S of A39)
phone (0643) 5970 *Mich* 403 (J30) Exeter 43 m.

POUNDSGATE
Leusdon Lodge

Simple restaurant with rooms (S)
Secluded/Gardens/Good value (meals)   ®

A granite house with glorious views stretching 20 miles to the
south. The enterprising efforts of the owners match the 'tonic'
panorama: Neelia Hutchins' traditional English cooking is honest
and fresh – no packets for her soups here and the tin opener is
rarely used. Helped by her daughter Carol, her menus are
studded with tasty treats: 'Farmers family lunch', Falmouth
toasties, Torbay smokies, beef cobbler and so on. Menus change
daily – husband Denis' word processor makes that easy. Families
are welcome – children's meals and family rooms.
menus **A** (lun-din) Bar lun also *rooms* 8 **C-D** *cards* A AE DC Visa
closed Open all the year. (Oct-Mar – booking essential)
post Poundsgate, Newton Abbot, Devon. (Nr Leusdon Ch.)
phone (036 43) 304 & 436 *Mich* 403 (I32) Exeter 26 m.

WRAFTON
Poyners

Simple restaurant with rooms (S)
Gardens

A series of mostly thatched cottages built around a paved
courtyard. The young owners, Geoffrey and Helen Benn, took
over in 1983; previously he had worked for large hotel groups.
They have done well because they give their local clients what
they appear to want – a formula based on classical concepts with
portions large enough to satisfy any appetite. If that style suits
you then choose from 50 alternatives like steak Diane, veal
cordon bleu, chicken Kiev and endless others.
menus **A** (din) *alc* **B-C** (din) *rooms* 10 **D** *cards* A Visa
closed Xmas-1st week Jan. Sun evg. Lunch-every day.
post Wrafton, Devon EX33 2DN. (100 yds off W side A361)
phone (0271) 812149 *Mich* 403 (H30) Exeter 45 m.
Readers recommend the Little Beach Hotel at nearby
Woolacombe: *phone* (0271) 870398. Remember also the
marvellous Castle at **Taunton** – east of Exmoor (see page 139).

NORTH YORKSHIRE MOORS

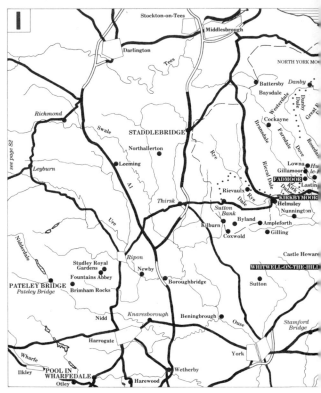

Little seems to have changed in the 831 years since St. Ailred – the third abbot of **Rievaulx** Abbey – wrote these words: 'everywhere peace, everywhere serenity and a marvellous freedom from the tumult of the world.' Why is it then that so many turn their backs on the **North York Moors National Park** – one of the most appealing in Britain? Southerners ignore it – hardly aware of its existence. The map above extends south and west from the North Yorkshire Moors – there are many exciting places to be seen beyond the Park's boundaries.

The North Yorkshire Moors are a self-contained group of hills rising to no more than 1400 feet – a mixture of open heather moors, each with its own name, and numerous dales. In the north small, deeply-cut valleys feed the River **Esk**; to the south much longer valleys carry water into the River **Derwent** – a series of picturesque, gentle dales provide a rich contrast to the flat-topped, bleak moors rising above them.

But Nature's attractions do not end there: the National Park's eastern boundary is a dramatic coastline of spectacular cliffs – ranging in height from 200 to 700 feet. Only three villages within the boundaries of the National Park provide direct access to the sea: **Staithes, Runswick Bay** and **Robin Hood's Bay**. See them all but particularly the last named; there's an exhilarating three-hour walk, only safe when the tide is out, from Robin Hood's Bay to **Ravenscar**, perched high above the sea.

76

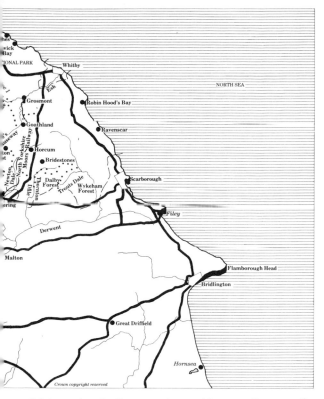

Driving and navigating present no problems; on the moors the roads are long and straight, but dive steeply down to the valley floors. There are many 'surprise views': examples are at **Gillamoor** (100–6890); at 100–7890; and, my favourite, at 100–5388 – drive 2 is a must. All the southern dales are worth exploring – from west to east in this order: **Rye Dale, Riccal Dale, Bransdale, Kirk Dale, Farndale, Rosedale, Newton Dale, Thornton Dale** and **Trouts Dale**. Use your legs!

Start in Rye Dale. Approach it from **Thirsk** – the home of the real-life 'James Herriot'; this allows you to climb the famous 'wall' of **Sutton Bank** – extensive views to the west. A mile south, on the same wooded Roulston Scar, is an essential diversion – the Kilburn White Horse; forest walks and more marvellous views – south this time. Rye Dale is rejuvenating walking country but matching Nature's treats are the stunning ruins of Rievaulx Abbey, considered by many to be the most beautiful in England – be sure to view it from the Temples and grass-covered Terrace above and to the east of it (see drive 2). Another abbey is at **Byland**, south-east of the White Horse; what a great size it must have once been. Visit Shandy Hall at nearby Coxwold (100-5377) – once the home of Laurence Sterne.

Bransdale is a 'hidden' dale – later to become Kirk Dale where it enters the Vale of Pickering to the south; few make the clockwise drive up to **Cockayne** (100-6298). Farndale is the home of the River **Dove**; the dale is famed for its annual show of wild daffodils – walk north from **Lowna** (100–6890) through the Farndale Nature Reserve (or park at Low Mill – 100–6795). **Hutton-le-Hole**, just east of the Dove, is a delight – the village is the site of the Rye Dale Folk Museum. Nearby **Lastingham** is another showpiece village – perhaps even prettier.

Don't miss Rosedale. Explore the old workings of the Rosedale Railway system in the dale – built in the last century when the area was the scene of a flourishing mining industry. So important was the Rosedale ironstone – first mined by the Cistercian monks of Rievaulx and Byland centuries ago – that 20 miles of standard gauge railway was built to transport the ore to **Battersby**.

For railway enthusiasts Newton Dale is the start of one of the best of all the privately-owned lines in Britain – the **North Yorkshire Moors Railway**. Starting at **Pickering** – visit the Beck Isle Museum of Rural Life – the line, built 150 years ago, runs north through Newton Dale for 18 miles to **Grosmont** in the Esk Valley. Every mile is a treat.

Thornton Dale and Trouts Dale are dominated by the great **Dalby**, **Wykeham** and, to the north, **Cropton** forests. Don't begrudge the small toll (£1) you pay to cross Dalby Forest – it's a fine drive with many marked trails. See drive 2.

Three spots on the high moors deserve your time: **Wade's Causeway** (a legendary giant) – a preserved stretch of Roman road (100–8097); the Hole of **Horcum** – a natural amphitheatre, below the A169 (100–8493); and the **Bridestones** – outcrops of weird-shaped rocks, sculptured by the elements (94–8791).

The northern dales are different in character from their southern counterparts – smaller, deeply-indented dales all feeding the Esk: **Baysdale, Westerdale, Danby Dale**, the quaintly-named **Great Fryup Dale** and **Glaisdale**. Access to them is easy. East of Danby is the Park's 'The Moors Centre' – 13 acres of pleasure. South of Grosmont, near **Goathland**, are two musts: the hamlet of Beck Hole – literally at the bottom of a hole; and the 70-ft high cascade of Mallyan Spout.

Another interesting railway route is the Esk Valley line that British Rail operate from **Middlesbrough** to **Whitby**. Join it at Battersby and enjoy the scenic run to Grosmont.

Scores of other man-made sites await you. On the coast there's the abbey at Whitby, the castle at **Scarborough** and, at **Bridlington**, the gardens of Sewerby Hall. Inland, within the Park, is the 12th-century castle at **Helmsley**; and the Mount Grace Priory – a Carthusian house, near **Staddlebridge**, in an attractive setting underneath a long, wooded hill.

Outside its boundaries are **Gilling** Castle – now part of **Ampleforth** College; **Nunnington** Hall, south-east of Helmsley; **Castle Howard** – the TV location for *Brideshead Revisited;* **Harewood** House and Bird Garden; **Fountains Abbey** and **Studley Royal Gardens; Ripon** Cathedral – a personal favourite (try to hear the choir); **Harrogate**; the Georgian house at **Sutton** Park; **Newby** Hall and **Beningbrough** Hall – both set in the river valleys between Ripon and York; and Kirkham Priory at **Whitwell-on-the-Hill**. Children will love Flamingo Land, south of Pickering. And if all that was not enough there's majestic **York**: its inspiring Minster, Castle Museum, National Railway Museum – and much else besides.

OS Landranger maps: 94.99.100.101.104.105
OS Routemaster map 6. Michelin map 402
Airport: Leeds & Bradford. Tees-side
Distance from London – York 204 miles.

Recommended Drives

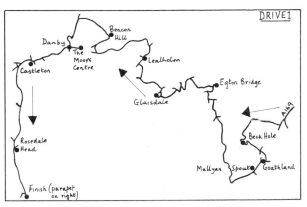

Drive 1 map 94 *Flat-topped, heather-blanketed moors, wooded dales, vast views, two smashing railway lines and two other man-made marks!*
Start 855034 (A169). 852028: NE North Sea; SE 3 Fylingdales 'Golf Balls'. W thru 8303. Beck Hole – 'big-dipper'. 827007 – walk to Mallyan Spout fall. N thru 8102. NW thru 7905. Glaisdale. N thru 7606. W thru 7508 – aeroplane-like views of Esk Dale. 736093 – panoramic view of sea and moors. Danby (detour 716084; The Moors Centre – Nat Park Centre). Castleton. S thru 684060 and 677020 (more extensive views). Finish 684989: note old Rosedale Railway line to E - parapet at junc. was a bridge (trace tracks on map); and spot those golf balls peeping over the moors. Approx. dist. 30 m.

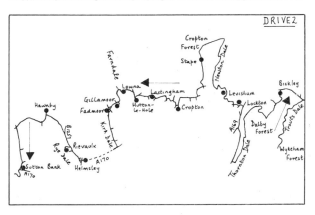

Drive 2 maps 94/100 *A succession of surprises: villages, 'surprise views', dales, woods and man-made treasures. The longest BofB drive.*
Start 94–914868 – walk/view. E thru 9490. S thru 9191. Dalby Forest. Detour 903907 – view in 8991. S thru 8586. N thru 8487. Levisham. N thru 8191. Cropton Forest – dusty! S thru 7992. Views at 788905/760897 (walk). Lastingham (see Norman crypt in church). Hutton-le-Hole. Farndale Nat. Res. at 687909 – walk N. 684902 – view. S thru 6786. 676858; detour tiny Saxon Kirkdale Minster! Map 100. A170 – Helmsley. B1257 to 583852; ent. Rievaulx Terr. and Temple. Detour Rievaulx Abbey at 576850. Back to B1257. NW thru 5588. View at 534882 – wow! S thru 5187 (walk to view at 509876). Finish view at Sutton Bank (A170). Approx. dist. 60 m.

Hotel and Restaurant Recommendations

FADMOOR
Plough Inn

Simple inn
Good value   ®

Years ago when my brother lived near Bridlington he pestered
me regularly to come north and enjoy the cooking skills of Kath
Brown. How right he was: Britain needs 500 more *cuisinières*
like self-taught Kath – with husband Don the two put on a super
show. An unpretentious welcome to greet you; a buzz of
contented diners in the cosy dining room; an amazing choice – at
bargain prices; and a kaleidoscope of ingredients – my
'Pickering' pink trout with lime and watercress cream and roast
duckling with a spiced caramel pear (influenced in part by their
Singapore spell) were masterly. You lucky Yorkshire folk!
menus **A-B** (din) (Rooms? Ask Don re B&B – or next entry)
closed 10 days in Feb, in May and in Oct. Sun. Mon.
post Fadmoor, Kirkbymoorside, North Yorks YO6 6HY.
phone (0751) 31515 *Mich* 402 (R21) York 35 m.

KIRKBYMOORSIDE
George and Dragon

Comfortable hotel (S)
Gardens/Good value (meals)

A family-owned, centuries-old inn – a listed building – but with 23
modern bedrooms in the hotel section at the rear which blends in
well with the old. Mum and Dad, Anne and Peter Curtis, daughter
Sheila and her husband Trevor Austin are the hosts: Peter's
garden is immaculate; Sheila's home cooking is tasty and Mum
and Trevor make sure you are made welcome. Value for money,
fresh produce: try the local 'Pickering' trout; local beef; York
ham; fresh Whitby fish; much above average vegetables; and
home-made treats like soups, pies and puddings.
menus **A** (lun) *alc* **A-B** (din) *rooms* 23 **C-D** *cards* A Visa
closed Christmas.
post 17 Market Place, Kirkbymoorside, North Yorks YO6 6AA.
phone (0751) 31637 *Mich* 402 (R21) York 33 m.

PATELEY BRIDGE
Sportsman's Arms

Comfortable restaurant with rooms
Quiet/Gardens/Good value (meals)   ®

The more I travelled through Britain in '84, the more I realised
how accurate the UK Michelin accolades are: this super, so-
attractively situated inn at the heart of Nidderdale, is a classic **M**
example. Ray Carter was a tutor at Leeds and York catering
colleges until five years ago. Now 35, he and his pretty wife, Jane,
and young partners John Topham and Simon Treanor have made
a big impression in Yorkshire; they and their staff alternate
between Pateley and Fountain House in Boroughbridge, owned
by them and off the A1, east of Ripon. Skill and style – at such low
prices – applied to Yorkshire produce: Nidderdale lamb and
trout; dales beef and duckling, and Whitby crab, lobster and fish;
venison from Westmorland. Simpler, low-cost Sunday lunch.
(See *Northern Dales* for Nidderdale details.)
menus **A** (Sun lun) **B** (din) Bar lun *rooms* 6 C-D cards A AE DC Visa
closed Rest: Sun evg 'non-res'; lun-ex. Sun. (2 m. N Pateley Br.)
post Wath-in-Nidderdale, Pateley Bridge, North Yorks HG3 5PP.
phone (0423) 711306 *Mich* 402 (021) York 34 m.

POOL IN WHARFEDALE

Very comfortable restaurant with rooms
Gardens/Good value (menu B)

Pool Court
BEST
MEAL
IN 84 ®

Yorkshire folk have got it made! SIP: Skipton, Ilkley and Pool –
three great restaurants within miles of each other. Owners
Michael and Hanni Gill should be bursting with pride. Why? At
the bubbling teamwork and skill of their all-British staff; chef
Melvin Jordan and his seven-strong kitchen *équipe* and a group
of young lads and lasses who do such a professional job in the
dining rooms. Brilliant touches from appetisers to *petits fours*: a
'variety of melons' – a firework of dazzling colour; a honey-glazed
roast breast of duck with duck galantine in a plum and brandy
sauce – second to none; and a 'Frédy Girardet lemon tart' which
the genius could not better himself. 'Reet champion' applies to
everything – including the ultra-modern, 'electronic' bedrooms.
Michelin: come on – where's the star?
menus B-C (din only served) *rooms* 4 **D2-D3** *cards* A AE DC Visa
closed 2 wks Aug and Xmas. Rest: Sun. Mon. Lun-every day.
post Pool Bank, Pool in Wharfedale, Otley, West Yorks LS21 1EH.
phone (0532) 842288 *Mich* 402 (P22) York 24 m.

STADDLEBRIDGE

Comfortable restaurant with rooms

McCoys at
the Tontine
®

A dismissive eight-line report, finishing with 'you either love it or
hate it' was to be expected from *The GFG*. The extrovert 30s
décor, with foot-tapping period music, may not be to the liking of
some but the Yorkshire welcome and what arrives on the plate
will be enjoyed by all. The cooking is polished: witness the
salmon in sorrel sauce, herb-scented baby lamb chops and many
innovative sweets. You have to admire the effort and energy the
three likeable McCoy brothers have put into establishing their
family inn over eight years. Fine wines and breakfasts.
(Junc. A19/A172; follow signs 'Cleveland Tontine'.)
alc C (din only) *rooms* 8 D2 *cards* A AE DC Visa
closed Xmas. Jan 1. Bank hols. Lun-every day.
post Staddlebridge, Northallerton, North Yorks DL6 3JB.
phone (060 982) 207 *Mich* 402 (P20) York 35 m.

WHITWELL-ON-THE-HILL

Comfortable hotel (S)
Secluded/Gardens/Swimming pool/Tennis

Whitwell Hall
Country House

I know of no better site for a hotel in the area: in a secluded,
wooded, hill-top setting at the doorstep of York, the coast,
Harrogate, the moors, and with Castle Howard a near neighbour.
Whitwell Hall has a quiet, winning appeal: comfortable, homely,
views of York Minster to the south, attractive well-fitted
bedrooms, a glorious staircase and stone gallery and a warm
welcome from the owners, Peter and Sally Milner. They have
worked wonders in eight years and are still making
improvements – '85 will see the new covered pool completed.
Thoroughly competent home cooking.
menus C (din only served) *rooms* 20 **D-D2** *cards* A AE DC Visa
closed Open all the year. (Lunches not served)
post Whitwell-on-the-Hill, York, North Yorks YO6 7JJ.
phone (065 381) 551 *Mich* 402 (R21) York 12 m.

NORTHERN DALES

J

see page 26
see page 27

Haltwhistle
Hadrian's Wall
Corbridge
Hexham
Tyne

South Tyne
East Allen
Allendale Town
BLANCHLAND
Consett

West Allen
Derwent

Alston
Allenheads

Hartside Cross
Garrigill
St. John's Chapel
Weardale
Stanhope
Crook
Kirkoswald
Westgate
Wear

Cross Fell
Drive 1
Hamsterley Forest

Temple Sowerby
Bowlees
Middleton-in-Teesdale

Teesdale

Eden Dale
Appleby
ROMALDKIRK
Tees
Staindrop

Brough
Barnard Castle

Kirkby Stephen
Tan Hill
Arkengarthdale
Richmond

Swaledale
Keld
Muker
REETH
Reeth

Butter Tubs
Grinton

Drive 2
Hardraw Force
Askrigg
Castle Bolton
Constable Burton

Sedbergh
Garsdale
HAWES
Bainbridge
Leyburn

Dentdale
YORKSHIRE DALES
Aysgarth
Wensleydale
Ure

Drive 3
Cam Houses
LOW GREENFIELD
Bishopdale
Jervaulx Abbey

Whernside
Langstrothdale
Cray
Buckden Pike

Hubberholme
Buckden

Kirkby Lonsdale
Ingleton
Ingleborough
Pen-y-ghent
Littondale
Wharfedale
Kettlewell
Nidderdale
Ramsgill

Bentham
Clapham
Horton in Ribblesdale
Arncliffe

AUSTWICK
NATIONAL PARK
PATELEY BRIDGE
Pateley Bridge

Malham Cove
Settle
Gordale Scar
Grassington
Stump Cross Caverns

Malham
Wharfe

Burnsall

Forest of Bowland
Ribblesdale
The Strid
Bolton Abbey

Drive 4
Skipton
SKIPTON
POOL IN WHARFEDALE

WHITEWELL
Ribble
Airedale
ILKLEY
Ilkley
Ilkley Moor

Clitheroe
Leeds-Liverpool Canal
Colne
Keighley
Bingley

Nelson
Burnley
Haworth
Shipley

Visitors to Britain often include only London and the south on their travels; in the process they miss some of our most rewarding countryside. Alas, vast numbers of southerners, too, born and bred in Britain, have yet to travel north!

Today, the Northern Dales are a kaleidoscope of beauty – an ever-changing landscape of sparkling facets: vast fells, stalking mists, limestone scars, swift streams, spectacular waterfalls and lush emerald dales. It was tens of thousands of years ago that Nature, at her most ferocious, sculptured and shaped this variety of scenery. To reap the best dividends from her majestic legacy do three things: use large-scale maps, your car and your legs – particularly the latter. It's a walkers' paradise; no other part of Britain is more popular with ramblers.

The words – Northern Dales – have been chosen carefully: they include not just the Yorkshire Dales but also the northern end of the Pennines – the undiscovered delights of **Teesdale, Weardale**, the twin arms of the Allen, the **South Tyne** and the **Derwent** Valley. Don't bypass this deserted terrain.

First seek out the Derwent Reservoir and the country around the historic village of **Blanchland** – the combination of woods, river, moors and the man-made reservoir is an ideal introduction to the area. Visit **Hexham** and its 13th-century abbey – and, of course, one of my favourite cathedrals at **Durham**. Then drive west across the high, bleak hills to **Allenheads** – the starting point for a tour of the 'English Alps'. This Victorian description was given to the twin arms of the River Allen because of the rocky landscapes, green, wooded valleys and gurgling streams. Head north from Allenheads to **Allendale Town**, once the centre of a lead mining community – the road follows the **East Allen** downstream; then strike west and south again, upstream on the **West Allen** (Catherine Cookson country).

Alston is a splendid, moorland town with steep, cobbled streets. From there you can drive north to **Haltwhistle** (see its church) and enjoy South Tynedale – **Hadrian's Wall** is another highlight (see *Border Country*); or south-west of Alston, via **Hartside Cross** (nearly 2000 ft high) with eagle-eye views of the fells in the English Lakes; to **Kirkoswald** and the Acorn Bank Gardens at **Temple Sowerby**, in quiet **Eden Dale**; or to nearby **Garrigill** – the scene of some of Turner's paintings.

Enjoy Weardale next – several villages are special highlights: **St. John's Chapel, Westgate** and **Stanhope**. Then make the 2000 ft plus climb over Chapel Fell to Teesdale. In the vicinity of **Bowlees** are a number of waterfalls: the fury of High Force – England's best; the gentler, scenic Low Force; the falls in the woods near Gibson's Cave; and Cauldron Snout – the longest cascade in England. (Do drive 1 – one of the very best.) See **Middleton-in-Teesdale**, especially at daffodil time.

Before leaving this undiscovered area complete a short circular tour which will take you in turn to **Hamsterley Forest** – pay the toll for the 4½ mile drive through the mixed woodland; then south to Raby Castle, near **Staindrop** – in a huge deer park; and, finally, to the astonishing Bowes Museum at **Barnard Castle** – housed in a massive French-style château.

However, it will be the famous Yorkshire Dales that most readers will want to enjoy – and rightly so; most of them are within the **Yorkshire Dales National Park**. One favourite is **Wharfedale**: I have set aside two extra pages so that my friend, Peter Harland, can describe its delights and the varying charms of the terrain encircling it. For me it's at its best near **Buckden**. South of **Grassington** the character of the dale changes – it's a gentler landscape. East of Wharfedale a dead-end road takes you from flower-filled **Pateley Bridge**, through **Ramsgill** to the head of **Nidderdale** – ignored by most visitors. (At Lofthouse pay the 50p toll and use the Yorks Water Authority private road – built on an old railway line; 99-100735.) Don't bypass **Stump Cross Caverns** – just west of Pateley Bridge.

To the north of Buckden are **Wensleydale** and **Swaledale**; subtle scenic changes give these dales a different character – both will already be familiar to those of you who have watched any of the James Herriot TV stories. Wensleydale has many man-made attractions along its length: the villages of **Hawes, Bainbridge, Askrigg, Aysgarth** and **Castle Bolton** among them; and **Jervaulx Abbey** – a Cistercian foundation where Wensleydale cheese was first made. Nature competes with Semer Water, south of Bainbridge; **Hardraw Force**, north of Hawes, is the longest single-drop waterfall in England; the various falls at Aysgarth and also Carter Force, north-west of Hawes; and the gardens at **Constable Burton**, east of **Leyburn**.

Various mountain roads climb north from Wensleydale to Swaledale; the most famous is **Butter Tubs** with its unusual limestone columns in huge pot-holes. **Reeth**, with its Folk Museum, makes a good centre to explore both Swaledale and **Arkengarthdale**, a subsidiary valley to the north. Complete the drive from the latter up to **Tan Hill**, where you'll find the highest inn in England. **Keld, Muker**, Gunnerside, Low Row and **Grinton** are other villages; **Richmond**, much further downstream, is famous for its 12th-century castle.

To the west is the fourth of the famous dales – **Ribblesdale**. What a dramatic change of scenery you'll find here – dominated as it is by Yorkshire's mighty Three Peaks: **Whernside** (2414 ft) and **Ingleborough** (2373 ft) to the west of the River Ribble and **Pen-y-ghent** (2273 ft) to the east. **Settle, Austwick, Clapham** and **Ingleton** are the most convenient centres to explore the vast scars, crags and the many pot-holes and caves that lie to the north of the **A65**. The glens at Ingleton (a superb but long walk) are famous for their waterfalls – Thornton Force is the best known; Clapham is renowned for Ingleborough Cave – reached by a nature trail walk. White Scar Cave (on the B6255) is easily accessible. **Dentdale**, my favourite (see drive 3), and **Garsdale**, both to the north of Ingleton, are ignored by visitors. Enjoy a run on one of the best-loved railway lines in Britain – from Settle to Carlisle; '85 may see it closed.

Nature's most unusual handiwork will be found north of **Malham**: the *cirques* of **Malham Cove** and **Gordale Scar**; many waterfalls; the limestone 'pavement' north of the cove and Malham Tarn – a bird sanctuary and nature reserve. There's an information centre at Malham; but use your legs in this terrain.

Seek out a remote corner of Lancashire – the **Forest of Bowland**. High fells, quiet streams, bluebell woods, sleepy villages – it's an isolated haven. (See drive 4.)

There's so much more to mention: Brontë country – based on the haunting museum at **Haworth**; the **Keighley** and Worth Valley Steam Railway – the location for the film *The Railway Children*; **Skipton** – with its castle and the Yorkshire Dales Railway; and ruined **Bolton Abbey**, in a riverside setting. Enjoy, too, the Victorian model mill village at Saltaire, near **Shipley**.

OS Landranger maps: 86.87.91.92.97.98.99.102.103.104
OS Routemaster map 5. Michelin map 402
Airports: Manchester. Leeds & Bradford
Distance from London – Keighley 208 miles

Recommended Drives

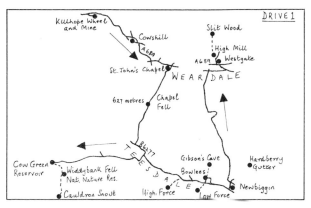

Drive 1 map 92 *More a series of joyous walks in Weardale & Teesdale. Man has left scars – Nature's mark is made in more pleasing ways.*
Start 885379. (First detour 5 m. NW on A689 – Killhope & 34 ft high wheel; Visitor Centre shows how lead mined 100 years ago.) S thru 8635 – one of England's two highest roads. E thru 8231 to Nat. Nature Res. (810308); even wheelchairs can make it to Cauldron Snout Cascade. Back to B6277. 885286; walk High Force – torrential rain made it a ferocious fury. 906281 (phone box); walk Low Force and suspension br. Bowless Info Cent. (906283); walk Gibson's Cave. N thru 9128; look E Hardberry Gutter – a 'hush' – man-made, using water to extract lead ore. Finish 906383 – walk past High Mill to Slit Wood (905390). Approx. dist. 33 m.

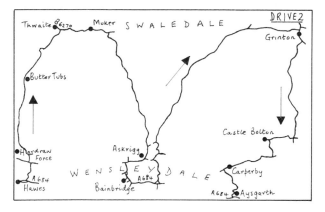

Drive 2 map 98 *Herriot Country: heather-clad moors; limestone scars; views – one a stunner; gentle, green dales; stone walls, trees and becks.*
Start Hawes (876899): Nat. Park Cent. for info; Upper Dales Folk Museum. N thru 8790. Access Hardraw Force at Green Dragon (868912). N thru 8695 (see Butter Tubs – limestone pillars). B6270. S thru 9394. S thru Askrigg. S thru Bainbridge (greens, stocks, falls). A684. N thru 9590. Note wall on left thru 9795. Stunning views thru 9896 and 0298. S thru 0395. Castle Bolton; 14th-cent. ruins and, in '84, at St. Oswald's Church, a fine exhib. on old Wensleydale Rlwy – now dismantled. '85 exhib? W thru 0290. Finish Aysgarth Falls (three of them). More info 012887. Approx. dist. 36 m.

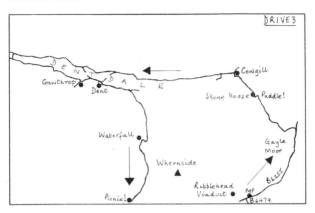

Drive 3 map 98 *Three great peaks; a man-made marvel under threat; and a chance to examine the 'anatomy' of a seductive dale. Super drive.*
Start milepost B6255 (769795): SE Pen-y-ghent; SW impressive Ingleborough; NW Whernside; behind you Ribblehead Viaduct – in need of repair, could be cause of '85 closure Settle-Carlisle line. W at 795836. ½ m. views far as Lakes' peaks. 771859 – narrow bridge – have paddle! N bank Dentdale – thru 720867 & 660900. Dee tree-lined most of length – ideal for walks. Dale best W end. Off map for 200 yds – keep turning left. SE thru 6788. Tea at Bridge Cott. Gawthrop? Surprising Dent – cobbles, too. S thru 7284. 723837 – waterfall and paddle! Finish 712800 (ideal for picnic). Approx. dist. 24 m.

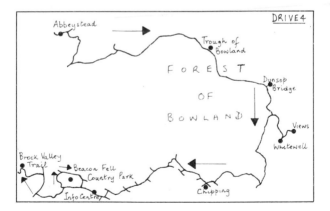

Drive 4 map 102 *The Forest of Bowland – ignored by so many. Desert the M6 for a couple of hours and surprise yourselves.*
Start Abbeystead (562544). Sharp right after bridge – walk in riverside woods. S to 565532 – then E. E thru 6053; bees do well – lots of honey for sale! Climb Trough of Bowland. Dunsop Bridge. Dome-topped hills, lovely woods. S thru 6548. Detour Whitewell (church 658469 – climb E for views). S thru 6446 & 6444. W to Chipping. Note trees at 627438. NW to 613443. SW thru 5942. Info Centre for Beacon Fell Country Park at 579422. Do clockwise circuit of Park – walk thru woods on hill. N thru 5542. Finish 548431 – Brock Valley Trail; naturalist's delight. Approx. dist. 26 m.

A Personal View of the Dales

Peter Harland

My love affair with the Yorkshire Dales began soon after I was born on the **Airedale** side of Rombalds Moor (**Ilkley Moor** to you) and continued through quiet childhood in wartime **Wharfedale** to early adult days cycling in **Swaledale**, then back to Wharfedale to raise a family. Yet in 50 years I cannot recall reading anything which truly conveys the native's deepest feelings for the place.

Perhaps guidebooks should not attempt to describe natural beauty but concentrate instead on facts. I could tell you what most locals prefer to keep to themselves – that the Dales are one of the true glories of the world. The Wharfe between **Bolton Abbey** and **Burnsall** is my own favourite spot, particularly when the leaves are yellow or the heather purple on the moors above; but you believe it not until you experience it for yourself, and a hundred different parts of the Dales (**Reeth** and **Arkengarthdale**, for example, **Fountains Abbey**, or **Brimham Rocks** – see page 76 – which so inspired the sculptor Henry Moore) easily excite similar passions.

But I will confine myself to advising motorists to beware of fine Sundays and bank holidays, when the weight of traffic makes it dangerous to gaze at anything but the road ahead and difficult to find a parking space at riverside beauty spots such as **Richmond** or Bolton Abbey, the latter the grouse shooting base of the Duke of Devonshire. At weekends, we used as a young family to dash up the dale with sausages and frying pan to hold a picnic breakfast on a deserted fell top and then drive back against the tide to spend the afternoon in our garden! However, pub lovers please note that the great homeward drift starts early, so that an evening spent in a Dales hostelry is still a genuinely hospitable experience.

Sadly, pub food in the Dales is not as it used to be. Many, presumably for economy, have abandoned home cooking in favour of commercial freezer food to be found in Cotswolds and Dales alike, so it is a joy to find a pub like the White Lion at **Cray** (a village of three homes), halfway up the Kidstones Pass into **Bishopdale**, where the Hirds, a former returning officer in the West Riding and his wife, insist on home cooking served in a small dining room with an open fire. And in the bar, you can play the rare game of bull's nose. Ask the landlord for a demonstration – he's a champion at it.

Yorkshire people travel the world but, liking home comforts, always return, so it will be no surprise to them that Richard Binns has included some really fine eating places there (see *North Yorkshire Moors* chapter as well). My one qualification is that the best of them are in the lower dales, whereas the dramatic sightseeing is usually in the middle and upper dales. One solution is to stay in a cottage or inn and drive down the dale when you feel like a really good meal.

We have stayed for many years in the excellently appointed Dalegarth cottages, in **Buckden**, at the head of Wharfedale, convenient for dales north and south, with superb views of the hills and even saunas to soothe tired muscles after a hard day's fell walking. Staying here now has the added advantage of being almost the only way a non-resident can reserve a table at **Low Greenfield**, in **Langstrothdale**, where the cooking and hospitality are remarkable but space is restricted.

But there are plenty of inns. At least two are nationally known. **Tan Hill**, on the moors above Swaledale, is reputedly England's highest pub – 1732 feet above sea-level. A great sheep sale is held here once a year. The other is the George at **Hubberholme**, in

Langstrothdale, which used to be the vicarage, and houses an annual land-letting every New Year's Eve. The home-made soup is more likely to catch the attention of most of us. A visit to Hubberholme Church is imperative. It is one of only a handful in the country whose rood-loft survived the Reformation, presumably because it was too isolated for Cromwell's men. The church is furnished with wooden pews made by Robert Thompson, the unique Yorkshire carpenter who carved a mouse as signature on all his work. Sheep graze in the graveyard and inside all is cool and quiet. (The Thompson workshops are at **Kilburn**, near Sutton Bank – see *North Yorkshire Moors*.)

The Dales can only be savoured fully by getting out of the car. The number of available sports is astonishingly high: pot-holing, fishing, particularly for trout, riding, canoeing, hang-gliding, sailing, rock climbing, fell-walking (and running – there's an annual Three Peaks race), motor-cycle scrambling, even skiing in winter. Believe me, you can sail over the Pennines, by taking a boat on the **Leeds-Liverpool Canal** from **Skipton**. Surprise your friends and sail into **Burnley**!

Even if such athletics are out, walking is necessary to reach many of the more dramatic Dales sights, such as **The Strid**, deep in Bolton Woods, where the **Wharfe** narrows to a raging torrent and many people have died trying to jump across. Other natural sights reached only on foot include **Gordale Scar**, far less intimidating than the James Ward painting in the Tate Gallery, **Malham Cove**, **Hardraw Force** (see drive 2), **Stump Cross Caverns**, or such simple but mind-stirring monuments as a Polish airmen's war memorial at the top of **Buckden Pike**, and Willance's Leap, near Richmond, making a cliff fall in 1606 that ended with only a broken leg but a dead horse.

Some birdwatching can be done from a car – oyster catchers in **Littondale** perhaps, curlews virtually anywhere – but you have to get out to find, as we have, Dippers behind a waterfall, yellow wheatears on a fellside, or a pair of heron on **Pen-y-ghent**. Locals say there are black pheasant now in the young forests above Langstrothdale.

You certainly see the wonders of the drystone walls from a car, winding over the mountain tops in the limestone areas. But you will not smell the history of the lead mines unless you climb steep, grass roads. I was concerned to discover recently that the old Roman road from **Cam Houses** Farm, high up on Dodd Fell, has been metalled, enabling cars to penetrate where previously we walked along ancient setts (now covered) to the sound of no more than skylarks and an occasional jet plane. Here, on a fine day, you can see as far as **Sutton Bank** (page 76) and the Lakeland peaks (page 60) on opposite sides of the country. No reason not to share this view of the dramatic ones of Pen-y-ghent and **Ingleborough** nearby; but cars do take some of the mystery from that loneliest of farms, often cut off by snow in winter.

The Dales have always attracted artists, of whom the most famous must be Turner, befriended and supported by a local squire at **Otley** (page 76). However, examples of good, modern Dales art are surprisingly hard to find. It is easier to study the crafts in museums at **Hawes**, Reeth and **Grassington**. See the Hartley-Ingleby collection in Hawes railway station.

For the rest, imagination plays its part as you think of ancient Brits living on top of mountains, of the centuries-long struggle of sheep farmers to make a living, or of the mystery of the Roman legion that marched out of York, into the Dales to subdue the natives and never returned. Good hunting!

Hotel and Restaurant Recommendations

▋AUSTWICK▐   Game Cock Inn

Very simple inn with rooms (S)
Gardens/Good value (meals)

One of my most modest recommendations – a totally
unpretentious country inn. For 45 years Mary Howarth – a gentle,
sweet soul – has been known far and wide for her homely
cooking; oh, if only there were more like her. She lost her
husband, Harry, in 1983, so times are tougher now: but the simple
formula of her renowned roast duck, or lamb (roast beef at
Sunday lunch), combined with home-made soups and pies
continues to please contented clients. Please ring ahead – the
dining room is small, so booking is essential; it also gives you a
chance to discuss the main course with Mary. Three basic
bedrooms (the quiet Traddock nearby has 11 rooms).
menus **A-B** (din-Sun lun) Bar lun *rooms* 3 **B-D**
closed Dec 25/26.
post Austwick, Lancaster, Lancs. (In fact in North Yorks.)
phone (046 85) 226 *Mich* 402 (M21) Keighley 29 m.

▋BLANCHLAND▐   Lord Crewe Arms

Simple hotel (S)
Quiet/Gardens/Good value (meals)

Blanchland richly deserves to please visitors from much further
afield than Northumberland or Co. Durham; it's a handsome
village centred around the 12th-century Blanchland Abbey – its
proud character makes a strong impression. The 13th-century
hotel was once the Abbot's home – itself full of intriguing corners
and legends: a priest's hole, stunning crypt and the ghost of
Dorothy Forster among them. Before your meal explore the
valley – the paths along the banks of the Derwent are the perfect
apéritif. Simple fare with melon, chicken broth, free-range
chicken and strawberries being typical alternatives.
menus **A** Bar lun (Mon-Sat: Oct-July) *rooms* 16 **D-D2** *cards* A AE DC Visa
closed Mon-Thurs (Jan-mid Mar).
post Blanchland, Consett, Co. Durham DH8 9SP.
phone (043 475) 251 *Mich* 402 (N19) Keighley 100 m.

▋HAWES▐   Cockett's

Simple hotel (S)
Good value (dinner)

Four years ago Brian and Cherry Guest pulled up their roots in
Welford-on-Avon (nr. Stratford) and made the courageous
decision to try their hands as hoteliers. The 17th-century, stone-
built Cockett's, once a Quaker-owned property, is a small 'home'
where Brian is the ideal front-of-house host and Cherry succeeds
admirably as the chef. It was particularly satisfying to see several
local young couples relishing Morecambe Bay shrimps; guinea
fowl flamed in Cointreau; and a cheese board with two different
Wensleydales, a Swaledale and a Ribblesdale. The dining room is
too dimly lit – which neither does justice to Cherry's talents nor
to the fine paintings, the work of local artists.
menus **A** (dinner only served) *rooms* 5 **D** *cards* A Visa
closed Jan. Feb. Lunch – every day.
post Market Place, Hawes, North Yorkshire DL8 3RD.
phone (09697) 312 *Mich* 402 (N21) Keighley 46 m.

ILKLEY   Box Tree

Very comfortable restaurant/Michelin ★★   Ⓡ

The classical-based cuisine is highly rated by Michelin. It's in the capable, experienced hands of Michael Truelove, who's so eager to please; the 26-year-old chef took over from Michael Lawson in July 1984. A visit is an experience every reader should relish – a series of pleasures: cottage rooms more like an art gallery; unpretentious, kindly staff – how magnificently they looked after two tiny tots in a party of six Canadians; faultless specialities – rarely-seen tuna with clever use of an artichoke base and baby ones, a 'North Sea' fish soup, and sorbets tasting of their menu descriptions. And, as a bonus, sparkling-eyed Christine. Rooms? Try Craiglands; **D-D2**, *phone* (0943) 607676.

alc **C-D** (dinner only served) *cards* A AE DC Visa
closed Dec 25/26. Jan 1. Sun. Mon. Lun-every day. (Book ahead)
post 35-37 Church St, Ilkley, West Yorks LS29 9DR.
phone (0943) 608484 *Mich* 402 (022) Keighley 10 m.

▌LOW GREENFIELD▐   Low Greenfield

Simple hotel (S)
Secluded/Gardens/Good value (dinner)

In their thirties, Austin and Lindsay Sedgley needed all the advantages of youthful energy and good health in their successful battle to turn this once sadly neglected 17th-century farmhouse into the happy home it now is. The setting is perfection: over 1000 ft above sea-level; up a dead-end road; and overlooking Green Field Beck, one of the two sources of the River Wharfe (98-847803). Fishermen, walkers, botanists and ornithologists will revel in the lonely streams and moors surrounding Low Greenfield. Wholesome, tasty fare – one highlight is a delicious port wine and redcurrant jelly.

menus **A** (dinner only served) *rooms* 6 **B-D** (Book ahead)
closed Dec-Feb. Lunch-every day.
post Langstrothdale Chase, Buckden, North Yorks BD23 5JN.
phone (075 676) 858 *Mich* 402 (N21) Keighley 34 m.

PATELEY BR./POOL IN WHARFEDALE (p. 80/81)

▌REETH▐   Burgoyne

Simple hotel (S)
Gardens/Good value (meals)   Ⓡ

The moment you step through the door, to be met by Penny Cordingley, you sense you are going to hate leaving this cheerful hotel – overlooking a green and the hillsides of Swaledale. She's a delightful soul – and a super cook; husband Chris is an enthusiastic helper with a sense of humour. They have the perfect personalities for hoteliers. Menus provide a choice: my meal of home-made bread, ham and pea soup, roast duckling in a cherry sauce with three veg and an orange salad, apricot and ginger ice cream and several local cheeses was first class – the equal of Mr Tovey. And 20 half-bottles of wine.

meals **A** (din-Sun lun) *rooms* 10 **B-D**
closed Nov-1 wk before Easter.
post Reeth, Richmond, North Yorkshire DL11 6SN.
phone (0748) 84292 *Mich* 402 (N21) Keighley 45 m.

ROMALDKIRK   Rose and Crown

Comfortable inn with rooms (S)
Good value (meals)

I would drive a long way to see Romaldkirk – in Teesdale, the
'lovely, sweet vale': space to breathe; several greens – with stocks
and water pump; solid, secure, grey-stone cottages; a 12th-
century church; and the Rose and Crown. David and Jill Jackson
have worked out a successful formula; a happy atmosphere and
tasty fare – usually local produce like grouse, sausages, pork,
beef and salmon. The words 'home-made' appear regularly.
Dinner can bring pork cooked with the fine local cheese,
Cotherstone. Of the 15 bedrooms, five are in a modern annexe;
one is a four-poster and one is purpose-built for the disabled.
menus **A-B** *rooms* 15 **D-D2** *cards* A AE DC Visa
closed Dec 25/26.
post Romaldkirk, Barnard Castle, Durham DL12 9EB.
phone (0833) 50213 *Mich* 402 (N20) Keighley 82 m.

SKIPTON   Oats

Comfortable restaurant
Good value (lunch)   ®

You'll not find better skills at such low cost in the north. Roger
Grime, after 14 years at Pool (page 81), and with the financial
backing of local printers, is putting Skipton on the culinary map.
A variety of delights: *salade Chinoise, crêpes au Camembert,*
local pigeon, duckling with honey and orange, local Gargrave
trout ('jaws' said a neighbour), Karen's (Roger's talented
assistant) open flan with Yorkshire rhubarb and summer
pudding are just a few of the kitchen's skills. No shortcuts: bread
from Skipton Bakery across the road – visit it and Stanforth's
shop (what pork pies); a Yorkshire-style welcome; *petits fours* –
better than the Box Tree's; all of it served in a listed building. At
least try lunch – rarely served in the north.
alc **A** (lun) **B-C** (din)
closed Sun. Mon. (Rooms? Speak to Martin Duce – their own soon)
post Chapel Hill, Skipton, North Yorks BD23 1NL. (B6265/A65)
phone (0756) 3604 *Mich* 402 (N22) Keighley 10 m.

WHITEWELL   Inn at Whitewell

Comfortable inn with rooms (S)
Quiet/Fishing/Good value (meals)

The picturesque riverside setting worked against Richard
Bowman three years ago – the River Hodder washed his kitchens
away! When Richard finishes arguing about compensation with
his landlords – the 'Duchy' no less – he can get back to financing
the improvements he has in mind for his country inn with such an
easy-going atmosphere; credit for that goes to the girls and
particularly Lisa, from Colorado, who loves it all so much she's
getting married to a lucky local lad. The words 'home-made' and
'local' appear often: they apply to salmon, ham, soups, bread, ice
cream and sausages. (Gents: enjoy the Gents?)
menus **A-B** (din) Bar lun *rooms* 10 **D** *cards* A AE DC Visa
closed Open all the year. (By church, 2 m. S of Dunsop Br.)
post Forest of Bowland, Clitheroe, Lancs BB7 3AT.
phone (02008) 222 *Mich* 402 (M22) Keighley 36 m.

SCOTTISH LOCHS

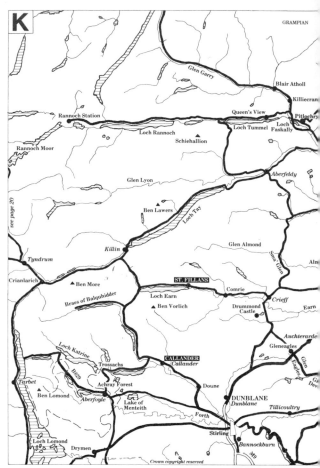

I pondered for a long time wondering what name to give this beguiling area of Scotland. I solved the problem as I prepared the artwork for the map above – it was then that I decided to give it my own idiosyncratic name – Scottish Lochs. There are numerous lochs – of every kind – to tempt you, surrounded by heather-clad hills, wonderful woods and emerald-green glens. It is a paradise for all of you who love Nature's handiwork.

Dunkeld would make a good starting point. The town itself is a small place – but, together with the wooded neighbourhood and the River **Tay**, it has, for me, a special appeal (see the recommended drive). Don't miss the delectable lochs to the east of the town; **Loch of Lowes** is a nature reserve.

From Dunkeld you can make several magnificent day drives. Two would take you up the deserted dead-end roads in **Glen Clova** and **Glen Esk** (detour first to **Edzell** Castle). Both are unusual in that the scenery changes so dramatically as you head north-west up their ever wilder valleys. A third drive could lead

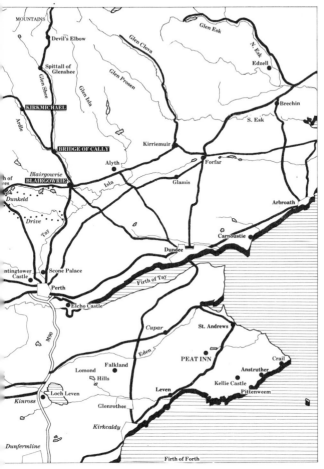

you over the mighty **Grampian Mountains** – via the **Devil's Elbow** – to Braemar and the incomparable Dee Valley – perhaps one of the most inspiring and beautiful in Europe.

Pitlochry is an old-established tourist centre with a modern Festival Theatre. Nearby **Loch Faskally** is man made; see the 'fish ladder' where 34 pools give salmon a helping hand as they head upstream past the dam.

North of Pitlochry is the start of the renowned Road to the Isles – a superb scenic drive. But don't be fooled: it's a dead-end road – though that's of no consequence as it will please enormously. But, before heading west, detour north to the wooded gorge at **Killiecrankie** – where the Jacobites routed the English nearly 300 years ago – and to the great Blair Castle at **Blair Atholl**. Return to **Loch Tummel** where, near its eastern end, you can admire the same stunning view that thrilled Queen Victoria – it's called **Queen's View**. Continue westwards – it's 40 miles of spellbinding terrain: pine and birch woods, lochs and mountains

93

– you'll want to stop often. Do so – use your legs and maps. The road comes to an end at **Rannoch Station** on **Rannoch Moor** – a desolate and dramatic landscape. On your return be sure to use the minor road on the southern side of **Loch Rannoch** – through the Black Wood of Rannoch.

At the eastern end of the loch continue on the minor road as it heads south-east under the huge brooding mass of the 3547 ft high **Schiehallion** – the contoured 'cone' made famous by Maskelyne's 1774 experiment (see plaque at 51 or 52–753557). As you head south towards Loch Tay you must be certain you have plenty of time to do justice to the many drives and walks that await you. (Try to use the minor road alternatives alongside lochs – the south side of **Loch Earn** is an example.) First there is the 30-mile diversion up **Glen Lyon** – famous for its 'Deer Forests' and the longest in Scotland. Don't miss **Aberfeldy** – use your legs to explore the Birks of Aberfeldy, set in the narrow ravine to the south of the town. Enjoy huge **Loch Tay**. The 3984 ft high **Ben Lawers** towers over the northern shore; in its shadow there's a Mountain Visitor Centre at Lochan na Lairige (51–608379) where nature trails allow you to enjoy some of Britain's finest arctic and alpine flora. At **Killin** you'll be thrilled by the Falls of Dochart – divided and step-like.

In the south-west corner of the map you'll notice another group of lochs; one of them is the most famous in Scotland – **Loch Lomond**. The northern end is a narrow strip of water, hemmed in by massive 3000 ft high peaks; the southern end is a broad expanse – dotted with islands. Explore the wooded eastern banks – where there are many fine forest walks. From **Aberfoyle** drive the **B829** to the eastern shore of Loch Lomond.

North of Aberfoyle are the romantic **Trossachs** – made famous by Sir Walter Scott. Use the Duke's Pass to enjoy **Achray Forest**, descending to the wooded lochside of **Loch Katrine** – don't miss the summer cruises on the ancient steamer named Sir Walter Scott. Detour to the **Lake of Menteith** – where, on a tiny island in 1547, the child Mary Stuart took refuge. See **Callander**, drive west up the picturesque dead-end **Braes of Balquhidder** – Rob Roy country – and then east to **Crieff**.

Near the latter visit the gardens at **Drummond Castle** and drive through **Glen Eagles** and **Glen Devon** to **Loch Leven** – a nature reserve and where, in 1567, Castle Island was the prison of Mary, Queen of Scots. To the east, and beyond the **Lomond Hills**, are several man-made sights: the 16th-century **Falkland** Palace and gardens; **Kellie Castle**; and the Hill of Tarvit House, near **Cupar**. Detour to the villages of **Pittenweem**, **Crail** and **Anstruther** (home of the Scottish Fisheries Museum) – all with examples of 'Little Houses' – restored cottage homes.

Elsewhere in the area are many other man-made treasures: the castle at **Stirling**; nearby **Dunblane** Cathedral and **Doune** Castle; at Perth there's the Black Watch Museum at Balhousie Castle and Branklyn Garden; close at hand are **Elcho Castle**, **Huntingtower Castle** and **Scone Palace** and park. To the north-east is **Glamis** Castle and the Angus Folk Museum at Glamis; nearby is J. M. Barrie's birthplace at **Kirriemuir.**

Golfers can enjoy the courses at **St. Andrews, Carnoustie, Gleneagles** and dozens of others. And there are enough lochs and rivers to give any angler a lifetime of pleasure.

OS Landranger maps: 42.43.44.50.51.52.53.54.56.57.58.59
OS Routemaster map 4. Michelin map 401
Airports: Edinburgh. Glasgow
Distance from London – Perth 449 miles.

Recommended Drive

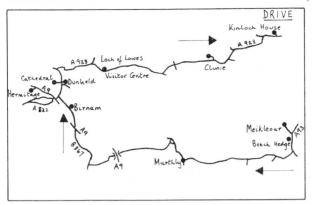

Map 53 *Dunkeld – and the immediate ring of country encircling it – is a favourite of mine: wood-capped hills; quiet, small lochs; and the ancient town itself, alongside the Tay. It will remain a deeply-etched picture in your subconscious mind for decades – as it has in mine.*

Start 163390 (app from NW) – read sign on right; Meikleour Beech Hedge – the world's highest. Cross Tay 160380 – in high season four rods for five days cost £6000 here! W thru 1238 and 0638. Thru 030420 – Macbeth's Birnam. W on A822 thru 0241 – views. Use 'yellow' back to valley – 020421. At 014424 – Hermitage Woodland Walk: folly, cave, waterfall, marvellous trees. Back to Dunkeld – park by Cathedral. The town's a jewel: a cathedral beside the Tay in a park setting; 17th-cent. restored 'Little Houses'; Stanley Hill Park; and the Tay. 040435 – Loch of Lowes Nature Reserve inc' ospreys (alas, in '84 only a male returned); Visitor Centre and super Observation Hide (ideal for disabled). E thru 0643 and 1043. Finish 135450 – enjoy the Highland herd (see hotel entry below). Approx. dist. 24 m.

Hotel and Restaurant Recommendations

BLAIRGOWRIE   Kinloch House

Comfortable hotel (S)
Secluded/Gardens/Good value (dinner)   ®

Perhaps the best way I can compliment David and Sarah Shentall is by recounting the story of one couple I met on my visit. They had been earlier in the week for one night, continued on their travels only to return, two days later, for a second dose of the Kinloch 'tonic': it's a family-sized house with a fine gallery and several bedrooms with four-poster beds; guests get to know each other quickly through David's efforts; Dunkeld and its woods and lochs are close at hand; and Sarah, helped by daughter Tessa, does sterling work in the kitchens, using Scottish produce with many traditional recipes like Cullen Skink and tipsy monk. Their version of marinated Highland salmon is a three-star winner. Be sure to make friends with their seven-strong Highland herd – all are family pets; and buy some of the mole catcher's super pure heather honey.

menus **A-B** (din) Bar lun *rooms* 9 **D** *cards* A AE DC
closed Open all the year.
post Blairgowrie, Perth PH10 6SG. (3 m. W on A923)
phone (025 084) 237 *Mich* 401 (J14) Perth 16 m.
Several readers recommended Lands of Loyal Hotel at Alyth – east of Blairgowrie; comfortable, secluded – *phone* (082 83) 2481.

BRIDGE OF CALLY

Bridge of Cally

Simple hotel (S)
Gardens/Fishing/Good value (meals)

The whitewashed hotel sits above the River Ericht at the southern end of Strathardle. It may be small and simple but certainly it's spotless – a credit to the Innes family. Grace Innes, with the help of her daughter, does the cooking – enjoyable fare with the sure hand of an experienced 'mum' who knows how to please. Enjoy delights like port and stilton pâté, tasty lentil soup, Tay salmon, local lamb and a feather-light hazelnut meringue gâteau. It's possible the family may move on soon: let's hope that will not be for a year or two.

menus **A** *rooms* 9 **B-D** *cards* A Visa
closed Open all the year.
post Bridge of Cally, Blairgowrie, Perth PH10 7JJ.
phone (025 086) 231 *Mich* 401 (J14) Perth 21 m.

CALLANDER

Roman Camp

Comfortable hotel
Secluded/Gardens/Fishing/Good value (meals)

Built in 1625 as a small hunting lodge, the small, château-like building is set in extensive and photogenic wooded grounds and gardens – all of it alongside the River Teith. Sami Denzler hails from Lausanne – like the great Frédy Girardet; though he would be the first to claim no comparison with that master. Cooking is typically Swiss: safe, nothing exciting, impeccably done, international in style and good value. Desserts like *apfel strudel* are highlights; and a mouthwatering, genuine *gâteau forêt noir*, made in the Roman Camp kitchens. No smoking allowed in the Swiss-style dining room; the taboo is spreading – let's hope it becomes the rule throughout Britain.

menus **B** rooms 11 **D-D2**
closed Mid Dec-Jan.
post Main St, Callander, Perth FK17 8BG.
phone (0877) 30003 *Mich* 401 (H15) Perth 40 m.

DUNBLANE

Cromlix House

Very comfortable hotel
Secluded/Gardens/Tennis/Fishing ®

It's at Cromlix where you realise why the Royal Family adore Scotland. The 'House' is at the heart of a 5,000 acre estate – owned by the same family for 400 years; private fishing and shooting are on the doorstep and there's golf at nearby Gleneagles. With a maximum of 20 guests *in situ* you're fussed royally in Balmoral-like luxury. A typical no-choice dinner menu – light and attractively presented – could be asparagus, lobster mousse, Angus beef (or game), 'Minty' cheeses (see next page) with tasty cheese and herb rolls, a Guérard-style sweet of fresh fruit and home-made appetisers and *petits fours*. Full marks to Stephen Coupe, the young general manager, his even younger staff and to Aileen Scott, so talented with flowers.

menus **D** (din only served) *rooms* 10 **D2-D5** *cards* A AE DC Visa
closed Christmas. New Year.
post Dunblane, Perth FK15 9JT. (3½ m. N – by A9/B8033)
phone (0786) 822125 *Mich* 401 (I15) Perth 28 m.

KIRKMICHAEL Log Cabin

Fairly comfortable hotel (S)
Secluded/Fishing/Good value (meals) ®

You are likely to awake to the sight of red squirrels or deer from your window, such is the nature of this isolated log cabin. No hoteliers could do more to promote their local region; the Sandells – Bryan, Liz and teenage daughters, Kate and Emma – are a fine example of what a happy 'hotel' family should be. They make great efforts to use Scottish produce and recipes: 'Harry's haggis wi' clapshot' (Harry's the butcher) or 'cranachan' – a delicious sweet – are examples. Try the daily roast – presented tantalizingly on the restaurant's Victor carver.
menus **B** (din) Bar lun *rooms* 13 **C-D** *cards* A AE DC Visa
closed Open all the year. (Ideal for the wheelchair disabled)
post Kirkmichael, Blairgowrie, Perth PH10 7NB.
phone (025 081) 288 *Mich* 401 (J13) Perth 28 m.

PEAT INN The Peat Inn

BEST
Comfortable restaurant **MEAL**
Good value **IN 84** ®

Michelin: why no star? It's absurd that David Wilson's marvellous cooking skills – a bearded Scottish culinary magician – should be ignored at lunchtime when such largesse is there for the taking. Readers know I don't give 'duff' advice – so please, will every visitor to Scotland make sure they seek out his isolated whitewashed inn, no more than 18 holes distance from St. Andrews. David and Patricia Wilson's clients profit from their fortuitous setting – the East Neuk (little corner) fishing villages of Pittenweem and Anstruther provide superb fish and shellfish. Then there's lamb and the world's best beef, game and salmon – David makes clever use of Scotland's bountiful harvests. He's a *cuisine moderne* master – one of Britain's best; light, artistically presented specialities.
menus **A** (lun) *alc* **B** (din) *cards* AE Visa (Rooms? Speak to Pat)
closed 1st wk Jan. 1 wk April. 1 wk Oct. Sun. Mon.
post Peat Inn, Cupar, Fife KY15 5LH.
phone (033 484) 206 *Mich* 401 (L15) Perth 28 m.

ST. FILLANS Four Seasons

Comfortable hotel (S)
Gardens/Good value (meals)

I can promise you one thing: you'll taste no better trout in Britain than the famous Loch Earn variety. Fresh from the lake, these unrivalled treats are more like salmon trout in texture, taste and colour. There's also a wide selection of fresh cheeses – from George Minty's remarkable 'Cheesemonger' shop in nearby Comrie (so many Scottish varieties). The owners – Carlo and Elizabeth Donetti and young Scotsman, Boyd Stewart – offer fine Scottish produce like Tay salmon and Arbroath smokies and many Italian dishes – *frittata al Parmigiano* is one example. Pretty lochside setting and views of Loch Earn.
menus **A** (lun) **B** (din) *rooms* 18 **D-D2** *cards* A AE
closed Nov-Mar.
post St. Fillans, Perth PH6 2NF.
phone (076 485) 333 *Mich* 401 (H14) Perth 29 m.

SUFFOLK

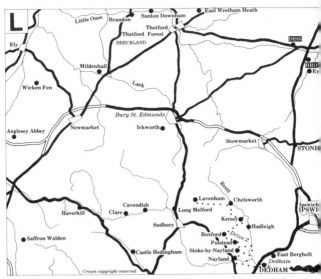

Crown copyright reserved

I have both happy and poignant memories of Suffolk. In 1947 my brother and I, together with our parents, returned to Britain from India. We spent six joyful months together in Suffolk, before setting sail to Canada – only to return again to England the following year in sad circumstances. Those six months were the last and only spell I ever spent with my father.

1947 was a brilliant, hot summer – considered perhaps the best this century. I still have vivid memories of those never-ending, shimmering days – I cannot remember one raindrop falling during the entire six months. Suffolk left many deeply-etched impressions which remain to this day: the lonely coast; the tinder-dry heathlands; the cool forests; and the first sight of some of England's most picturesque villages. Suffolk is ignored by too many; please give the county some of your time.

Start at the coast. Over the centuries the **North Sea** has been nibbling away at the shoreline and high tides constantly flood the many salt marshes. **Dunwich** is perhaps the best example where you can see how the waves have taken their toll; once a prosperous village it started to disappear six centuries ago – the ancient Church of All Saints sank as recently as 1919. Nearby Westleton Heath is a nature reserve and the village of **Westleton** is one of many irresistible Suffolk villages – it has a large green, duck pond and pastel-shaded cottages. South of Dunwich is the world-famous **Minsmere** Bird Reserve (see drive 1).

Ancient **Southwold** has many scattered greens and walks alongside the **Blyth** Estuary. To the north is **Covehithe**; at 156-529819 the road ends dramatically – see for yourself how the sea is eating away at the cliffs. **Aldeburgh** has a special charm – not least because of its happy connections with Benjamin Britten; visit The Maltings at **Snape**, alongside the **Alde** and a few miles inland – it's one of the finest concert halls in Europe. Painters, too, love the marshes of the Alde to the east.

Orford, further south, is an exception to the rule, because here the sea has receded. Once a busy port, now it's a quiet village – each year the massive gravel bank of Orford Ness grows by 20

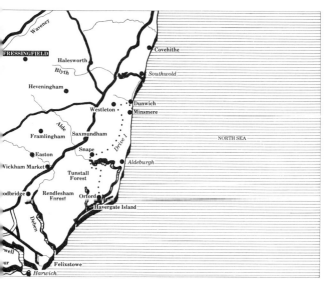

yards. The castle with its huge keep is a fine sight. The
surrounding semicircle of countryside is a favourite of mine.
There are two forests, each with its own character: **Tunstall**,
north of Orford, has a mixture of pines; **Rendlesham**, towards
Woodbridge, is an older, darker forest. Between them and the
sea is where you feel the spirit of Suffolk most strongly: remote,
muddy estuaries and salt marshes – havens for birds, like the
reserve at **Havergate Island**; huge shingle banks; and the
rejuvenating tonic of peace and sea air.

Four estuaries – the Alde, **Deben**, **Orwell** and **Stour** – point
inland like fingers, suggesting to visitors that they desert the
solitude of the coast and give time to some of man's ancient
skills. **Ipswich**, the biggest town, has many fine parks – including
Christchurch Park with its mansion, now a museum - medieval
churches and buildings. Woodbridge is another old favourite of
mine; be certain to visit the restored Tide Mill (access near
station) – an ingenious working mill that uses the tides of the
Deben. **Framlingham**, to the north, is an unspoilt market town –
proud of its small, handsome 12th-century castle (the first
English castle I ever saw). South-east of Ipswich, on the coast, is
the seaside resort of **Felixstowe** – ideal for children.

The Stour is famous enough. John Constable was born at **East
Bergholt**, north of **Dedham**; his father owned the mills at
Flatford and Dedham – two of the subjects the painter
immortalised with his work in the Stour Valley. Today it's known
simply as Constable Country. **Sudbury**, further upstream, was
the birthplace of Thomas Gainsborough; the house where he was
born is a museum and attached to it is an exhibition gallery. Seek
out the 200-year-old Quay Theatre, alongside the Stour.

Sudbury is one of a great number of towns and villages in the
area that prospered over the centuries through the wool trade;
today silk is woven in the town. The De Vere Mill at nearby
Castle Hedingham is another site where silk is woven – you can
visit it; see, too, the historic, 12th-century castle with its
marvellous keep. **Lavenham** is richly endowed with glorious

99

centuries-old timber buildings; the Guildhall (a museum telling the 'wool' story) is the most superb timber-framed building. Melford Hall, at **Long Melford**, is a Tudor mansion with fine furniture; spare time for the nearby church – one of so many fine examples in Suffolk. Nearby Kentwell Hall is another Tudor structure – famous for re-creating scenes of Tudor domestic life.

In the circle of countryside surrounding Sudbury are numerous other alluring villages: **Boxford** – a mixture of Tudor and Georgian; **Cavendish** – a green, 14th-century church and a modern-day enterprise in the form of Cavendish Manor Vineyards all combine to please; **Chelsworth**, alongside the River **Brett**, is an idyllic jewel – an attractive riverside setting and a timeless peace; **Kersey** – a captivating example of the rich heritage created by prosperous weavers centuries ago; **Nayland** beside the Stour; **Polstead** – renowned for its orchards, its large, pretty duck pond and the scene of the infamous murder of Maria Marten; and **Stoke-by-Nayland** – a tiny medieval treasure. **Hadleigh** is a bustling market town – famed for its medieval buildings; **Bury St. Edmunds** is considerably larger – its cathedral, the romantic ruins of a 11th-century abbey and its Theatre Royal all deserve your time and attention.

Elsewhere in Suffolk are more man-made sites to explore: at **Ickworth**, south-west of Bury St. Edmunds, is a most unusual house – built in the 18th century and in a parkland setting; **Heveningham** Hall, north of Framlingham, is a Palladian-styled house built in 1779 (alas, badly damaged by fire in '84); **Easton** Farm Park, south of Framlingham, was opened ten years ago and has a collection of old farm machinery; Letheringham Mill Gardens, at **Easton** – the site of a mill since Saxon times and surrounded by acres of water-meadows and gardens (156-280582); at **Stowmarket** is the museum of East Anglian Life – much of what you see in the county is explained at the museum; and, at **Clare**, there's Clare Castle and a country park.

In the north-west corner of Suffolk is an unusual part of the county called **Breckland** – sandy heathland, meres and covered, to a large extent, by the huge **Thetford Forest**, one of the biggest in England. Within the forest is **Brandon** House and, surrounding it, a 30-acre country park. Seek out a fascinating bit of countryside in the middle of the forest – **Santon Downham**, alongside the **Little Ouse**; an endearing mixture of riverside and forest walks. At **East Wretham Heath**, north-west of Thetford (2nd layby on A1075) is a typical bit of Breckland terrain: woods, heathland and meres – it's a nature reserve.

To the west of the county boundary are four further essential diversions. Detour first to inspiring **Ely** Cathedral – its towers a landmark for miles around in flat fen country. Then head south to **Wicken Fen**; now a nature reserve and owned by The National Trust since 1899, it is an incomparable example of what the fens must have been like thousands of years ago – full of superb flora and fauna. It's an ornithologist's delight, too. West of **Newmarket** is **Anglesey Abbey** – in an inviting setting – and, further south, near **Saffron Walden**, is huge Audley End House – set in a magnificent Capability Brown park.

Try, if you can, to do both the recommended drives – either in full or in part; they show off the contrasting faces of Suffolk in an appealing, rewarding way.

OS Landranger maps: 143.144.154.155.156.168.169
OS Routemaster map 9. Michelin map 404
Airports: Stansted (Essex). Norwich
Distance from London – Ipswich 68 miles

Recommended Drives

Drive 1 maps 156/169

Take walking shoes and binoculars: heaven for ornithologists.

Start 169-409490; walk SE (unmarked island is Havergate – famous bird reserve). Orford Castle at 419499. Quay at 425496 – walk S and see notices for Havergate access. Map 156-427505. Detour Sudbourne Church 421520. N thru 4253. Iken Church at 412566 (mainly ruined but part still used). Park 400563 – Iken Cliff; super river walks. Snape Maltings – don't bypass it; river boat trips, too. Use B1069 to Leiston, B1122 and B1125 to Westleton (green/duck pond). S thru 4768 – to car park on NT Dunwich Heath (WC). Walk ½ m. S to public 'hides' at Minsmere Bird Reserve – incomparable site and sight! Approx. dist. 26 m. If time permits detour to Dunwich (4770) – where sea eating cliffs. Westleton Nature Reserve at 460695 – limited access.

Drive 2 maps 155/168

Seductive Suffolk: Constable Country; ancient 'wool' villages; glorious churches; half-timbered buildings; pastel-coloured and thatched cottages.

Start 168-065322; Truman Heavy Horse Centre. E to Castle House – Munnings Art Coll. Dedham (see Stour). Detour 042335 (Le Talbooth). W thru 0333. N 0133. Map 155. 013344 – view from bridge. Map 168. W thru 9833. Map 155. Nayland. N thru 9735. Stoke-by-Nayland Church. E thru 9936 (thatched cotts). S thru 0236. Detour Higham Church. N thru 0337. Polsted from SE; pond and 12th-cent St. Mary's Church. W thru 9639. Boxford. NE thru 9741. Hidden Kersey and its ford. N thru 9845. Finish Chelsworth (view from bridge). Approx. dist. 35 m. Now visit nearby Lavenham to see marvellous half-timbered buildings – particularly the Guildhall; a museum tells the 'wool' story.

Hotel and Restaurant Recommendations

BROME   Oaksmere

Comfortable hotel (S)
Quiet/Gardens/Good value (meals)

Brothers Bill and Mike Hastead, helped by Ann McGovern, are
working hard to establish their old family home as a viable
country house hotel. Many 'benefits' please clients: an unusual
building – a mixture of 16th-century and Victorian; a lively 'pub'
atmosphere in the bar – where the 400-year-old timbers are
shown off to great advantage (eyes down for the folly); a wooded
park with a long tunnel of welcoming lime trees; a topiary garden
of ancient yews; attractive dining rooms and a conservatory for
'outdoor-like' meals; modernised, not-too-expensive bedrooms;
and sound, above-average cooking.

alc **B** Bar meals *rooms* 5 **D-D2** *cards* A AE DC Visa
closed Open all the year.
post Brome, Eye, Suffolk IP23 8AJ. (E side A140)
phone (0379) 870326 *Mich* 404 (X26) Ipswich 20 m.

DEDHAM   Le Talbooth

Very comfortable restaurant-hotel/Michelin ★
Quiet (hotel)/**Gardens/Good value** (lunch)   ℝ

The setting of the Tudor half-timbered restaurant, alongside
Constable's Stour, is as appealing as ever. Scots chef, Sam
Chalmers, proves that a Michelin star can be won without
following an all-French path: a young team of British lads and
lasses in the kitchen; an 'English' menu; first-rate produce; and
simplicity on the plate appeals, too – marinated cod, unknown
English cheeses and a passion fruit *brûlée* as examples. Sam:
you're a talented chef – sign your letters, like Girardet, *cuisinier*
rather than 'Director & General Manager'; show off your skills
with pride. 'Hotel' – Maison Talbooth – towards Dedham.

menus **B** (lun) *alc* **B-C** *rooms* 10 **D2-D4** *cards* A AE DC Visa
closed Open all the year.
post Gun Hill, Dedham, Colchester, Essex CO7 6HP. (W A12)
phone (0206) 323150/322367 (hotel) *Mich* 404 (X28) Ipswich 11 m.

DISS   Salisbury House

Comfortable restaurant with rooms
Gardens   ℝ

The Victorian-styled 'home' with its Victorian furnishings and
old-fashioned garden – full of herbaceous borders, roses and
colourful plants – is, for me, a winning combination. I like the
bedrooms, lounges and dining rooms (particularly the 30 framed
fans) – cosseting and not a thing missing; the small garden is a
surprising pleasure – make friends with the abacot rangers and
Dutch frillbacks; and the four-course dinner (plenty of choice)
using various permutations of ingredients – prawns, cucumber,
yoghurt and mint in one dish, lamb's liver, butter, Dubonnet and
orange sauce in another. (But some ½ bottles please.) Jonathan
Thompson and Anthony Rudge – the chef and an ex-Michelin
inspector – have worked marvels in their five years at Diss.

menus **C** (dinner only served) *rooms* 3 **D-D2**
closed 1 wk Spring. 1 wk Autumn. Xmas. Sun. Mon. Lun-every day.
post 84 Victoria Rd, Diss, Norfolk IP22 3JG. (E on A1066)
phone (0379) 4738 *Mich* 404 (X26) Ipswich 25 m.

FRESSINGFIELD   **Fox and Goose**

Simple inn

The 16th-century inn (in 'Giles' country) has long been famous
for 'Clarke' cooking; today 25-year-old Adrian is at the stoves – a
decade ago his mother, Betty, won a Michelin star. If you have an
old-fashioned appetite and your stomach aches for old-fashioned
classical cooking, served in vast portions, then head for *bœuf en
croûte*, *pintadeau au Cognac* and similar dishes. It's worth the
trip for the smoked eel; Adrian's father, Philip, catches them in
the nearby Waveney – gigantic pike, too (used for *quenelles*).
Over 200 wines with formidable clarets and sweet Anjou Moulin
Touchais varieties (1929-59).

alc **B-C** *cards* A AE DC Visa (Rooms? Speak to Philip)
closed 1 wk Xmas. Tues.
post Fressingfield, Eye, Suffolk IP21 5PB.
phone (037 986) 247 *Mich* 404 (X26) Ipswich 30 m.

IPSWICH   **Marlborough**

Very comfortable hotel
Gardens/Good value (meals)   ℞

Lucky Ipswich! If only all county towns had a Marlborough.
Enterprising owners, Dick and Mary Gough (they also run The
Angel at Bury St. Edmunds), together with young managers,
David and Wendy Brooks – a lively, interested, professional
couple – have created a client-pleasing recipe: comfortable
bedrooms – in a site away from the busy town centre; a flower-
filled garden; and a wide choice of light specialities – a Stilton and
tomato soufflé quiche and chicken *quenelles* with tarragon and
lime are typical representatives. Bravo Andrew Townend – the
Yorkshireman chef. Try the Cavendish white wine – see
introductory notes. Exceptional value, fixed-price menus.
menus **A-B** *alc* **B-C** *rooms* 22 D2 *cards* A AE DC Visa
closed Open all the year.
post Henley Rd, Ipswich, Suffolk. (S of A12-between A45/B1077)
phone (0473) 57677 *Mich* 404 (X27).

STONHAM   **Mr Underhill's**

Comfortable restaurant with rooms   ℞

Celebrate and enjoy Chris Bradley's talented cooking; like
Stephen Bull at Richmond, he has had no formal training but
already he has the skill and confidence to be considered one of
our best *faites simple* chefs. It's a joy to share Chris and Judy's
sensible formula: a no-choice menu (except sweets) but
whatever produce is served – perhaps salmon, lamb in a sorrel
and mint sauce and a fruit tartlet – it will demonstrate the
increasing emergence in Britain of young couples brave enough
to risk all and follow their own instinctive culinary noses. *French
Leave* readers will relish the excellent varied wines – including,
amazingly, a Chardonnay Vin du Bugey! First-class cheeses from
Shirley Webster-Jones of Oulton Broad – a Totnes 'Garland' was
new to me. Why Mr Underhill's? Ask Frodo Baggins – the cat!
menus **C** *rooms* 2 **D** (Lunches by arrangement)
closed Sat lun. Sun. Mon. Bank hols.
post Stonham, Stowmarket, Suffolk. (S junc. A140/A1120)
phone (0449) 711206 *Mich* 404 (X27) Ipswich 10 m.

VALE OF SEVERN

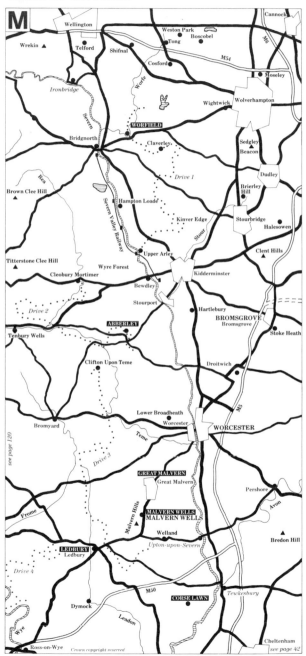

M

Cannock

Wellington

Weston Park

Boscobel

Wrekin ▲

Telford

Tong

M54

Shifnal

Cosford

Moseley

Ironbridge

Worfe

Wightwick

Wolverhampton

Severn

WORFIELD

Bridgnorth

Claverley

Sedgley
Beacon

Rea

Dudley

Brown Clee Hill ▲

Drive 1

Brierley
Hill

Severn Valley Railway

Hampton Loade

Kinver Edge

Stourbridge

Halesowen

Stour

Titterstone Clee Hill ▲

Wyre Forest

Upper Arley

Clent Hills ▲

Cleobury Mortimer

Kidderminster

Drive 2

Bewdley

Stourport

Hartlebury

BROMSGROVE

ABBERLEY

Bromsgrove

Tenbury Wells

Stoke Heath

Clifton Upon Teme

Droitwich

M5

Lower Broadheath

Worcester

WORCESTER

Bromyard

Teme

see page 120

Drive 3

GREAT MALVERN

Great Malvern

Pershore

Avon

MALVERN WELLS
MALVERN WELLS

Malvern Hills ▲

Frome

Welland

Bredon Hill ▲

LEDBURY

Ledbury

Upton-upon-Severn

Drive 4

M50

CORSE LAWN

Tewkesbury

Wye

Dymock

Leadon

Ross-on-Wye

Crown copyright reserved

Cheltenham
see page 42

The Vale of Severn is a part of Britain that I love dearly. It was my home for 25 years: initially as an eleven-year-old schoolboy – after returning to the UK with my mother and brother from a short, unhappy spell in Canada; then in our early married days when Anne and I made our first home in Shropshire. Both our children were born in Shropshire – there's no better county in Britain to claim as your birthplace.

As you can imagine I know the area more intimately than any other part of the world. There was a time when I may have admitted to personal prejudice in claiming that this was perhaps one of the most interesting parts of Britain; I make no apologies for making that statement now – time has cemented those feelings in a determined way. It is the heart of Britain; it was the birthplace of British Industry and the crucible of the Industrial Revolution; it has links with so much British history; and it is a chess-board of lovely countryside – rivers, hills, woods and gentle pastoral scenes, handsome villages, a dozen or more fascinating museums, many architectural treasures and lots more besides. Yet, it's an area that is ignored by visitors to Britain and by all but a few of the people living in our islands.

I implore all readers to give this marvellous area some of their time. You are going to be surprised just how much there is to see and do; I want to leave you in no doubt whatsoever why I claim this to be one of the most rewarding parts of Britain. What is also going to surprise you is that the culinary scene in the Vale of Severn is of a higher standard than many of the other British areas in this book.

The western edge of the area is guarded by four formidable landmarks: the dome-shaped **Wrekin** in the far north; then the long line of **Brown Clee Hill** – closely followed by the angular face of **Titterstone Clee Hill** on its southern flanks; and, finally, the hypnotic humps of the brooding **Malvern Hills**. The eastern borders of the Vale of Severn have their own high hills: **Sedgley Beacon** and the **Clent Hills** offer extensive views of the industrial conurbation to the east and a green landscape to the west; **Bredon Hill** overlooks the rich Vale of Evesham. All those hills, and the varying terrain between them, is Nature's contribution to the enticing mixture of pleasures awaiting you.

It is the Malvern Hills that I remember most clearly from those early days. Elgar's music had already made a big impression on me at the age of nine or so – at my school high in the Himalayas. When I got my first cycle at twelve I made the round trip of 80 miles or so from **Wolverhampton** to **Great Malvern** to see for myself the captivating bit of England that had meant so much to that genius; even today the Malverns still have an emotional effect on me. They provide vast views (the highest point is 1395 ft above sea-level) to both east and west; drive the entire circuit and desert your car as often as you can.

Drive the lanes that lead northwards from **Ledbury** to **Tenbury Wells**. Some of the prettiest hills in England lie in that swathe of green to the south of the River **Teme** – full of tiny, isolated churches; it's superb in the spring when the first blossom covers the trees in the orchards. One of my drives takes you through the best of it. North of the Teme is another hilly bit of country, climbing steadily until you reach the high Clees – another drive winds through a series of quiet villages. The 6,000 acres of the **Wyre Forest** and ancient **Bewdley** are to the east – the latter beside the **Severn**.

There's a captivating triangle of country to the east of the Severn – with Bewdley, **Bridgnorth** and Wolverhampton at the three angles: **Kinver Edge** is the site of Kingsford Country Park; **Claverley** is an old Shropshire village; and **Hampton Loade** and **Upper Arley** are two riverside villages on the east bank of the Severn. Bridgnorth itself is a great favourite of mine; the 'Low Town' is alongside the Severn – it's connected to the 'High Town' by the Castle Hill Railway which has a 2 in 3 gradient. The myriad lanes in the triangle are full of pretty aspects and extensive views. Don't miss them.

Adults and children alike will be thrilled by a trip on the **Severn Valley Railway** – one of Britain's best privately-owned steam railways which runs from Bridgnorth to Bewdley. For most of the trip you have unique river views because no roads run alongside this stretch of the Severn.

History has played its part in the Vale of Severn over the centuries. **Dudley** Castle is a ruin today – but it was one of the most impregnable in the land 500 years ago. The Battle of Worcester in 1651 was the start of Charles II's escape back to France; you can follow the first stages of it from **Worcester** north to **Boscobel** House – the 'Royal Oak' there now is only a descendant of the 1651 tree. Visit nearby **Tong**, marvellous **Weston Park** and **Moseley** Old Hall, north of Wolverhampton, where Charles II fled after leaving Boscobel.

Worcester is one of England's most English towns: the 900-year-old cathedral is a splendid one – but it suffered badly during the Civil War; the site of the cricket ground is second to none; and spare an hour or so for the ancient Commandery. Medieval **Tewkesbury** is another highlight – particularly its Abbey Church and the dozens of half-timbered buildings.

A collection of intriguing museums and a number of pottery and glass works are additional bonuses. Admire the fine bone china work done at the Boehm studio in Malvern and the incomparable creations of the Royal Worcester factory at the Dyson Perrins Museum in Worcester. Musts are the fine crystal glass factories: the Royal Brierley Works at **Brierley Hill** and the four in the **Stourbridge** area – Thomas Webb Crystal, Webb Corbett, Tudor Crystal and Stuart Crystal. Of the museums, pride of place must go to the **Ironbridge** Gorge Museum – the birthplace of British Industry; Abraham Darby developed the process of smelting iron ore with coke rather than charcoal at Ironbridge. Today it's a fascinating complex of museums. A second industrial museum very dear to my own heart is the remarkable Black Country Museum – sitting in the shadow of Dudley Castle. There's a complete village – chapel, shops, workshops, pub and even a working tram; don't miss a trip on one of the narrow barges on the subterranean waterway called the Dudley Canal Tunnel adjoining the museum.

The Avoncroft Museum of Buildings at **Stoke Heath**, near Bromsgrove, is an ever-growing, enterprising affair: it's a series of buildings – including a working chain workshop, an ancient pub, a blacksmith's forge and a working windmill. There are other more conventional museums at Bewdley, **Hartlebury** and at **Wightwick** Manor, west of Wolverhampton. Finally, three quite different museums appeal to me: Elgar's birthplace at **Lower Broadheath**, near Worcester; the Midland Motor Museum and Bird Garden, two miles from Bridgnorth on the A458 Stourbridge road; and the **Cosford** Aerospace Museum.

OS Landranger maps: 127.138.139.149.150
OS Routemaster map 7. Michelin map 403
Airport: Birmingham
Distance from London – Worcester 124 miles

Recommended Drives

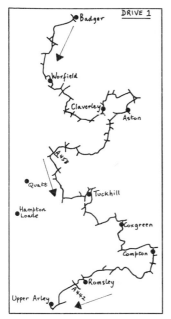

Drive 1 map 138

Secret Shropshire: sandstone buildings and churches; extensive views. Surprise yourself.

Start at Badger Church – see the pools. At 766995 walk down to Badger Dingle. Thru Worfield Village – see church (758958). Views west at 770934. Claverley from SW. Explore village. Admire Ludstone Hall (800944). Aston. S thru 7991 and 7990. Cross A458 in 7690. Care at ford at 769890. S to Kingsnordley. Then E. Tuckhill Church. Lindridge. Coxgreen. S thru The Hollies. E thru 8185 – super views south-eastwards, this time towards Kinver Edge. Compton. Greyfields Court (8182). Cross A442 at 779823. Finish at Upper Arley. Cross river by modern footbridge to Severn Valley Railway station. Approx. dist. 28 m. If time allows detour to Quatt Church (7588) and Hampton Loade beside the Severn (7486). Visit Kinver Edge, too.

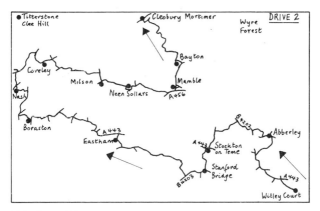

Drive 2 map 138

The quiet Teme Valley and, later, hilly ups-and-downs.

Start at 770650 – Witley Court's 1735 Baroque church is a stunner and a well-kept secret. In its day Witley Court must have been a sight. 750674 to Abberley. Extensive views. Past church to B4202. SW thru 730686. Stockton on Teme. Stanford Bridge. Orleton. A443 to Newnham Bridge. Past church to 625705 from SE. Boraston Church. N to Nash. B4214 to Knowlegate. Coreley Church. Milson. Neen Sollars. Mamble. Bayton – don't miss the church. NW to Cleobury Mortimer. Approx. dist. 30 m. Later drive to Titterstone Clee (5977); good walks in Wyre Forest (753740).

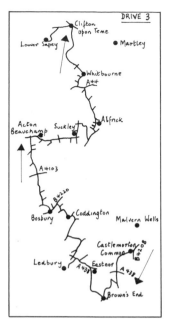

Drive 3 maps 149/150

Hills, orchards and woods; England at its loveliest.

Start at 150-780387. Head SW. Cross A438. Whiteleaved Oak. Brown's End. NW to Eastnor. A438. Map 149. N thru 7239. Coddington. Bosbury. N thru 6844. Acton Beauchamp (detour church). Stocks Farm (7251) – see Cottage in the Wood entry. Suckley Church. Map 150 at 730526. S thru 7351. Alfrick Pound. Knightwick (7355). A44. Map 149. N thru 7257. Clifton upon Teme. Finish at Lower Sapey (700603). Approx. dist. 40 m. Enjoy the views – particularly in the early miles. Don't bypass the churches. Walk the woods NW of Alfrick. Near Clifton see the view back to the Malverns. Later explore the Teme Valley; seek out Shelsley Walsh (famous hillclimb), Shelsley Beauchamp and Martley – drive the B4197 S to the Teme (views). What superb countryside.

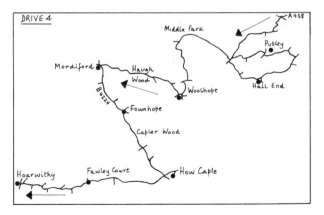

Drive 4 map 149

A hidden corner of Herefordshire – hills, woods and the River Wye.

Start at 649392 on A438. S thru 634380. E thru Putley. Clockwise circle thru 6436 to 631372. NW. Then S thru 6137 and 6136 to Woolhope. Haugh Wood – walk the nature trails – to Mordiford. S on B4224 to Fownhope. S thru 5833 and Capler Wood - high above the Wye. How Caple – detour to church. West to Fawley Court (5730); on the open ground beyond it, stop, and admire the view back. Approx. dist. 21 m. Now continue west to Hoarwithy where you will 'discover' an Italianate church that will both surprise and delight you. Thank you Mr Lines for leading me to it.

Hotel and Restaurant Recommendations

ABBERLEY
The Elms

Very comfortable hotel
Secluded/Gardens/Tennis

Built in 1710, and the work of Gilbert White, the Elms has a long-established reputation in the Midlands – I first visited it 25 years ago. Chefs come and go; the present man behind the stoves is a young Englishman, Nigel Lambert. He has an eye for presentation – and though he satisfies Midlanders' hearty appetites with sizeable portions, nevertheless, he manages to give his primarily English-styled specialities a light touch. Particularly noteworthy is the high standard of friendly service from the young English team of staff – all under the watchful eye of the experienced manageress, Rita Mooney.
menus **A** (lun) **C** (din) *rooms* 27 **D-D2** *cards* A AE Visa
closed Open all the year.
post Abberley, Worcestershire WR6 6AT. (2 m. W on A443)
phone (029 921) 666 *Mich* 403 (M27) Worcester 15 m.

BROMSGROVE
Grafton Manor

Very comfortable restaurant with rooms
Quiet/Gardens
®

Desert the M5 and see for yourself how this historic treasure is being brought to life again by John and June Morris. It has been John's home for 40 years but the present substantial changes were started four years ago when the couple opened it as a restaurant. With their children, Stephen, Simon and Nicola (who helps dad in the kitchen), they have already made an impression on the local culinary scene. Though John is a self-taught cook, the secret of his success is his eye for detail – not surprising as he was trained as an engineer. His plans for the development of the manor and its vast gardens (and a lake, too) are so exciting. They have an unusual herb garden – put to effective use in the kitchens. Visit this enterprising family – enjoy their fine fare and their fine home.
menus **B** (Sun lun) **C** (din) *rooms* 6 **D2** *cards* A AE DC Visa
closed Sun evg. Mon. Lunch-every day except Sun.
post Grafton Lane, Bromsgrove, Worcs B61 7HA. (2 m. S on A38)
phone (0527) 31525 *Mich* 403 (N26) Worcester 11 m.

CORSE LAWN
Corse Lawn House

Very comfortable restaurant with rooms
Quiet/Gardens/Good value (lunch)

Exceptional value for money and a wide range of enterprising desserts are highlights; menus, based on French-style specialities, are of a high standard. Denis Hine, a Frenchman from Cognac country, and Baba, his English wife who does the cooking, first met at Aston Clinton (see *Chilterns*) where they both worked in their early days. They have made a great success in re-establishing Corse Lawn in the six years since they took it over. Excellent wine list with a wide choice. Much of Baba's fresh produce comes from Sullivans, Abergavenny.
menus **A** (lun) **B** (din) *rooms* 4 **C-D** *cards* A AE DC Visa
closed Sun evg. Mon.
post Corse Lawn, Gloucestershire GL19 4LZ.
phone (045 278) 479 *Mich* 403 (N28) Worcester 17 m.

VALE OF SEVERN

GREAT MALVERN   Walmer Lodge
Simple hotel (S)
Gardens

In France Maurice Bunton would possibly win a Michelin red 'R'
recommendation – for good food at moderate prices. But do not
compare Maurice with the category 3 entries in this section; he
uses basic produce like sole, steak and duck – cooked either
simply or in rich sauces – with plenty of vegetables. To finish
there's Shropshire Blue, home-made sweets (with a glass of
sweet Jurançon) and *petits fours*. Well done Maurice!
alc **B-C** (dinner only served) *rooms* 9 **C-D**
closed Xmas. New Year. Sun. Bank hols. Lunch-every day.
post 49 Abbey Road, Great Malvern, Worcestershire WR14 3HH.
phone (068 45) 4139 *Mich* 403 (N27) Worcester 8 m.

LEDBURY   Hope End Country House
Comfortable hotel
Secluded/Gardens   ®

Seek out John and Patricia Hegarty's home – lost in a secret fold
of wooded hills on the south-western flanks of the Malverns.
Their ten years of prodigious effort have brought about a minor
miracle; once the childhood home of Elizabeth Barrett
Browning, Hope End has been restored from a derelict state into
a most enchanting small country hotel. No couple in Britain or
France do more to promote their local terrain; garden-grown
herbs, fruit and vegetables and other fresh produce from the
bountiful larder of Herefordshire grace their table. Marry all this
to Patricia's light cooking style – such a welcome treat – and
John's magnificent cellar, where the value/quality ratio (and 40
half-bottles) is second to none, and the result is a formidable
recipe of pleasure. Spectacular redwood trees, a fascinating
walled garden, charming hosts: what more can you want?
menus **C** (din only served) *rooms* 7 **D-D2** *cards* A AE DC Visa
closed Dec-Feb. Lunch-every day.
post Hope End, Ledbury, Herefordshire HR8 1DS.
phone (0531) 3613 *Mich* 403 (M27) Worcester 18 m.

MALVERN WELLS   Cottage in the Wood
Comfortable hotel (S)
Secluded/Gardens/Good value (lunch)   ®

What the accurately described 'hotel' name does not tell you is
that the Georgian dower-house (built about 1800) sits high up on
the steep slope of the Malverns – extensive views stretch
eastwards far across the Severn. My warmest congratulations to
Michael Ross for his success in promoting English dishes,
produce, cheeses and wines. Three cheeses come from Laurel
Farm at Dymock, near Ledbury – Cloisters and Single Gloucester
are superb. Three Choirs wine is from Dymock, too – and Stocks
from Stocks Farm at Suckley (see drive 3). Value-for-money
menus and a bargain weekday buffet lunch (£3) are great
attractions. Bedrooms are small: remember it really is a 'cottage'.
menus **A** (lun) **B** (din) *rooms* 21 **D-D2** *cards* A Visa
closed Open all the year.
post Holywell Rd, Malvern Wells, Worcestershire WR14 4LG.
phone (068 45) 3487 *Mich* 403 (N27) Worcester 10 m.

110

MALVERN WELLS   Croque-en-Bouche

Comfortable restaurant/Michelin ★   Ⓡ

Amazing! I know of no other Michelin-starred restaurant that can match the unique efforts of Marion and Robin Jones. Robin organises, **on his own,** all the ordering and serving of food and drinks for about 20 diners – and, what is more, supervises with immense pride one of the most comprehensive cellars in Britain (over 350 wines on his superb list). Marion? This attractive, vivacious *cuisinière* – in her thirties, self-taught, and a secretary in London just a few years ago – works **on her own** in the kitchen with only washing-up help. Every detail is immaculate – from the *apéritifs* to the coffee; that includes Marion's light, personalised touch with her specialities. Don't arrive late – you can see why. Rooms? Holdfast Cottage Hotel, Welland, Malvern – *phone* (0684) 310288; quiet/gardens.
menus **C** (dinner only served) *cards* A Visa (Book ahead)
closed Sun. Mon. Tues. Lunch-every day.
post 221 Wells Rd, Malvern Wells, Worcs WR14 4NF. (On A449)
phone (068 45) 65612 *Mich* 403 (N27) Worcester 10 m.

WORCESTER   Brown's

Comfortable restaurant   Ⓡ

I hope Worcester appreciates just what Bob and Pam Tansley are doing at their riverside restaurant – a pleasing and clever conversion of an old cornmill where ancient and modern combine in perfect harmony. Among their many attractive specialities, little things stand out like beacons: new potatoes and green beans which are so fresh and tasty that they would merit being served as a separate course; and sorbets which for once taste of the fruits they are made from – the passion fruit is particularly good. You may be lucky and have the chance to try some salmon from the Teme. Attention to detail – from start to finish – is a way of life for Bob and Pam. *Best of Britain* readers should ensure they do not bypass splendid Brown's.
menus **B** (lunch) **C** (dinner) *cards* A AE Visa
closed Xmas-New Year. Sun. Sat lunch. Bank hol' Mon's.
post 24 Quay St, Worcester WR1 2JM. (By river, nr. Cathedral)
phone (0905) 26263 *Mich* 403 (N27)

WORFIELD   Old Vicarage

Comfortable hotel (S)
Secluded/Gardens

On the hill above the village with extensive views to the east across the Worfe Valley. The trauma of redundancy three years ago was the catalyst for Peter and Christine Iles to convert their Edwardian home into a family-run hotel – you really do feel at ease with the couple and their three children. Enjoy well fitted-out bedrooms – named after local villages; two acres of grounds; a large lounge with a log fire; and simple cooking – treats like home-made soups, pies and sweets. Enjoy *The Wandering Worfe* – a super book; each bedroom has a copy.
menus **A** (lunch) *alc* **B** *rooms* 10 **D** *cards* A AE DC Visa
closed Open all the year.
post Worfield, Bridgnorth, Shropshire WV15 5JZ.
phone (074 64) 498 *Mich* 403 (M26) Worcester 32 m.

WELSH LAKES

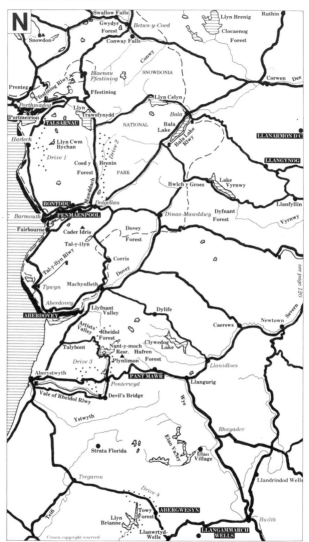

Of my four grandparents, two were English, one Irish and one Welsh. I was born in India and spent the first ten years of my life in the high Himalayas and the next year or so in North America. I was 12 before I first set foot in Wales and ever since I have had a strong intuitive feeling that Wales is my spiritual home. So don't be surprised if I enthuse about Wales – particularly its mountains, lakes and forests, all of which have a strong attraction for me. No wonder then that it is the land of song: the irresistible landscape is the catalyst that fires Welsh hearts – out pours their love for home, family and country in overwhelming melody and music.

One thing I will not enthuse about is the cooking; apart from an odd oasis or two, Wales remains a culinary desert. The Wales Tourist Board should take the initiative to improve standards.

You may think my choice of name for this area a strange one; but it isn't because there are so many lakes dotted throughout the mass of mountain country. They vary in size; some are man-made and some were created by Nature. Linking them together are bleak mountains, many now blanketed with forests of pine – most of which have been planted since the last War; green, secluded valleys with rushing, crystal-clear streams (but not in '84's drought conditions); remote, dark-stone villages; and hundreds of miles of lonely lanes and tracks. Use those lanes and stop at some of the isolated hill farms; talk to the friendliest of farmers that you'll meet anywhere. The more remote the track, the better – particularly dead-end ones (see drives and recommendations); opening farm gates will become a way of life – but be certain to close them behind you, too.

Let me start with the lakes. Consider first one of the smallest of them all – a gem and unknown by all but a handful of people. On map 136, it's called Marsh's Pool; see square 9281, south-west of **Llanidloes** – access is from the A470 at the 233 spot height. A whole series of small natural lakes encircle **Dolgellau**: **Tal-y-llyn** is the most famous, just west of the main A487 to **Machynlleth**; also easily accessible by car are the two lakes in the hills south-west of Dolgellau and **Llyn Cwm Bychan**, east of **Harlech**. There are dozens of other small lakes.

Of the bigger lakes, **Bala** is the largest natural sheet of water. Others have been formed by the creation of huge reservoirs: the five **Elan Valley** reservoirs (four dams), west of **Rhayader**, are the most famous (see **Elan Village** – use the road through 147–9463); recently-built dams have formed new lakes at **Llyn Brianne**, west of **Llanwrtyd-Wells**; at the **Nant-y-moch Reservoir**, north of **Ponterwyd**; at **Clywedog Lake** – drive the scenic roads encircling the winding arms of the reservoir – north-west of Llanidloes; at **Lake Vyrnwy**, perhaps the prettiest of them all; and the lakes in the huge **Clocaenog Forest**.

The work of the Forestry Commission in Wales has done much over the last few decades to bring a refreshing green aspect to the otherwise barren landscape. I am not on the side of the critics who 'knock' man-made forests; I welcome them – though I have some reservations. The hundreds of miles of forest tracks and walks are easily accessible (other than in fire-risk, drought conditions) and the Commission has done much to create trails, picnic places and to making their forests interesting for all visitors – adults and children alike. (The terrible present-day 'scars' on many hillsides are created by farmers – 'roads' paid for by EEC grants!)

There are so many forests I can only do justice to a few. The **Dovey Forest**, between Dolgellau and Machynlleth, is one of the biggest. The **Coed y Brenin Forest**, north of Dolgellau, is another old favourite; seek out the Visitor Centre just off the A470 before starting drive 2 (see the drive details). The giant **Hafren Forest** (Welsh for 'Severn') is another must for all visitors; various walks, including the Cascades Forest Trail, start from 136–857870. **Llyn Brenig** in the huge Clocaenog Forest has a whole series of trails around it – particularly absorbing for those interested in archaeological sites.

Gwydyr Forest, to the immediate west and south of **Betws-y-Coed**, has a number of marked trails, an arboretum and a visitor centre. A bonus is some of the best river country in Wales, particularly the **Swallow** and **Conway** falls, west and south of pretty Betws-y-Coed. Other favourites of mine, all of which I know so well, are the vast **Towy Forest** in the south; the **Rheidol Forest**, north of Nant-y-moch Reservoir; the **Dyfnant Forest**, south of Lake Vyrnwy; and the forests lining the Rheidol Valley, near **Devil's Bridge**, the site of fine waterfalls.

Several museums require your time and attention. Two are sited just a mile apart on the main A44 west of Ponterwyd: the first is the Llywernog Silver-Lead Mine – a fascinating place based on old mine workings; a mile up the road towards **Aberystwyth** is the Rheidol Forest Visitor Centre – it explains the work done in the forest in a splendid visual way and as a bonus there are fine views. A mile or two due south is the Rheidol Hydro Electric Power Station – open to visitors; seek it out and its clever 'fish ladder'. A museum with a real difference is the Centre for Alternative Technology; it's three miles north of Machynlleth at 135–754045 – you'll learn much about alternative forms of natural energy, like wind and solar power.

Mother Nature has created her own 'attractions'. The highest peak in Wales is **Snowdon; Cader Idris** – a sleeping giant – dominates the landscape to the south of Dolgellau; and there are many more high peaks throughout the area I have chosen to call Welsh Lakes. There are miles of beaches for children's pleasure – the best are at **Fairbourne** and north from Harlech.

Of other man-made sites I would highlight these: **Portmeirion**, an Italianate dream village created by the late Sir Clough Williams-Ellis in 1926; the ruins of the Cistercian abbey at **Strata Florida** with an isolated, tranquil setting; the formidable fortress at Harlech with its unforgettable views to the north; and the privately-run railways that have the evocative name 'The Great Little Trains of Wales'.

Those little lines are a delight. Much the more exciting is the **Ffestiniog Railway** that runs from the coast at **Porthmadog** for 15 miles along the Vale of Ffestiniog to its inland terminus at **Blaenau Ffestiniog**. In the process it climbs several hundred feet through forests, tunnels and even a Swiss-style spiral where the line crosses over itself. Other less spectacular lines are the **Tal-y-llyn Railway** – from **Tywyn**, on the coast, for 7¼ miles inland towards the Tal-y-llyn Lake; the **Bala Lake Railway** – on the lake's south-east shore; the Snowdon Mountain Railway – from Llanberis to the 3559 ft high summit; the **Vale of Rheidol Railway** (run by British Railways) from Aberystwyth to Devil's Bridge; and the Fairbourne Light Railway which has been given a new lease of life. All are great fun.

The recommended drives that follow only scratch the surface – I could list scores. In addition to the four drives it is imperative you try these: the mountain road from **Abergwesyn** west to **Tregaron**; the mountain road from Llanidloes, via **Dylife**, to Machynlleth; the road north from Ponterwyd, past the Nant-y-moch Dam, and then west to **Talybont**; the wooded run encircling Lake Vyrnwy, then west to **Bwlch y Groes**, taking great care on the drop to **Dinas-Mawddwy**; the enchanting **Llyfnant Valley** road (135–7297 and also 740000 – views), south-west of Machynlleth; the climb west from **Prenteg** (124–5841); and the beguiling **Artists' Valley** run (to 135–707941).

OS Landranger maps: 115.116.124.125.135.136.147
OS Routemaster map 7. Michelin map 403
Airports: Birmingham. Cardiff. Liverpool
Distance from London – Dolgellau 221 miles

Recommended Drives

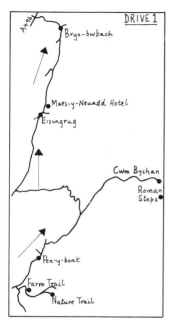

Drive 1 map 124

Stone walls, for a change 'Welsh' oak woods, one of the most stunning views in Britain – and the 'Harlech Hairpins'. Use your legs, too.

Start 600273. Detour S – ½ m. to Bluebell Wood. Then detour to 603273 – Farm Trail (Welsh Hill Farm) takes 1 hr. Continue to 608270 – Nature Trail & Waterfall takes ½ hr. NE to Cwm Bychan (6431). Walk SE to 'Roman Steps' – reckoned to date from pre-Roman times. Return to 621298 (site of carpark). N & E to 615309 – one of the most exciting short rally stages in UK. At night, in thick cloud, it's a shocker; it's called 'Harlech Hairpins'. Standing Stone at 602314 – get the camera out. What a view at 607323 – one of the best in Britain; use the camera again. Can you see Portmeirion?: 5937; visit it later. N thru 6134 & 6236 to finish at A496. Approx. dist. 17 m.

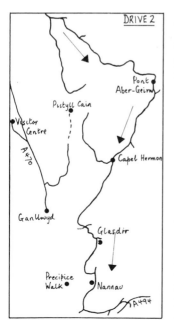

Drive 2 map 124

Coed y Brenin – my favourite Welsh forest: start and finish with vast mountain views; but for the most part relish gorgeous woodland aspects – in the valleys and on hills.

Before you start call at Visitor Centre at 715277 – for info and map on forest walks and views. Start 726318. Detour to dead-end in 7428 – view! Return to 726318. SE thru 7529. At 750257 detour to 744273. S thru 7423 – what a pretty valley. Arboretum at 743226. If you are energetic park at 746212 and 'do' famous Precipice Walk. SE thru 7419. Finish at 754196 (A494). Approx. dist. 23 m. One worthwhile walk: park at 735264 – access from A470 at 727247; walk to waterfall – Pistyll Cain – & smaller Rhaeadr Mawddach. A little way N of latter gold is being mined today! In fact area near Capel Hermon has deposits of copper, lead and gold. Will it ever be mined?

115

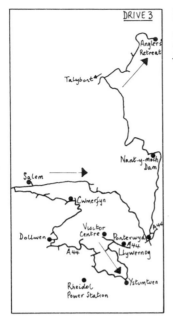

Drive 3 map 135

Wildest Wales at its wildest – desolate heights and moorlands, extensive views, forests and lakes.

Before you start seek out Rheidol Forest Visitor Centre (718813) – walks, views, museum; Llywernog Silver-Lead Mine (733808); and Rheidol Power Station, Info Centre and 'fish ladder' (707794). Start 725812. S thru 7379 – views. View of Rheidol Valley at 728788. Sharp right 715797. A44. N thru 7082 – hairpin bends and old mine. W thru 6883. E thru 6884. Nice lakes 7183 and walks. S thru 7481. N thru 7583 and W thru 7586. Nant-y-moch Reservoir is part of Rheidol Hydro-Elec scheme; created in '62/63 I saw it full then – half empty in '84. At 723909 NE to finish at Anglers' Retreat – a deserted dead-end 'white' road. Approx. dist. 33 m. Descend to Talybont via 723909 and 7089.

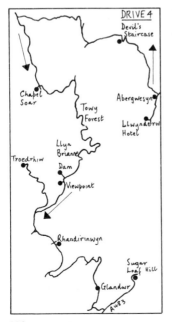

Drive 4 map 147

One of Britain's greatest drives – it has everything! Mountain roads, walks, rare birds, entrancing 'natural' woods, conifer forests, a huge lake, a monster dam and at the finish one of the best dead-end roads.

Start 850518 – Llwynderw Hotel. N thru 8453 – a Nature Reserve; look out for birds – particularly red kite. Devil's Staircase – hairpins. W thru 7757. S thru 7755. Stop at Chapel Soar (7853). S thru 8150; Llyn Brianne was created in '74 – marvellous views. Be sure to see spectacular dam from 794480 and also 794485. At 773459 head N thru 7746; one of Wales best-kept secrets. Natural woods and exciting river gorge view at 777466. Do exhilarating clockwise walk from 783464 (Nature Reserve). Approx. dist. 30 m. More? S thru 7843 – and NE thru 7942 – serried ranks of hills to far S. Walk? Sugar Loaf Hill; 837429.

Hotel and Restaurant Recommendations

ABERDOVEY
Plas Penhelig

Comfortable hotel (S)
Secluded/Gardens/Good value (meals)

Much the most enticing benefit of the Richardson's family-run hotel is its elevated site – just east of Aberdovey and overlooking the Dovey Estuary and the high mountains to the south. Fine trees and flowering shrubs, plus a south-facing, sun-trap patio and garden, make it a place where putting your legs up is a pleasure. Oak plays a big part in the panelled entrance hall and gives it a welcoming feel. Young David Richardson, the son of the owners (they hail from Solihull), is the chef. Commendable fare with home-made soups, Dovey salmon, Dovey crab and smoked mackerel (David catches the mackerel himself).
menus **A** (lun) **B** (din) *rooms* 11 **D** *cards* A AE DC Visa
closed Jan–Mar.
post Aberdovey, Gwynedd LL35 0NA.
phone (065 472) 676 *Mich* 403 (H26) Dolgellau 25 m.

ABERGWESYN
Llwynderw

Comfortable hotel
Secluded/Gardens   Ⓡ

Of the many remote hotels I have sought out over the years this jewel must be in as captivating a setting as any. Llwynderw is in a secret fold of isolated hills, flanked by splendid trees and yet it's a southerly-facing sun-trap, too. In effect you are the pampered guest of Michael Yates in his elegant 18th-century home where comfort and good taste come first. A high standard of cooking: three separate courses, with no choice, followed by a variety of sweets – dishes of the sort you would be proud to serve at home. A typical menu would be cheese soufflé, sorrel soup, roast duckling (superb), lemon flummery, mango fool and damson sorbet. A welcome plus: there's no 'bar' – so no locals pop in for drinks. An ornithologist's paradise.
menus **C** *rooms* 10 **D2-D4** (dinner included)
closed Nov-Mar. Lunch unless by prior arrangement.
post Abergwesyn, Builth Wells, Powys LD5 4TW. (See drive 4)
phone (059 13) 238 *Mich* 403 (J27) Dolgellau 65 m.

BONTDDU
Bontddu Hall

Comfortable hotel (S)
Gardens

This favourite of some *FL3* readers has a lot going for it: the view across the wooded Mawddach Estuary to the sullen mass of Cader Idris; comfortable lounges; a sun-trap terrace; attractive gardens; and attentive young receptionists. The cooking is done by two young ladies – Kim Cartledge and Susan Lewis: straightforward classics based, in the main, on local produce – salmon, lamb, beef – with one or two commendable efforts such as salmon mousse, scrambled eggs with Morecambe Bay shrimps and *millefeuille* of hot prawns. Girls: concentrate less on the conventional and develop your own creations.
menus **A** (buffet lun) **B** (din) *rooms* 24 **D-D2** *cards* A AE DC Visa
closed Nov-Easter.
post Bontddu, Dolgellau, Gwynedd LL40 2SU.
phone (034 149) 661 *Mich* 403 (I25) Dolgellau 5 m.

LLANARMON D C   West Arms

Simple inn with rooms (S)
Gardens/Fishing/Good value (meals)

'Duck or Grouse' is the warning given on the low beams of this
16th-century hostelry. The character of its remote country
setting is best described by the pheasant's nest and her eggs that I
saw in the garden which runs down to the River Ceiriog. Lovely
hill views, the friendly Edge family and modest but wholesome
food: what more could you want? Exciting, scenic drive? Map 125
– NW thru' 1638 and 1439 – ignore 'unsuitable' signs.
menus **B** (din-Sun lun) Bar lun *rooms* 15 **C-D** *cards* A AE DC Visa
closed Open all the year.
post Llanarmon Dyffryn Ceiriog, Llangollen, Clwyd LL20 7LD.
phone (069 176) 665 *Mich* 403 (K25) Dolgellau 42 m.

LLANGAMMARCH WELLS   Lake

Comfortable hotel (S)
Quiet/Gardens/Fishing/Tennis/Golf   ®

The new owner, Pierre Mifsud, is breathing rejuvenating life into
this beguiling 'Heart of Wales' hotel with its list of attractions: a
50-acre park, studded with lovely trees; a short 9-hole golf
course; a lake full of trout; tennis; and river fishing. Pierre is
making many improvements: extra bathrooms are being fitted;
and the cooking is much improved – wholesome, fresh produce
with excellent local meat and luxuries like guinea fowl and
pheasant. Lunches served Sat and Sun. (The local countryside
was the setting for BBC TV's *The Magnificent Evans*.)
menus **B** (din) Bar lun *rooms* 25 **D-D2** *cards* A Visa
closed Open all the year.
post Llangammarch Wells, Powys LD4 4BS. (1 m. E village)
phone (059 12) 202 *Mich* 403 (J27) Dolgellau 75 m.

LLANGYNOG   New Inn

Simple inn with rooms (S)
Good value (meals)

Don't have great expectations at this 200-year-old inn. The 'heart'
of any good pub is the family – here it's the Williamsons: Alex (an
ex-computer man), Vera and daughters Christine and Elizabeth.
Smart, simple bedrooms, bargain-price food and Border beer.
Ask for directions to get the key to Pennant-Melangell Church (2
m. to W) and its association with St. Melangell, the patron saint of
hares! Don't miss Pistyll-Rhaeadr (125-0729) – a high waterfall, at
its best after heavy rain. Is the boat launched yet?
menus **A** *rooms* 8 **B-D**
closed Open all the year.
post Llangynog, Powys.
phone (069 174) 229 *Mich* 403 (J25) Dolgellau 32 m.
Other nearby recommendations
An old favourite is the Lake Vyrnwy Hotel. In 1984 I could only
spare an hour for a coffee – but the welcome was as charming as
ever. Victorian character, glorious views, seclusion, tennis, lift,
heaven for fishing and shooting and 'country house' cooking.
post Llanwddyn, Salop. *phone* (069 173) 244.
Some *FL3* readers recommended Rosalind and Arfon Jones' tiny
Valentine's Restaurant at Corwen, north of Llangynog.

PANT MAWR

Glansevern Arms

Simple hotel (S)
Fishing/Good value (meals)   Ⓡ

Bill Edwards and his team of local ladies should be proud of the job they do at this much modernised 18th-century hostelry – alongside the A44 and overlooking the young River Wye. You see it in the attention that little things get: comfortable lounges; immaculate table linen and flowers; and the treats from the kitchen. Modest fare but done with loving care – with six courses at dinner: simple starters, fish, a sorbet, main courses like veal or chicken, a choice of sweets and then finally cheese and fruit. Do the lovely, lonely high drive (a dead-end run) from 136–895802 to 843773. Book ahead for meals.

menus A *rooms* 7 **B-D**
closed 1 wk Christmas.
post Pant Mawr, Powys SY18 6SY.
phone (055 15) 240 *Mich* 403 (I26) Dolgellau 50 m.

PENMAENPOOL

George III

Simple inn with rooms (S)

Bags of character and an extra special setting give this tiny, whitewashed pub two big 'plus features'. It's on the north side of the A493 at the point the toll bridge crosses the Mawddach – the view across the estuary is most attractive. Cooking, too, is a great deal better than run-of-the-mill 'pub grub': local fish – trout, mackerel, lemon sole and plaice – feature strongly as does lamb and sirloin steak prepared in various ways. Ensure you do this drive: S through 124–6816 and NW through 6514 – look out for the peacocks at 688152.

menus **B** *rooms* 12 **C-D2** *cards* A AE DC Visa
closed Rest: Sun evg to 'non-res'.
post Penmaenpool, Dolgellau, Gwynedd LL40 1YD.
phone (0341) 422525 *Mich* 403 (I25) Dolgellau 2 m.

TALSARNAU

Maes-y-Neuadd

Comfortable hotel
Secluded/Gardens/Good value (meals)   Ⓡ

Hurrah – an oasis of exceptionally flourishing promise in the Welsh culinary desert. Marry this bubbling good news with a devastatingly enticing setting – towards the end of drive 1 (read it and do it!) with Snowdon to the north and the Lleyn Peninsula to the west – and you will understand why I was bowled over. When you see the care the Horsfalls and the Slatters have put into little details – like the conservation of their handsome boundary stone walls, the preservation of wild flowers, and the fitting out of their centuries-old granite and slate country house, then you will not be surprised if I vouch for the same detailed attention in the mouthwatering cooking. Dishes are cooked to order and, thank heavens, many Welsh delights earn, on merit, a place on the menus. Visit this oasis – and help it blossom further; even if you can only afford a meal.

menus **B-C** (din/Sun lun) Bar lun *rooms* 12 **D-D2** *cards* A AE DC Visa
closed Open all the year.
post Talsarnau, Harlech, Gwynedd LL47 6YA. (3 m. NE Harlech)
phone (0766) 780200 *Mich* 403 (H25) Dolgellau 24 m.

WELSH MARCHES

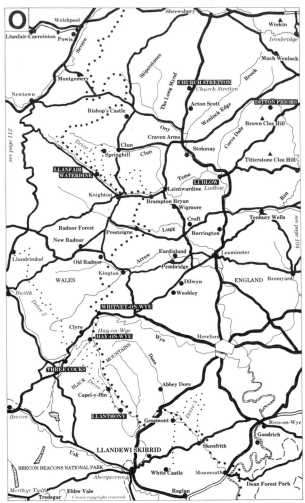

see page 112

see page 124

Crown copyright reserved

For the past 15 years my family and I have lived in leafy Bucks, just outside London. Many benefits accrue from living in the Chiltern Hills – but nevertheless all of us regret that we had to leave the idyllic Welsh Marches behind us when we moved south from the Midlands. We spent hundreds of happy hours in that rejuvenating terrain – studded as it is with so many pleasures to entice the visitor; it's one of Britain's most pleasing 'undiscovered' corners. Seek it out!

All my readers know by now how often I write about my great passion for maps; I have motor rallying to thank for that. At some stage or other I must have travelled down possibly every lane west of the **Severn**; this as a result of competing on scores of rallies and through organising some of Britain's most important events. I love the Welsh Marches dearly and I regret that so few people enjoy them.

The Welsh Marches is the border country of England and Wales. Centuries ago it was the scene of considerable fighting – as a consequence there are many castles in the area, from complete ruins to spectacular structures like **Ludlow** and **Raglan**. Man also brought his architectural influence to bear in other ways: the majestic cathedral at **Hereford**; many ancient churches and abbeys; and a series of unspoilt villages – many with picturesque half-timbered buildings – are just some of them. My plan is to first highlight the many man made treasures and then to concentrate on what I enjoy most – Mother Nature's pleasures; both abound in great numbers in the Marches.

Consider the castles first. Ludlow is as exciting a fortress as any – built, centuries ago, by the English kings to keep the fierce Welsh at bay (see it from 137–505743); the town itself is a treasure-chest of medieval buildings. In the hills east of **Abergavenny** are three Norman Marcher strongholds – all built in the 13th century to keep the troublesome Welsh to heel: **White Castle** is the largest – my favourite; **Skenfrith** and **Grosmont** are its near neighbours. Ruined **Goodrich** Castle, built 700 years ago, has a fine site overlooking the River **Wye**. Raglan Castle lies a few miles south of White and is one of the best Border fortresses. **Powis** Castle, near **Welshpool**, is best described as a stately home; it has an impressive site and outstanding gardens. **Stokesay** Castle is in fact a 13th-century fortified manor house and **Croft** Castle is a restored 14th-century mansion in a huge 1,000 acre estate.

Hereford Cathedral is a mixture of styles and within it are many treasures – a 700-year-old map of the world and a chained library amongst them. Explore the old town – it has had a turbulent history. **Shrewsbury**, too, is steeped in history: various churches, a castle, a riverside setting and streets full of half-timbered houses are highlights. Both **Leominster** and **Ross-on-Wye** are small market towns and well worth visiting.

Of the ruined abbeys two require your time: **Llanthony** Priory – dating from its Augustinian foundation in 1108 – has an enchanting valley site in the **Black Mountains**; and the 12th-century **Abbey Dore**, part of which is still used today. North of Llanthony is the monastery at **Capel-y-ffin** – the home of Eric Gill, the stone carver, from 1920–24.

Captivating villages abound – I could list scores of them. Seek out the following: **Bishop's Castle, Clun** and **Leintwardine** are three gems in south Shropshire; **Pembridge** and **Eardisland** – in the **Arrow** Valley, west of Leominster – are two of the particularly alluring villages noted for their black and white houses; others are **Dilwyn** and **Weobley**; so, too, are **Brampton Bryan** and **Wigmore** – east of **Knighton**. Of all our English counties, Herefordshire is as fortunate as any to have such a great number of ancient, timeless villages.

There are several museums: the Museum of Cider in Hereford where cider brandy will soon be distilled; the Textile Museum at **Newtown** – once a centre of the Welsh woollen industry; the Ludlow and Abergavenny museums which tell the story of their local communities; and the **Acton Scott** Working Farm Museum where a re-creation of a Shropshire upland farm of 100 years ago will please adults and children.

Of other diverse man-made sites, some are worth bringing to your attention. First there's King Offa's Dyke, built in the 8th century to protect the Marches from those worrying Welsh – sections north of Knighton can still be seen today (137-2580 –

Springhill – is best); the outstanding Hergest Croft Gardens are at **Kington** – magnificent at rhododendron time; the towns of **Old Radnor** and **New Radnor** – the latter founded 700 years ago; and **Berrington** Hall with its Capability Brown landscaped parkland. **Hay-on-Wye** is the world's largest second-hand 'bookshop' and for railway enthusiasts there's the Welshpool and Llanfair Light Railway – a narrow gauge line between Welshpool and **Llanfair-Caereinion.**

As much as I have enjoyed detailing some of the area's man-made pleasures I have been impatient to turn to what I consider makes the Welsh Marches so appealing – the irresistible handiwork of Nature. I'll describe my favourites in a series of small pen pictures – detailing river valleys and groups of hills; but I cannot do justice to it all. Get out your maps!

The River Wye cuts right across the bottom half of the Welsh Marches; here it is a quieter, more alluring version than the torrent you'll discover further west. It flows fast enough between **Builth** and Hay – but later, beyond Hereford, it's a tranquil, sleepy river before it enters its most famous section south of Ross-on-Wye and adjacent to one of my favourite forests, the **Dean Forest Park.** The Wye near **Clyro** is my favourite stretch; I had been bewitched by the hills lining both sides of that part of the river long before I knew of the writing of the Revd Francis Kilvert who spent seven happy years at Clyro (1865-72). *Kilvert's Diary* is compulsive reading (Jonathan Cape Publishers) – it contains references to two inns included in the recommendations. The **Teme** Valley, too, is an enchanting stream – pretty as a picture every inch of the way as it travels east from its source. So, too, is the Arrow in its upper reaches; and **Corve** Dale, lying under the gentle sloping side of marvellous **Wenlock Edge** – much loved by A. E. Housman.

Mountains dominate the landscape throughout much of the area. Like thousands of young children I was a great fan of Malcolm Saville and his 'Lone Pine Five': remember the **Stiperstones**? It's a spooky bit of countryside, south-west of Shrewsbury (137-3697 and 3698). The Stiperstones' neighbour is **The Long Mynd** – another mysterious, but higher ridge with a hypnotic effect much like the Lubéron Mountain in Provence; drive through 137-400915 – but not the faint-hearted please.

The mountains between Newtown, **Llandrindod**, Ludlow and Leominster are rallying country. Narrow lanes dive, helter-skelter like, from one lonely ridge down to a green valley and then climb again to the next desolate hill-top. There are miles of tracks where you will have no neighbours but the area's wildlife – drive the lanes adjoining the **Clun**, Teme, **Lugg** and Arrow valleys. Explore the high **Radnor Forest** – access from Kinnerton (148-2463) and Bleddfa (148-2068).

Finally, I implore you to give time to the Black Mountains south of Hay – to the northern slopes overlooking the Wye Valley and to the many high, wild ridges running like fingers from north to south and the endearing valleys lying between them; and to Wenlock Edge – Mary Webb country. Read two of her books – *Gone to Earth* and *Precious Bane*. Mary, a distant relation of my wife, was born near the **Wrekin** and lived for many years near **Much Wenlock** and the Stiperstones – she had an ironic link with Jonathan Cape. All of it is inspiring countryside.

OS Landranger maps: 126.136.137.138.147.148.149.161.162
OS Routemaster map 7. Michelin map 403
Airports: Birmingham. Cardiff. Liverpool
Distance from London – Hereford 133 miles

Recommended Drives

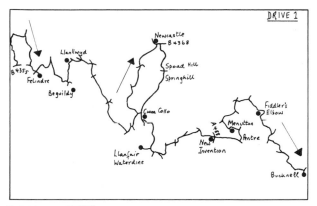

Drive 1 maps 136/137

Spectacular views – in all directions; a stunning drive that proves 'white' roads are worth using. See the best of Offa's Dyke at Springhill. You will see few cars on this drive.

Start on B4355 at 136-148822. N thru 1483. S thru 1682. E thru 1781. Llanllwyd (1981) from S. Map 137. S thru 2080. 220780. N thru 230790. NE thru 2481 to B4368. S to Spoad Hill. Offa's Dyke. S thru 2477. Detour Llanfair Church. Ignore 'unsuitable' sign at 254758 – but care! NE thru 2676. X A488 in 2976. N thru Pentre. NW thru Menutton. NE to 306784. E thru 310792. Fiddler's Elbow (Roy filleted his funny bone here). 325775. SE thru 3376. Finish Bucknell Church. Approx. dist. 33 m.

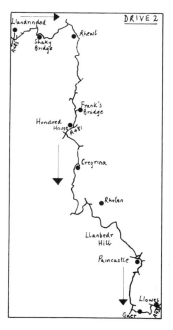

Drive 2 maps 147/148

Deserted hills: and an exciting climb of a newly-metalled 'white' – with a reward of fine views from Llanbedr Hill.

Start junction of A4081/A483 (117 060610). E thru 0761. At Shaky Bridge enjoy nature trail walk and detour N to 13th-cent St. Michael's Church. Map 148. S thru 1160 and 1155. S on white at 120507. SE on new 'white' thru 1349. Extensive views at 1448. Paincastle from N. S thru 1643. E thru 1741 (Gaer). Views from common at 187416. Llowes from NW. Approx. dist. 24 m. One obvious change these days from two decades ago is the huge number of new 'roads' on farm property – climbing up and down in the most unlikely places. Most of them are paid for by grants from the EEC. Alas, also, so many woods are being cleared – 1159 is the saddest example. Overgrazing, too, is causing all sorts of problems for the future.

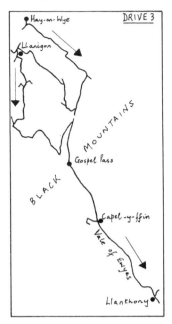

Drive 3 map 161

Contrasting terrain – all of it loved by Kilvert (curate at Clyro) over a century ago and by Eric Gill, some 50 years later.

Start at 227420 – junction with B4350. SE thru 2340. S thru 2438. N thru 2338. NW thru 2239 to Llanigon. Explore St. Eigen's Church – traces of Norman work. Near E end of church is grave of Frances (Daisy) Thomas – her father (the vicar) rejected Kilvert as future son-in-law. S thru 2138. Nice picnic spot at 231357. S thru 2335 – Gospel Pass. Change of scenery – long, steep-sided Vale of Ewyas. Capel-y-ffin: a phone box, St. Mary's Church (ancient yews), Baptist Chapel to the east, and detour to The Monastery at 252314 (Roman Catholic Chapel) – Eric Gill, the sculptor, lived here 1924-28. Pony trekking at Capel-y-ffin. Finish Llanthony Priory – founded 1108. Approx. dist. 20 m.

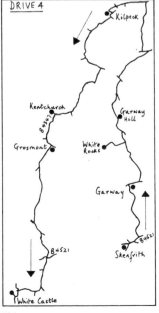

Drive 4 map 161

The Welsh Marches at its most alluring – green, gentle country. Norman Marcher castles and, at Kilpeck, a stunning Norman church with stone carvings.

Start at Skenfrith Castle (4520). N thru 4521 – lovely river valley. Garway Church. N thru 4523. Detour to White Rocks (post box) for views S. N thru 4425 NE thru 4527. Vast views N and S. N thru 4528 – duckponds! Kilpeck Church – 445305; what a treasure. SW thru 4226. Grosmont Castle. S thru 3921; more extensive views. S and W thru 3917 to finish at White Castle (379167). This is a must – with moat, walls and towers; children will love it. Approx. dist. 27 m. If time permits head due S to the well preserved Raglan Castle (4108). But one essential, not-to-be-missed detour is the Walnut Tree Inn at Llandewi Skirrid (337165) – three m. west of White.

Hotel and Restaurant Recommendations

CHURCH STRETTON   Stretton Hall

Comfortable hotel (S)
Quiet/Gardens/Good value (meals)

A pleasant hotel – in tiny All Stretton, just north of Church Stretton and away from the busy A49; on one side are the high 'bumps' of Caer Caradoc and The Lawley and on the other The Long Mynd – all of it super walking terrain. Modest fare – home-made soups and sweets and basics like lamb and chicken; but what modest prices – at the bottom end of band **A**. Try the straightforward meals at this ideal 'base' hotel – but for far more ambitious cooking make the short drive to Ditton Priors.
menus **A** *rooms* 12 **C-D** *cards* A AE DC Visa
closed Open all the year.
post All Stretton, Church Stretton, Salop SY6 6HG.
phone (0694) 723224 *Mich* 403 (L26) Hereford 40 m.

DITTON PRIORS   Howard Arms

Comfortable restaurant with rooms
Quiet/Gardens   ®

Come on my Salop, Staffs and Worcs readers: make the thoroughly enjoyable diversion to out-of-the-way Ditton Priors and relish the enterprise and eye for detail that Jane Marsh puts to such good use in her culinary repertoire. Self-taught and quick to learn, she took over the responsibility of the kitchen some ten years or so ago when her two girls, now aged 12 and 10, were toddlers. Menus provide a wide choice of alternatives: examples are cream of finnan haddock soup – with an authentic aroma; pork *rillettes* – as good as any in Touraine; skilfully-prepared desserts; and other much appreciated details include splendid fresh bread from nearby Cressage, crunchy vegetables, home-made yogurt and tasty *petit fours*. Husband Richard looks after all the ordering and is justly proud of a first-rate wine list. Two basic, comfortable bedrooms.
menus **B** (din/Sun lun) *rooms* 2 **B-C**
closed Sun evg. Mon. Lun (not Sun). 1 wk July. 3 wks Aug.
post Ditton Priors, Bridgnorth, Salop WV16 6SQ.
phone (074 634) 200 *Mich* 403 (M26) Hereford 38 m.

HAY-ON-WYE   Old Black Lion

Simple inn with rooms (S)

Rosemary and Colin Vaughan – an ex-Army career man – took over the 13th-century hotel two years ago. Full marks to them both for including several Welsh specialities on their à la carte menu: Welsh lavercakes and bacon – a must for all visitors; Wye salmon cured in Armagnac and herbs – tasty, but why do so few order it?; Welsh salted duck; Welsh lamb in pastry with laverbread stuffing; Welsh oatmeal dumplings and potato cakes are accompaniments to some dishes; and, apart from handsome-looking meringue *gâteaux*, bonus marks for wild plum ice cream (a recipe legacy from Dorothy Adler, the previous owner). Well fitted-out bedrooms – the Cromwell Room is a 'historic' surprise.
alc **B-C** *rooms* 10 **C-D** *cards* A
closed Open all the year.
post Lion St, Hay-on-Wye, Powys HR3 5AD.
phone (0497) 820841 *Mich* 403 (K27) Hereford 21 m.

LLANDEWI SKIRRID   Walnut Tree Inn

Simple inn   ®

I made a nostalgic but joyous return in 1984 to the whitewashed
home of Franco and Ann Taruschio. 20 years earlier it didn't take
us rallying lads long to discover the newly-arrived couple at their
minuscule inn – at the door of so much fantastic motoring
country. (I didn't know it then but I had already enjoyed Franco's
talents at The Spinney in Wolverhampton!). Today it's an
institution – living proof that each year thousands of happy
clients will flock vast distances for character, bubbling
informality, friendly service and enterprising, skilful cooking.
Everything imaginable is on the huge menu – including
remarkably fresh fish and shellfish. If 500 couples like Franco
and Ann graced Britain, the cross channel ferries would go bust.
Sleep at Angel Hotel or Llanwenarth Arms – Abergavenny.
alc **B-C**
closed Sun.
post Llandewi Skirrid, Abergavenny, Gwent NP7 8AW.
phone (0873) 2797 *Mich* 403 (L28) Hereford 26 m.

LLANFAIR WATERDINE   Red Lion

Simple inn with rooms (S)
Quiet/Gardens/Good value (meals)

The Red Lion nestles besides the young River Teme – the
opposite bank is Wales! A variety of charms beguile you at
Llanfair: a 300-year-old whitewashed inn – originally farm
cottages; deserted hills; the warm welcome of experienced hosts,
Jim and Joan Rhodes – soon to retire in two or three years time;
and basic fare like home-made soups, sweets, local lamb and
free-range poultry. Other than in summer, there's a blazing fire in
the cosy bar lounge. Bear in mind that your hosts do it all with no
help – 364 days a year. Essential to book meals ahead.
menus **A** *rooms* 3 **C-D**
closed Christmas Day.
post Llanfair Waterdine, Knighton, Powys LD7 1TU.
phone (0547) 528214 *Mich* 403 (K26) Hereford 34 m.

LLANTHONY   Abbey

Simple restaurant with rooms
Secluded/Gardens/Good value (dinner)   ®

If you worry about such things as amenities and style then don't
stay overnight. But all of you should be prepared to drive a long
way to enjoy Susan Fancourt's cooking. The Abbey is the west
front of the 12th-century Llanthony Priory – the hostelry was
'reconstructed' 200 years ago and incorporates an original
Norman spiral staircase. Susan is a talented cook – her repertoire
covers the globe, from Japan via Mexico to Wales. Try *cawl lafwr*
– a delicious soup based on seaweed and vegetables; *brythll chig
moch* – Welsh-style trout; and *rhostio eog* – a Welsh salmon dish.
Delightful, informal service from Maureen. Read the visitors'
books. Book ahead.
alc **A-B** (dinner only served) *rooms* 4 **B-C**
closed Nov-Mar. Sun. Mon. Lunch-every day.
post Llanthony, Abergavenny, Gwent.
phone (087 382) 487 or 559 *Mich* 403 (K28) Hereford 25 m.

LUDLOW   Feathers

Very comfortable hotel (S)
Good Value (lunch)

For those of you who want – and can afford – luxury accommodation, then the 400-year-old Feathers is the ideal base to explore the Marches. The hotel's superb Jacobean façade makes an important contribution to Ludlow's medieval atmosphere. For other visitors with less-deep pockets the low-cost menus, based entirely on English cooking, are bargains: home-made Ludlow broth, lamb, pork, duckling, beefsteak and kidney pie, bread and butter pudding, numerous sweets, conventional English cheeses and good coffee are typical.
menus **A** (lun) **B** (din) *rooms* 35 **D-D2** *cards* A AE DC Visa
closed Open all the year.
post Bull Ring, Ludlow, Salop SY8 1AA.
phone (0584) 5261 *Mich* 403 (L26) Hereford 24 m.

THREE COCKS   Three Cocks

Comfortable restaurant with rooms
Gardens

Barry and Jill Cole bought the 15th-century hostelry from the Hines in 1979 (see *Vale of Severn* – Corse Lawn). Several *FL3* readers recommended it – my visit confirmed their praise. The highlight was the exceptional efficiency – coupled with the right balance of friendliness – of the young receptionist, Heather; she and her waitress colleagues do a fine job. Cooking is well above average – mainly French classical but there's always a Welsh dish on the menus; I enjoyed *cig cen a mel* – Welsh lamb, roasted with honey, cider and ginger. Several comfortable lounges; take note French restaurateurs!
menus **B** (din only served) *rooms* 7 **D** *cards* A AE DC Visa
closed Mid Dec-mid Feb. Lunch-every day.
post Three Cocks, Brecon, Powys LD3 0SL.
phone (049 74) 215 *Mich* 403 (K27) Hereford 25 m.

WHITNEY-ON-WYE   The Rhydspence Inn

Comfortable inn with rooms (S)
Gardens   ®

I 'discovered' this gem of an inn by chance. I had been reconnoitring drive 2 in the hills to the north and I used the 'yellow' road from Newchurch to reach the A438 at 148-243473 (the inn has an attractive setting – the Wales England border is the brook that runs through the gardens). There's a fine view overlooking the Wye and the Black Mountains – Kilvert's descriptions of river ice and flooding near the inn make interesting reading. During the hour I was there I also 'discovered' it had won Ronay's 1984 'Pub of the Year' award. A ravishing 16th-century black and white timbered building, coupled to the enterprise of David (the cook) and Flo Wallington make it an outstanding treat. Duckling, steaks, roast sucking pig (order ahead) and excellent breakfasts are highlights.
alc **B-C** *rooms* 3 **C-D**
closed Sun evg. Mon. Two wks Nov.
post Whitney-on-Wye, Herefordshire HR3 6EU.
phone (049 73) 262 *Mich* 403 (K27) Hereford 19 m.

Favourite London Restaurants

BATTERSEA London SW8 — L'Arlequin

Comfortable restaurant/Michelin ★

BEST MEAL IN 84 ®

Good value (lunch)

Christian and Geneviève Delteil opened their tiny restaurant in unfashionable Battersea three years ago – a few paces from Chez Nico. Christian, just turned 30, and attractive, dark-haired Geneviève live over the 'shop' with five-year-old Laurianne – a typical young family fighting hard to make their culinary mark. At least one *French Leave 3* reader reckons this is one of the best London restaurants – I'll not dispute that. Evidence? Consider a *fricassée de champignons sauvages en feuilleté* – marvellous; a stunning and rarely seen *courgette à fleur farcie beurre de tomate* – amazing; or a *feuilleté de langoustines* – a cleverly-designed patterned pastry; and excellent fresh vegetables.
menus B (lunch) *alc* C-D *cards* A DC Visa
closed 3 weeks Aug. Sat. Sun. Bank hols.
post 123 Queenstown Road, London SW8 3RH.
phone (01) 622 0555 ('85 move north of river seems likely)

BATTERSEA London SW8 — Chez Nico

Comfortable restaurant/Michelin ★★

BEST MEAL IN 84 ®

Good value (lunch)

A major article on London restaurants in *The New York Times* ran this headline: 'One tip: be suspicious of places called 'Chez'.' Poppycock, my American friends. If you took that advice you would miss one of London's best chefs. Nico Ladenis is a 50-year-old, self-taught, human dynamo – crackling with energy, enthusiasm and exciting talent. Kenyan-born Nico, together with his wife, Dinah-Jane, won their richly-deserved second star in 1984 – remarkable in unfashionable Battersea. His cooking is very much in the modern style – sauces are three-star quality. Personal creations include a *ragoût de coquille St-Jacques à la crème légère de poireaux* – where attention to detail results in a mouthwatering masterpiece; and a smooth, light *parfait fondant de foie de canard au beurre de foie gras*. Bravo Nico!
menus B-C (lunch) *alc* C-D *cards* A Visa
closed Easter. 3 wks July-Aug. Xmas. Sat (lun). Sun. Mon.
post 129 Queenstown Road, London SW8 3RH.
phone (01) 720 6960

CHELSEA London SW1 — Chelsea Room

Luxury restaurant/Michelin ★

Good value (supper menu – see text)

You pay a price for the pampering luxury that complements the cooking skills of Bernard Gaume: space, light, comfort, flowers, a tree-filled view, superb Wedgwood china, fine wines (40 half-bottles) and a pianist in the evenings. Light classical and modern specialities: Bernard is particularly talented with fish – the *petite soupe* is cleverly presented and tasty. If you want real value try the 'Supper Menu' (band C) – served between 10.30 and 11.45 p.m.; *apéritif* and coffee included.
menus C (lunch and see text) *alc* D *cards* A AE DC Visa
closed Open all the year.
post 2 Cadogan Place, London SW1X 9PY.
phone (01) 235 5411 (Part of the Hyatt Carlton Tower Hotel)

CHELSEA London SW3   Dan's

Simple restaurant

'Dan's' is Dan Whitehead's small, colourful restaurant and garden – the latter is a minuscule patio but a delight on a warm summer's day. *FL3* readers recommended it – and, true enough, I enjoyed the informal atmosphere with no stuffy pretentiousness of any sort. Lunches are 'quick, original and fun' – dinners are 'relaxed, sophisticated and romantic': I'll not quibble with Dan's descriptions. I overheard a diner's remark: "Often elsewhere you don't know what to choose – because you fancy nothing; here the difficulty is it all sounds nice." That sums it up well.

alc **B-C** *cards* AE Visa
closed Sat. Sun.
post 119 Sydney St, London SW3 6NR.
phone (01) 352 2718

CHELSEA London SW1   Gavvers

Comfortable restaurant
Good value

One of four London restaurants owned by the Roux brothers – this was the original home of Le Gavroche, before the move to Mayfair. It's a comfortable dining room – managed by Bruno Ricard and his delightful wife, Anne, who hails from Scotland. Add the capable skills of long-serving chef, Denis Lobry, and a pricing policy where everything is included – *apéritif*, wine and coffee – and you have one of the best quality/price bargains in London. Modern-style, light classical cooking with a choice of seven to eight alternatives for each course – fish is particularly good. The French menu should have English notes – too much valuable time is spent explaining dishes.

menus **C** (dinner only served)
closed Sun. Bank hols. Lunch-every day.
post 61-63 Lower Sloane St, London SW1W 8DH.
phone (01) 730 5983

CHELSEA London SW3   Waltons

Luxury restaurant/Michelin ★
Good value (supper menu & lunch)   ®

Lack of consistency is the greatest problem with most London restaurants; Waltons is a typical example. Ignored by Ronay and *The GFG*, it's awarded a star by Michelin. Anne and I had a faultless meal; great friends, checking out for us, had a miserable evening. I'll describe ours. The newly-arrived chef, 29-year-old David Nicholls (a protégé of Mosimann), has found the perfect home. Attention to detail is David's greatest hallmark: you see it in his appetisers, bread, vegetables, *petits fours*, his specialities like 'moneybags' of salmon trout, terrine of orange-fillets and Walton's caramel pudding. A bonus is the list of good-value wines – some amazingly so. If there is a weakness it's service – slow and with some rough edges. Bargains? At lunch an **A** menu; after 10 p.m. and Sun. lun. a **B** menu.

menus **A-B** (see text) *alc* **C-D** *cards* A AE DC Visa
closed Xmas. 4 days Easter. Bank hols.
post 121 Walton St, London SW3 2HP.
phone (01) 584 0204

CHELSEA London SW3   La Tante Claire

Comfortable restaurant/Michelin ★★
Good value (lunch)

A score of London restaurants failed to pass the 'acid test' I describe on page 14. Pierre Koffmann was a member of that club for a time – and though I revisited more out of respect for the reputation he has with his fellow chefs, I nevertheless must qualify my recommendation. I spent a lot of money in 1984 giving him the benefit of the doubt.

A chef who wins two Michelin stars, gets rave reviews from *The GFG* and enjoys a Ronay three-star rating (the same as the incomparable Girardet) must expect his skills as a chef **and** restaurateur to be measured against the very **highest** standards. My first 1984 visit, together with Anne, was a miserable evening. Of the scores of Michelin two and three-star restaurants I know, Koffmann's small dining room is among the most uncomfortable – so much can go wrong when it's busy because of the overcrowding: you feel like a sardine in a tightly-packed can; it's poorly lit; and the waiters have a difficult task trying to do an efficient job. Of the six courses we tried not one was outstanding. The appetiser, the *petits fours*, the bread and the vegetables were all of average standard – I can think of many one-star chefs who do better with those 'little details'.

I revisited two weeks later – on my own at lunchtime. This was more like the innovative master matching his reputation: the famous leek terrine (*terrine de poireaux aux truffes*) and pig's trotter (*pied de cochon aux morilles*) were unusual, tasty and unique creative specialities.

So, if you must, go in the evening when the place is packed – but I would not recommend it. I suggest you visit at lunchtime when you have space, light, the entire *équipe* working efficiently and the chance to enjoy a value-for-money menu. Pierre: make the owners of the shop next door an offer they cannot refuse!

menus **B** (lunch) *alc* **D** *cards* AE DC (Essential to book)
closed Sat/Sun. Easter. 3 wks Aug-Sept. Xmas. New Yr. Bk hols.
post 68 Royal Hospital Rd, London SW3 2HP.
phone (01) 352 6045

COVENT GARDEN London WC2   Café Pélican

Comfortable restaurant
Good value   ®

Anne and I were thrilled by the impact the Café Pélican made on London during 1984. We have known Carolyn Lewendon (née Hall) for over 20 years – since she was a young girl. From 1981-83 we followed with great interest the detailed planning and fantastic energy that she and husband Richard put into their efforts to transform electricity board showrooms into such an authentic 1920s Parisian *brasserie* – with its remarkable 'meandering' bar. Chef Gérard Mosiniak and his brigade have high standards. A range of light, enjoyable treats come from the 'computerised' kitchen and are served by a youthful, friendly band of waiters. In the evening there's a variety of musical entertainment. Seek it out – and ensure Pélican is a success.

alc **A-C** *cards* A AE DC Visa
closed Open all the year.
post 45 St. Martin's Lane, London WC2N 4FJ.
phone (01) 379 0309

COVENT GARDEN London WC2 Interlude de Tabaillau

Comfortable restaurant/Michelin ★
Good value (lunch) ®

Every restaurateur could learn a great deal from 34-year-old Jean Louis Taillebaud – one of four famous Roux protégés (others are Koffmann at La Tante Claire, Chandler at Woburn and Germain at Montreuil). His 'inclusive' menu charge is just that: VAT, service, *apéritif*, coffee and wine are all included. The balance between quality and value for money is in perfect tune: there is no cutting of corners with specialities such as *mousseline de gibier aux herbes – quenelle*-like and light; *tronconnette de turbotin au safran* – a dozen mouthfuls of fish; cheeses from Philippe Olivier in Boulogne; and tasty *tarte passion*.
menus **C** (lunch) **D** (dinner) *cards* A AE DC Visa
closed Easter. 3 wks July-Aug. Xmas. Sat (lun). Sun. Bk hols.
post 7-8 Bow Street, London WC2.
phone (01) 379 6473

MARYLEBONE London NW1 Sea Shell

Simple restaurant (S)
Good value ®

For years I lived with the daily chore of commuting to and from London – in my case via Marylebone Station. Consequently there were many late evenings when a quick, cheap meal was the order of the day before catching a train home; the Sea Shell, 100 yards or so from the station, became a favourite – unknown in those days. Now it's London's best-known fish and chip shop. You must queue to get in. It's unlicensed, so bring your own wine – though that's hardly necessary; and it's very simply furnished. But John Faulkner, Mark Farrell and manageress Agatha Tiernan work wonders with fresh fish – halibut, Dover sole, cod, skate, haddock, plaice, lemon sole and, occasionally, salmon.
alc **A** (no reservations – queue on the pavement)
closed Xmas. Sun. Mon.
post 33-35 Lisson Grove, London NW1.
phone (01) 723 8703

MAYFAIR London W1 Gavroche

Luxury restaurant/Michelin ★★★ ®

Albert Roux has had his fair share of criticism during the last few years. Ignore it. Instead, rejoice in the consistent effort and skill he has applied in establishing Britain's only Michelin three-star restaurant. Despite other culinary business interests, Albert is rarely absent from his kitchens – unlike some superstar French chefs. Visit at lunchtime when you can enjoy a 'bargain' menu (£20 or so) and see what three-star standards are: no compromises in quality, produce, service, wines or furnishings. You will have a better chance, too, to quiz Silvano, the marvellous *maître d'hôtel*, and Peter Davies, the English *sommelier*. Albert's style is best defined by the title of his book, *New Classic Cuisine*: light, creative – but often so rich.
menus **D** (lunch) *alc* **D** *cards* A AE DC Visa (Book ahead)
closed Xmas-New Year. Sat. Sun. Bank hols.
post 43 Upper Brook Street, London W1P 1PS.
phone (01) 408 0881

MAYFAIR London W1   Langan's Brasserie

Comfortable restaurant
Good value

Michael Caine and Peter Langan are the more famous of the three
partners behind the Brasserie. My tribute is to the third – Richard
Shepherd, the chef, who does so much for trainee *cuisiniers*.
Every day his brigade serves 600 meals; the huge menu has 30
starters, 30 main courses and 30 desserts and cheeses. Keeping a
balance between those numbers and quality is like walking a
tightrope. A reasonably high standard of cooking emerges from
Richard's balancing act: typical treats are 'Langan's seafood
salad' with perfectly cooked vegetables and a delectable *crème
brûlée*. It's a no frills, value-for-money formula.
alc **B-C** *cards* A AE DC Visa (Book ahead)
closed Sat (lunch). Sun. Bank hols.
post Stratton Street, London W1X 5FD.
phone (01) 493 6437

MAYFAIR London W1   Le Soufflé

Luxury restaurant/Michelin ★

Five London hotel restaurants won Michelin stars in 1984 – two
for the first time. German-born Peter Kromberg, the chef at Le
Soufflé, was one of the two – a long overdue accolade. The art
deco-styled basement restaurant may not be to everyone's liking
– but few will dispute the skills of Peter's team. He is renowned
for his superb soufflés – Gruyère, crab, sole and salmon as
starters and main courses; and a variety of sweet ones – rum and
banana and orange and Grand Marnier are just two. A host of
other innovative specialities are no less delicious – particularly
Peter's seafood and shellfish dishes. Service is precise – a
necessity when timing of soufflés is so critical.
menus **C** (lunch) *alc* **C-D** *cards* A AE DC Visa
closed Open all the year.
post Inter-Continental Hotel, 1 Hamilton Pl, London W1V 0QY.
phone (01) 409 3131

MAYFAIR London W1   BEST MEAL IN 84   The Terrace ®

Luxury restaurant/Michelin ★

Anton Mosimann and Frédy Girardet share several things in
common: both are Swiss; both are immensely talented chefs with
individual styles; and both manage to win astonishing admiration
and respect from the fortunate few who work for them. Anton
won his long overdue first star in 1984; if you want to discover
just what the modern style of today means try his 'menu surprise'
– a favourite culinary 'trick' of many Swiss chefs. It may include
delights like *salade aux artichauts et brocoli aux homard rôti* –
fresh, light and pretty as a picture; *consommé de bœuf aux
julienne de betteraves* – a ruby-like gem; and some melt-in-the-
mouth fillets of *St. Pierre*. One of the world's great dining rooms
– what cosseting comforts. (At lunch try Anton's Grill Room –
British produce and dishes at their best.)
menus **D** (dinner only served) *cards* A AE DC Visa
closed Sun. Lunch-every day.
post Dorchester Hotel, Park Lane, London W1A 2HJ.
phone (01) 629 8888

NORTH KENSINGTON London W11   Leith's
Very comfortable restaurant

Leith's is a flourishing example of restaurants I enjoyed in France a decade ago – now rarely seen. You'll know what I mean: a tantalising choice of 15 or so super hors-d'œuvre – a really clever scallop terrine and smoked haddock pâté among them (bigger plates would help presentation); main courses with classic sauces like *béarnaise* and *beurre blanc*; and an eye-popping, 'real' *chariot de desserts*. All prepared by a Yorkshireman, chef Gordon Lang, and a team mainly staffed by Britons in the kitchen and long-serving Spaniards in the dining room: Bravo management! A favourite of many *FL3* readers.
menus D (dinner only served) *cards* A AE DC Visa
closed 4 days Xmas. Lunch-every day.
post 92 Kensington Park Rd, London W11 2PN.
phone (01) 229 4481

RICHMOND (see page 138)

ST. JAMES'S London SW1   Suntory
Comfortable restaurant

Many European chefs – including Mosimann – consider Japanese cuisine is the greatest of all. Perhaps, though it's not to my liking. It is healthy! Try it for yourself – and discover why some aspects of modern French cooking are so Japanese in style. Reserve a table in the Shabu-Shabu room and enjoy *sushi* – the famous 'picture' dish – a selection of lightly-cooked fish wrapped round hammocks of rice; *sashimi* – various raw fish with a soy sauce dip (it comes with *wasabi*, green horseradish: mix it into the dip because if you taste it 'neat' you'll hit the ceiling – it's like rocket fuel); *shabu-shabu* – wafer-thin beef cooked at the table; and *tempura* – shrimps and vegetables in a crispy covering (use your fingers). First visit? Ask for a fork.
menus B (lunch) C-D (dinner) *cards* A AE DC Visa
closed Sun. Bank hols.
post 72-73 St. James's Street, London SW1A 1PH.
phone (01) 409 0201

SOHO London W1   L'Escargot Brasserie
Comfortable restaurant (S)
Good value

I long ago gave up spending hard-earned pounds in most of Soho's 'strip-off' restaurants; this is one of the exceptions. Fare is very modest – so are prices. Grilled goat's cheese, black pudding, Cumberland sausages, rack of English lamb, *crudités* and treacle tart are the sort of basics any of us can do at home. But it's worth a visit for the wines alone; 50 of them, chosen and described by Jancis Robinson, the wife of the owner, Nick Lander. A mixture of French, Italian, Australian and Californian – one of the best price/quality ratios in London; the presentation of the list is a model – more should copy it.
alc B *cards* A AE DC Visa
closed Easter. Xmas. Jan 1. Sat (lunch). Sun. Bank hols.
post 48 Greek Street, London W1V 5LQ.
phone (01) 437 2679

SOHO London W1   Swiss Centre

Comfortable restaurants
Good value   ®

For 17 years the four Swiss Centre restaurants have been great favourites with my family. Ask my children "Where?" – and you can be sure of their reply. A huge basement brasserie-style place houses four restaurants: the Rendez Vous for quick Swiss German-style snacks; the Locanda for a selection of traditional *fondues;* the Taverne for Swiss French-style treats, including *raclette;* and the Chesa – a more expensive, ambitious corner. The best test of its popularity is to look around you - always full of European folk who know a good thing when they see it. Service can at times be snail-pace slow.

alc **A-C** *cards* A AE DC Visa
closed Open all the year.
post 10 Wardour Street, London W1V 3HG.
phone (01) 734 1291

SOUTH KENSINGTON London SW7   Hilaire

Comfortable restaurant
Good value (lunch)

Guide inspectors can become successful chefs! Simon Hopkinson, an ex-Ronay inspector, has already made a considerable name for himself as a talented chef in the year since he and John Solway, both in their late twenties, opened Hilaire. It was Greta Hobbs, at Inverlochy, who led us to this new, enterprising restaurant where professional touches stand out like beacons. Simon certainly took careful note of details on his 'inspector' travels: immaculate linen, fresh rolls, a succulent *rosette* (Lyonnais pork sausage) appetiser, a delicious spring vegetable *feuilleté au beurre d'asperges* and a light passion fruit *bavarois* are examples. Simpler lunches.

menus **A-B** (lun) **C** (din) *cards* A AE DC Visa
closed Mid-end Aug. Sat lun. Sun.
post 68 Old Brompton Rd, London SW7.
phone (01) 584 8993

SOUTH KENSINGTON London SW5   Read's

Comfortable restaurant   ®

Through prodigious hard work Caroline Swatland and Keith Read (they were married in August 1984) have quickly established themselves in London – after their initial success at Sandbach in Cheshire. At 26, and self-taught, Caroline is already a talented *cuisinière*. Bubbling originality and burning nervous energy are so evident in her work: pink calves' liver with a green peppercorn aspic; a *millefeuille* of frogs' legs; red mullet with stem ginger and fresh orange; home-made chocolates; just a few examples of her delicate skills. As time passes Caroline will learn how to balance exuberant creativity with those magic words *faites simple*: when it happens London will have a truly brilliant *cuisinière* – the match of any in France.

alc **B-C** *cards* A AE DC Visa
closed 2 weeks Xmas-New Year. Sun. Mon.
post 152 Old Brompton Rd, London SW5 0BE.
phone (01) 373 2445

BATH   The Hole in the Wall

Comfortable restaurant with rooms

Sue and Tim Cumming have worked tirelessly for two decades.
They first met when they worked for Perry-Smith who owned the
'Hole' in the 60s (p.137); they married in 1972 and then opened
their own restaurant in Salisbury. Holidays in those days were
spent in France seeking inspiration; French cooking influences
their own personal cooking style though they do put their fingers
in other culinary pies, too. They bought the 'Hole' in 1980. The
couple were away in Scotland on my September '84 visit: my
meal – *soupe de poissons, rouille et croûtons*, sea bass *en
papillote* and some home-made ice creams and sorbets – was of a
high category two standard. Super Yapp Loire and Rhône wines.
menus C *rooms* 8 **D-D2** *cards* A AE DC Visa
closed 3 wks from Xmas. Rest: Sun/Bk hols – 'non-res'.
post 16 George St, Bath, Avon BA1 2EN.
phone (0225) 25242 *Mich* 404 (M29) (Near 'Circus')

BRISTOL   Les Semailles

Comfortable restaurant
Good value (lunch)   Ⓡ

René and Jillian Gaté took the big plunge into the culinary deep
end in July '84 when they opened their own 'home' in a Bristol
suburb. René, 28, is an innovative master: his basic training came
from chef Campion at Avranches, sharpened by a stint with
Guérard and followed by two years with Raymond Blanc at
Oxford. He met Jill at Avranches – they had been pen-friends
since 1968. A summer lunch put the offerings of my Connaught
visit the previous evening to shame: light, personal creations like
gently-roasted *langoustines* with basil and mango and calf's liver
in a beetroot sauce were artistically presented specialities. Give
the courageous couple your support.
menus **A** (lun) *alc* **B-C** *cards* AE Visa (Rooms? Speak to Jill)
closed Sun. (Use junc 17 on M5: S of A4162 & W of B4054)
post 9 Druid Hill, Stoke Bishop, Bristol, Avon.
phone (0272) 686456 *Mich* 404 (M29)

CANTERBURY   Seventy Four

Comfortable restaurant
Good value   Ⓡ

All of you who speed through Kent, impatiently waiting for your
first 'French' meal, should think again. Instead, detour to
inspiring Canterbury and support Ian and Jane McAndrew in
their brave gamble to be their own bosses. Ian, a 32-year-old
Geordie and a Mosimann protégé, won many accolades when
'employed' at nearby Ashford; he's better than most chefs in
France's *North* (see *FL3*). His style is in the Roux mould: duck
liver mousse tartlet was three-star excellence; and a chicken and
lobster 'sausage' with a spring onion sauce, though rich, was
brilliant. Encourage and enthuse at 74: ask them about their
efforts to convert the 400-year-old house to a restaurant!
menus **A-B** (lun) **B-C** (din) *cards* A AE Visa
closed Sun. (Rooms? Speak to David Egerton or Jane)
post 74 Wincheap, Canterbury, Kent CT1 3RX.
phone (0227) 67411 *Mich* 404 (X30) (A28-100 yds SW station)

EAST GRINSTEAD   Gravetye Manor

Very comfortable hotel/Michelin ★
Secluded/Gardens   Ⓡ

Peter Herbert's 16th-century Gravetye Manor is endowed with a
string of impressive features which, in turn, offer seductive, but
expensive benefits for visitors: surrounded by Gravetye Forest,
the park-like garden was the work of William Robinson, a
previous owner and one of the greatest gardeners of all time;
panelled rooms use wood from the estate; and Allan Garth, the
Cumbria-born chef, who uses his native language on the menus,
has a light, innovative style – like the scallop mousse wrapped in
strudel dough. Home-smoked venison, smooth-as-silk honey and
almond ice cream, freshly-baked bread and a fine cellar with
dozens of half-bottles are other bonuses.

alc **C-D** *rooms* 14 **D2-D4**
closed Open all the year.
post Gravetye, East Grinstead, West Sussex RH19 4LJ.
phone (0342) 810567 *Mich* 404 (T30) (S of B2110 – 5 m. SW town).

FRESHFORD   Homewood Park

Very comfortable restaurant with rooms
Quiet/Gardens/Tennis/Good value (lunch – not Sat)   Ⓡ

Bernard Levin, in his book *Enthusiasms* (a remarkable c.v. of a
happy man), called Homewood Park 'what I imagine Paradise to
be and warmly hope is'. I visited on a dazzling April day when it
truly sparkled. Overlooking the Limpley Stoke Valley – for long a
favourite of mine – this country house 'home' is an informal gem.
Penny Ross has an eye for gentle shades and delicate textures –
her bedrooms are stunners. Husband Stephen, a skilful chef, is
full of clever ideas: innovative appetisers, wild rabbit sausage,
Cornish shark, maize-fed chicken in the Chinese style and
grapefruit and campari sorbet (sensational) are typical. You'll
linger long at 'Home'wood.

menus **B** (lun-not Sat) *alc* **B-C** *rooms* 10 **D-D3** *cards* A AE DC Visa
closed Xmas-mid Jan.
post Hinton Charterhouse, Freshford, Bath, Avon BA1 6HH.
phone (022 122) 2643 *Mich* 404 (M29) (On A36 – 7 m. S Bath)

GULLANE   La Potinière

Simple restaurant
Good value   Ⓡ

Book well ahead; reserving a table can present Girardet-like
difficulties – the best compliment I can pay Hilary and David
Brown. It's unbelievable that such beguiling skills can be
savoured at such low cost. Be on time; Hilary does **all** the
cooking herself and David **all** the serving (his wine list rivals
Croque-en-Bouche – page 111). A meal could be a mint-flavoured
tomato soup; a feather-light mousseline of sole and smoked
salmon; chicken as good as any in Bresse with, sensibly, just a
potato gratin and avocado salad; and Brie or an encore-satisfying
strawberry soup. Don't miss this super restaurant.

menus **A-B** (lunch and Sat dinner only served)
closed 1 wk June. Oct. Xmas. New Yr. Wed. Sat lun. Evgs (not Sat).
post Main St, Gullane, East Lothian EH31 2AA.
phone (0620) 843214 *Mich* 401 (L15) (19 m. E of Edinburgh)

HAMBLETON
Hambleton Hall

Very comfortable hotel/Michelin ★
Secluded/Gardens/Tennis/Fishing ℝ

The 100-year-old Hall's setting is a stunning surprise – on a wooded, island-like hill in the middle of Rutland Water. From the suntrap terrace you look down, through the tops of handsome trees, to the still surface of the man-made lake (1976). The hotel is as beguiling as the setting – cosseting and pleasing. Nick Gill, a young British chef, provides polished culinary touches: grisle with samphire, lamb's kidneys with wild mushrooms in a tarragon cream sauce and a clove-perfumed mango *sablé* are a few of the many choices available on fixed-price menus. Desserts and presentation are Nick's strongest talents. Expensive it is but a 'budget' lunch allows you a 'taste' of the Hall.
menus **C** (lun) **D** (din) *rooms* 15 **D2-D4** *cards* A AE DC Visa
closed Open all the year.
post Hambleton, Oakham, Leics LE15 8TH
phone (0572) 56991 *Mich* 404 (R25) (3 m. SE – off A606)

HELFORD
Riverside

Comfortable restaurant with rooms
Gardens ℝ

During the last 30 years George Perry-Smith has done as much as anyone to ensure that the British culinary 'seedling' he helped to sow would flourish. Readers will know of my great admiration for Elizabeth David and her significant influence in changing British attitudes: George, more than anyone else, was the chef who turned her concepts into restaurant reality – using a natural, imaginative style. With his partner, Heather Crosbie (how happy they are with life), George still knows how to beguile, just as he did when I first visited him at Bath over 15 years ago. Comfortable cottages in an 'absurdly pretty village'.
menus **D** (din only) *rooms* 6 **D2-D4** (Booking essential)
closed Nov-Feb. Lunch-every day.
post Helford, Helston, Cornwall TR12 6JU.
phone (032 623) 443 *Mich* 403 (E33) (50 yds from main car park)

HORTON
French Partridge

Comfortable restaurant
Good value ℝ

The GFG can be as fickle as the British weather; of the 20 '83 'distinctions' awarded in the English counties, 40% got the chop in '84! This was one: but why? It hasn't stopped contented locals flocking in; nor should it stop my readers seeking out this attractive country restaurant where outstanding value for money and skilful cooking will bowl you over, too. For Anne 'every mouthful was a delight': gravlax – in a mustard cream sauce; *œuf Argenteuil* – poached egg with asparagus in a crisp, thin pastry; superb sliced steak; light *crépinettes* of lamb sweetbreads and spinach; and tasty, rosemary-perfumed *courgettes*. Bravo David and Mary Partridge!
menus **B** (dinner only – book) (Rooms? Speak to Mary)
closed 1 wk Easter. 2 wks Xmas. 3 wks July-Aug. Sun. Mon.
post Newport Pagnell Rd, Horton, Northampton NN7 2AP.
phone (0604) 870033 *Mich* 404 (R27) (6 m. S N'hampton-B526)

LEAMINGTON SPA   Mallory Court

Very comfortable hotel/Michelin ★
Quiet/Gardens/Swimming pool/Good value (lunch)   Ⓡ

Come on businessmen from Coventry, Warwick and Leamington: try the value-for-money lunch that chef Allan Holland (self-taught and with a 100% British kitchen team) offers for £12 including service and VAT (in '84). My readers, looking for bargains, will not be so slow to accept such largesse. Cuisine is rich, Roux-style 'new classic' (see page 131): chicken *quenelles*, stuffed with liver mousse plus a leek and cream sauce – and truffles – is typical. Excellent sorbets and sweets. Gardens are the highlight of the setting and the panelled dining room has an authentic Warwickshire feel about it – real England.

menus **B** (lun) *alc* **D** (din) *rooms* 8 **D3-D4** *cards* A AE Visa
closed Sun din for non-residents.
post Harbury Lane, Tachbrook Mallory, Leamington Spa.
phone (0926) 30214 *Mich* 403 (P27) (2 m. S on A452 – 'Harbury' sign)

LIMPSFIELD   Old Lodge

Comfortable restaurant/Michelin ★
Good value

Within three years of opening, Brian Clivaz and chefs David Nicholls (now at Waltons – see page 129) and John Mann won their first star in 1984. How? By applying basics to the task at hand: light, modern cooking – without vast portions and with plenty of choice; fresh, daily-changing produce – mainly British; an eye for detail; young, skilled and friendly English staff; and, above all, by giving real value for money. Three fixed-price menus are inclusive of VAT, service and coffee. Brian should write his menus entirely in English – to complement his excellent team and the fine, panelled 'English' dining room.

menus **B-C** *cards* A AE DC Visa (Rooms? Speak to Brian)
closed 1st 3 wks Jan. Sat lun. Sun din. Mon.
post High St, Limpsfield, Surrey RH8 0DR.
phone (088 33) 2996 *Mich* 404 (U30) (N A25 – turn at T.Ls)

RICHMOND   Lichfield's
                                                      BEST
Comfortable restaurant/Michelin ★   MEAL
Good value (lunch)   IN 84   Ⓡ

Please – make the short detour from London to Richmond: enjoy the tantalising skills of 40-year-old, self-taught Stephen Bull – Britain's own Marc Meneau. What that means is that this half-Welsh, half-English chef is a master of the difficult art of *faites simple*. It takes carefully developed experience, confidence and good taste to acquire that talent – you see it in all sorts of ways: the succulent appetisers; a delicious mixture of a *millefeuille* of salmon, leeks and chives; the simplicity of *langoustines* wrapped in basil with a red pepper sauce; and the thoughtful, 'different' presentation of breast of duck with sweet and sour onions. Like Marc, the intelligent, creative Stephen Bull will go on to greater success. That's certain!

menus **B** (lunch) *alc* **C-D** *cards* A AE
closed 1 15 Sept. 1 wk Xmas. Sat lun. Sun. Mon.
post 13 Lichfield Terr., Sheen Rd, Richmond TW9 1DP.
phone (01) 940 5236 (Richmond is 8 m. W of London)

STORRINGTON
BEST MEAL IN 84   Manleys   ℝ

Very comfortable restaurant

There's something 'missing' from the line above – the fact that Karl Löderer thoroughly deserves his first Michelin star. This 45-year-old, Austrian-born chef has spent 20 years establishing his reputation in England; for the past six years at his charming country home and previously during a 13-year stint at Gravetye Manor, East Grinstead. Anne and I fell in love with Manleys: a well-lit dining room full of fresh flowers; a friendly, professional *maître d'hôtel* in 'Tom', scallops and shellfish as 'fresh-as-daisies,' and mouthwatering Scottish beef that could not be bettered anywhere (note the frequent use of 'fresh' *GFG*); masterly pastry; and magnificent desserts. Don't 'miss' Manleys. *alc* **B-C** *cards* A AE DC Visa (Rooms? Speak to Tom) *closed* Sun evg. Mon. 3 wks Aug-Sept. 1st wk Jan. *post* Manleys Hill, Storrington, West Sussex RH20 4BT. *phone* (090 66) 2331 *Mich* 404 (S31) (N of Worthing – W of A24)

STRATFORD-UPON-AVON
Hill's

Simple restaurant
Good value

Seek out Hill's – it's another enterprising venture that needs your support. Less than 12 months ago, after years of working for others – at Carrier's, the Capital and the Lygon Arms – Shaun and Anja Hill took the plunge and opened their new 'home', the minuscule restaurant previously called Marianne (the smallest in Britain?) – a longtime favourite of ours. Aided by old friends Colin Pope and his fiancée, Jackie, Shaun's talents should ensure they survive the gamble. It's not a glamorous, status-satisfying spot; but if you appreciate the creative, light efforts of a skilled chef you'll enjoy yourself hugely. *alc* **B-C** *cards* A AE DC Visa (Rooms? Plenty of hotels & B&B) *closed* 1 week Aug. Sun. Mon. *post* 3 Greenhill St, Stratford-upon-Avon, Warwickshire. *phone* (0789) 293563 *Mich* 403 (P27) (Near Station)

TAUNTON
Castle

Very comfortable hotel/Michelin ★
Gardens/Lift/Good value (lunch)   ℝ

Britain needs hundreds of go-ahead hoteliers like Kit Chapman, the Castle's MD: like any experienced businessman he knows full well that success doesn't just happen. The Chapman family's 'Castle' attracts in many ways: there's fine country on hand (see pages 54/68); the hotel has bags of character; and, best of all, 29-year-old Chris Oakes, Felixstowe-born, is in the kitchens. (He studies diligently – his honeymoon included a Girardet visit.) One of Britain's best young cooks, he puts his own culinary good sense to great use – modern, light, well presented specialities. Fresh fish from Lyme Regis is particularly good – thanks to Phil Bowditch, their Taunton supplier. Gents: enjoy the Lichfield 'loos'; a bit more plush than Richard Bowman's (p. 91). *menus* **A** (lun) **C** (din) *rooms* 40 **D2-D4** *cards* A AE DC Visa *closed* Open all the year. *post* Castle Green, Taunton, Somerset TA1 1NF. *phone* (0823) 72671 *Mich* 403 (K30) (Follow 'Castle Museum' signs)

For many years between the wars my parents lived in China – they left Shanghai a few months before I was born in New Delhi. During those years they got to know just a small part of the immense cuisine repertoire that goes under the ubiquitous and much-devalued word 'Chinese'. I recall from an early age the great fondness my mother had for duck – prepared in all sorts of ways; for vegetables, too – eaten almost raw and chopped in delicate slices; and for lightly-cooked fish. All those examples of her life-long favourites first took root in China.

She always stressed that to understand Chinese cooking fully was an impossible task. How could anyone, she would ask, master such a complex subject when one considered the vast size of the country (only Russia is larger); the huge population – one-third of the world's total; and the scores of dialects, religions and the diversity of cultures. The climate, too, varies from the cold north to the tropical south and the land mass has a coastline thousands of miles long – yet the western borders are themselves over one thousand miles from the sea. To understand Chinese cooking, she would emphasise, you must first get to grips with the regions. Add improvisation – a great Chinese talent – and you end up with a variety of cooking that makes the range of French cuisine seem limited in comparison.

During the last three decades the number of Chinese restaurants in Britain has mushroomed. Many are only capable of providing 'junk' food – quantity and low prices are their simple objectives. Few Chinese restaurants in Britain match those found in New York, Hong Kong or Singapore – though standards have picked up dramatically in London and the big cities during the last few years; three first-class examples follow on the next page. One thing I can guarantee: you will not find the dreaded MSG (monosodium glutamate) – that curse of flavouring ingredients – at any of them. What you will find is a subtlety and a lightness in their repertoires which comes as a welcome surprise.

What of the main regional cuisines? There are four:

Cantonese Most Chinese restaurants in Britain are run by Cantonese Chinese – so this is the style that predominates. South China has a tropical climate and a long coastline. Fish and shellfish feature strongly; great stress is placed on freshness and, in the best traditions of modern French cuisine, they're cooked for a very short time. Much Cantonese food is savoury – sometimes very peppery. Duck, pork and beef all appear in a multitude of ways. *Dim sums* are a favourite of mine – a selection of fried and steamed, savoury and sweet dumplings, buns, rice-flour rolls and paper-wrapped fillings of prawns, pork, rice, etc.

Peking The cold northern climate influences the region's recipes: it's famous for Peking Duck, served in thin pancakes; its roast and barbecued dishes; its Mongolian hot-pots; its prawns and its mutton. Spring onions, garlic and soya paste play an important part in many specialities.

Shanghai The eastern coastline is renowned for its delicate, light flavours – where freshness counts most. Because of the proximity of the sea, numerous ponds, streams and the mighty Yangtze, freshwater fish, crabs and seafood feature strongly. Nanking ducks are justly renowned.

Szechuan This is the western part of China. Its hot, spicy cooking is much to my liking; the use of chillies, ginger, pepper and onions are common – in pork, chicken and beef dishes.

One thing I find hard to get used to in Chinese restaurants in Britain is the take-it-or-leave-it attitude of waiters. Business like it may be – but it's rarely friendly.

EARL'S COURT London SW5   Tiger Lee

Comfortable restaurant/Michelin ★   ℝ

A remarkable restaurant by any standards. Michelin in Britain showed great courage and foresight in awarding the rare accolade of one star in 1980. To the best of my knowledge it's the only Chinese restaurant in Europe that wins a star. Seafood predominates – served in a small, smart dining room, with a maximum of 30 clients for dinner only. 'Tiger Lee stuffed fish' is a magnificent speciality – a reconstructed trout that requires a lot of preparation, any top French chef would be proud of it. 'Classic monk's vegetables' include five types of Chinese fungi – a delight and 'fried rice with steamed prawns wrapped in lotus leaf' is a big square of superbly cooked rice.

alc **D** (dinner only served) *cards* AE DC Visa
closed Christmas Day. Lunch-every day.
post 251 Old Brompton Road, London SW5 9HP.
phone (01) 370 2323

█ VICTORIA █ London SW1   Ken Lo's
                                  Memories of China

Comfortable restaurant
Good value (lunch)

At 71, Ken Lo has done more to popularise Chinese cuisine in Britain than anyone else. Dozens of books have come from his pen during the 50 years he has lived here. His restaurant is the ideal place to try a range of regional Chinese dishes. A menu called 'Gastronomic Tour of China' is a classic: it includes a 'Shanghai quick-fry' – scallops, chicken and prawns in a peppery sauce; a 'Peking salt-&-pepper three-spiced pork choplettes'; a delicious 'Szechuan aromatic and crispy duck'; and a flavoursome, spicy 'Cantonese chilli beef in black bean sauce'. Lattice-like screens divide the large dining room up cleverly.

menus **A** (lunch) **C** (dinner) *cards* A AE DC Visa
closed Sun. Bank hols.
post 67-69 Ebury Street, London SW1W 0NZ.
phone (01) 730 7734

MANCHESTER   Yang Sing

Simple restaurant
Good value   ℝ

The tips started years ago – from *FL* readers and old rallying mates: nose out Yang Sing. I did just that – for a Sunday lunch; it was one of my most enjoyable ever treats – you should do the same. The 60-seater, basement dining room was packed – mainly with happy Chinese families. Talent, innovation, freshness, variety – chef Harry Yeung deserves his culinary fame. 20 or so incomparable *dim sums*: tiny dumplings, paper-thin pastry rolls and puffs and other coverings with tasty fillings. Main dishes of beef, duck, scallops, crab and so on with accompaniments like seaweed, deep-fried for a second (Chapel fashion), and coconut cream *beignets*. Leave it to Vincent Wong to put together a 'surprise' menu. '85 will see a move to nearby bigger premises.

menus **A-B** *cards* A AE
closed Christmas Day.
post 17 George St, Manchester M1 4HE. (34 Princes St during '85)
phone (061) 236 2200 (Between Piccadilly and Town Hall)

Indian Cuisine

I spent the first ten years of my life in India – half of them in the high Himalayas where a boarding school 'year' meant nine long months spent far away from home. As much as the pupils loved Sherwood College in Naini Tal – 7000 ft above sea-level – nevertheless we all used to wait impatiently for the brief three-month break when we were allowed to 'escape' back home. Five or six years of age I may have been, but I can still recall the mediocrity of wartime boarding-school fare.

During those holidays I remember accompanying my mother on many a market expedition – when she would buy, from a vast selection, a variety of spices, herbs, different types of rice, lentils, vegetables and fruit. Even today, 40 years later, I can picture the colourful palettes of spices – and then, back home, watching how they were painstakingly ground down on an old grinding stone. Making your own fresh 'curry' powder, *masala* paste and *garam masala* was, and still is, a great art.

My mother was an excellent cook and she had a great understanding of and sympathy for Indian regional cooking – she had lived at various times in many parts of the sub-continent. She cooked rice perfectly (liking the *Patna* and *Basmati* varieties most) and presented it at the table in scores of different ways. 15 years later she passed the trick on to Anne; I have yet to find any restaurant, anywhere, that prepares rice better. Today, of course, we have the benefit of being able to use different varieties from all parts of the world, including the United States.

She made great use of a variety of *dals* – split peas, lentils and dried beans – and numerous chutneys, pickles and other accompaniments, all of which she made herself. Of the many excellent vegetables that she adored she had a special knack with the *brinjal* – the humble aubergine was made to work wonders in myriad ways; so were onions, limes and others. Mutton, lamb, chicken, fish – of all types, eggs and particularly vegetables were made into delectable treats. Don't think that meant they were always hot 'curries'. Far from it – the permutations possible when using turmeric, chillies, cardamom, cumin, cloves, coriander, mint, ginger, saffron, mace, cinnamon and many others are endless. In India variety is the spice of life!

The names of a host of Indian breads, snacks, favourite dishes, sweets and fruit remain embedded in my mind: *chapatis, parathas, naans, pooris* among the breads (*rotis*) – what treats they were; *samosas, poppadums, pakoras, kababs, chaat*, 'curry-puffs' and 'Polly's dirt' were some of the marvellous snacks; *koftas, kormas, kheemas, khichri, Jalfrazie* and *tundooris* were some of my favourite dishes; and *halva* – of all types, *jalebis, rasgullas, gulab jamuns, kulfi*, mangoes, guavas and lychees – to name only a few of the sweets and fruits we relished. Anne can prepare most of the above – my family love them all.

During the last 35 years I have visited scores of Indian restaurants in Britain. All but a few have been a disappointment – frankly we do better at home. The majority offer dishes that are a pale shadow of what I consider 'real' Indian cooking. My uncles always considered that no 'curry' (a non-existent term in Indian cuisine) passed the test unless their foreheads glistened with sweat – though that sort of 'rotgut' has never suited me. Most Indian restaurants in Britain have a very simple philosophy: make it plenty; make it all taste the same; and make it hot! Overspicing is rampant.

On the next page I recommend some of the better Indian/Pakistani restaurants in Britain. One tip: never drink wine with Indian food. Water is all you need – and plenty of it!

Favourite Indian Restaurants

HYDE PARK London W2 · Bombay Palace

Comfortable restaurant
Good value (lunch – weekends) ®

The Bombay Palace opened in a blaze of publicity a year ago – it won no less than 36 column inches in the two *Telegraph* papers alone! Attention to detail is a great feature here – and waiters are as sharp-eyed as any I have met. Starters are remarkably good – 'assorted snacks' include a lamb *kabab*, a crisp vegetable *samosa*, an exceptional *murgh tikka* and super vegetable and chicken *pakoras*. An onion *kulcha* (*roti*) is both tasty and different. Beware the description 'mild spices' – read it as 'hot'; both a Patiala *gosht* (lamb) and a *murgh keema masala* (chicken) are fiery. The Palace is one of a chain – there are seven others in North America and Sant Singh Chatwal, the owner of them all, has recently opened a Bombay Palace in Paris.
menus **A** (lunch-weekends) *alc* **B-C** *cards* A AE DC Visa
closed Open all the year.
post 2 Hyde Park Square, London W2.
phone (01) 723 8855/0673

KNIGHTSBRIDGE London SW7 · Shezan

Comfortable restaurant ®

It's Pakistani cooking at the Shezan – for long one of the better Indian sub-continent restaurants in London. The basement dining room is much too dark – though the dinner-jacketed waiters are first class, measured by any standards. Starters are abysmal – of the grapefruit and shrimp cocktail type. *Naans* and the various *tandoori* grills and barbecues are excellent. *Karahi kabab Khyberi* is a succulent chicken dish though the 'delicious' sauce with *kofta Kashmiri* proved to be too peppery. (Some of the menu descriptions are over the top – in the best advertising copy style.) *Halwa yakoti* and *kulfi* are authentic, tasty desserts.
alc **B-C** *cards* A AE DC Visa
closed Xmas. Sun. Bank hols.
post 16-22 Cheval Place, London SW7 1ES.
phone (01) 589 7918/0314

SOUTH KENSINGTON London SW7 · Bombay Brasserie

Very comfortable restaurant
Good value (lunch)

High-ceilinged rooms, tables set well apart and expensive furnishings – including overhead fans – give the restaurant an authentic air; you could be in India. A buffet lunch is remarkable value – there's a choice of eight to ten dishes. Specialities at dinner include chicken *dhansak* – a Parsee dish where *dal* plays an important part; chicken *tikka* – a *tandoori* favourite; a pork *vindaloo* – a fiery alternative from Goa; a Punjabi *thali* (a huge dish) for vegetarians; and, for those with real appetites, a house *thali* – made up of no less than three main courses. Despite five phone calls I still await some information I asked for; as I said, you could be in India itself.
menus **A** (lunch) *alc* **B-C** *cards* A AE DC Visa
closed Open all the year.
post Courtfield Close, 140 Gloucester Road, London SW7.
phone (01) 370 4040

Index of Hotels and Restaurants – by Village/Town

French Leave 3 amendments

page 52: **Vannes** please delete entry.

page 87: **Montchenot** now restaurant only – no rooms.

page 98: **Fayence** new owners – standards very much lower.

page 100: **Mouans-Sartoux** closed – André & Tricon are now in Tours.

page 114: **Alvignac** new owners – standards not as high.

page 122: **St. Pardoux** new owners – standards not as high.

page 165: **Onzain** *phone* (54) 20.83.88.

page 181: **Chauffailles** cancel entry. page 186: **Priay** closed.

page 221: **Thury-Harcourt** open all the year – except Dec 24/25.

page 238: **Bourganeuf** *phone* (55) 54.92.72.

page 242: **La Rochelle** Jacques Le Divellec is now in Paris.

page 254: **St. Rémy** new owners – standards not as high.

        delete 'no showers or baths' for entries on pages 215/293.

Paris? Use Patricia Wells' *The Food Lover's Guide to Paris* – a super book (published by Methuen in the UK and by Workman in North America).